E7/80

J. D. Atlas
School of Historical Studies
The Institute For Advanced Study
Princeton, New Jersey 08540
U. S. A.

An Introduction to the Philosophy of Language

Jay Atlas
Wolfson College
Oxford
July 1980

D0701277

Modern Introductions to Philosophy
General Editor: D. J. O'CONNOR

PUBLISHED

R. J. ACKERMANN, *Modern Deductive Logic*
R. F. ATKINSON, *Knowledge and Explanation in History*
⁂ D. W. HAMLYN, *The Theory of Knowledge*
BERNARD HARRISON, *An Introduction to the Philosophy of Language*
W. D. HUDSON, *Modern Moral Philosophy*
RUTH L. SAW, *Aesthetics*
J. TRUSTED, *The Logic of Scientific Inference: An Introduction*

IN PREPARATION

KAI NIELSEN, *An Introduction to the Philosophy of Religion*

An Introduction to the Philosophy of Language

Bernard Harrison

© Bernard Harrison 1979

All rights reserved. No part of this publication
may be reproduced or transmitted, in any form
or by any means, without permission.

First published 1979 by
THE MACMILLAN PRESS LTD
London and Basingstoke
Associated companies in Delhi Dublin
Hong Kong Johannesburg Lagos Melbourne
New York Singapore and Tokyo

Filmset in Great Britain by
Vantage Photosetting Co. Ltd,
Southampton and London
Printed in Great Britain by
REDWOOD BURN LIMITED
Trowbridge & Esher

British Library Cataloguing in Publication Data

Harrison, Bernard
   An introduction to the philosophy of language.
   – (Modern introductions to philosophy).
   1. Languages – Philosophy
   I. Title   II. Series
   401   P106

   ISBN 0–333–12043–4
   ISBN 0–333–12044–2 Pbk

This book is sold subject to the standard conditions of the Net Book Agreement

The paperback edition of this book is sold subject to the condition that it shall not,
by way of trade or otherwise, be lent, re-sold, hired out, or otherwise circulated
without the publisher's prior consent in any form of binding or cover other than
that in which it is published and without a similar condition including this
condition being imposed on the subsequent purchaser.

Contents

Preface

I was asked by Professor D. J. O'Connor, some years ago, to write for Macmillan a short introduction to the philosophy of language. I promised to do so, and was foolish enough to think that it would be quite easy to write such a book. I discovered my mistake. The present book, rather later and rather longer than I originally intended, is the outcome of that promise.

Philosophical discussion of language this century has been almost conterminous with philosophy itself. (It is often supposed that this is true only of philosophy in English-speaking countries and that continental European philosophers are properly above such demeaning and unphilosophical concerns. Those who think this have not read Husserl's *Logical Investigations*, or Merleau-Ponty's *Le Prose du monde*.) There is thus a bewildering variety and quantity of philosophical writing about language and it does not, even within the loose collection of philosophical outlooks called analytical philosophy, exhibit community of what is called 'approach'. To the uninitiated reader the writings of Donald Davidson and those of, say, the later Wittgenstein would scarcely appear at first sight to be contributions to the same discipline, let alone to the same discussion.

One solution to the problem of representing this diversity would have been to make the book a catalogue, or book of sketches, devoting a chapter to each major writer but not paying too much attention to the connections, or the gulfs, between them. This would have been easy, but ultimately unhelpful to the reader, whose false sense of familiarity with each writer would not go very deep. And I think it would have involved a misrepresentation of the subject. There *are* connections which bind the writings grouped under the heading of philosophy of language together to form a single 'subject' and even a single discussion: it is just that they are complicated, ramifying and hard to state simply and clearly.

The problem was therefore to find a thread in the labyrinth. In the end I chose three. The first is the current dispute between those – a very diverse group in themselves – who think that the concept of truth is the key to the understanding of meaning, and those who think that meaning has more to do with the implicit conventions by appeal to which speakers understand each other's intentions in concrete contexts of communication. The second is the problem of the autonomy of language and the creativity of language use: the fact that speakers of a language are able to read off, simply from the sentential sign, the meaning and syntactic structure of sentences they have never encountered before. The third is the fate of verificationism as a theory of meaning. In terms of these three topics, which are related to one another in many ways, I have tried to give the book a firm spine of argument, around which to group apparently diverse and unrelated discussions so that their status as contributions to a single discussion becomes, I hope, rather clearer.

One considerable problem which the book presented was the treatment of Wittgenstein. Wittgenstein is arguably the greatest philosopher to have written this century about language. At the same time his influence on current philosophy of language is comparatively slight. A fairly common conventional view of his work is roughly that the *Tractatus Logico-Philosophicus* contains an early and outmoded realism, and that his later work progresses by way of a swiftly discarded, or at any rate publicly disavowed, verificationism to a generally 'operationalist' theory of meaning founded on an obscure and largely unexplained notion of a *criterion* or *rule of use*.

This view is, I think, wholly mistaken, and its prevalence serves to distract attention from a writer of genius who in fact, I believe, addressed the central concerns of present-day philosophy of language.

The best, and indeed the only way, to counteract this view seemed to be to present Wittgenstein's views in their proper stages of development from one another and from the work of Frege. To do this properly, however, would be an enormous exegetical task, and one which it would be quite impossible to attempt within a book of this length. I therefore had to choose between the alternatives of leaving Wittgenstein out, offering a guarded and conventional account of his work which would divorce him from the mainstream of philosophical discussion of language, or giving a very bald and crude sketch of how I believe Wittgenstein should be read.

With some trepidation I have chosen the third, as the least unsatisfactory, of these options, and offer such a sketch in the concluding chapters of the book. For reasons of space I have made no attempt either to address the now quite large exegetical literature on Wittgenstein or to acknowledge, except in the Bibliography, the multifarious sources, in that literature, of my own interpretation.* I hope, however, that these chapters, despite their manifest defects, may serve some useful purpose in suggesting a reading of Wittgenstein which brings his work back into connection with current concerns.

The book as a whole is intended to make things as clear as possible for undergraduate and graduate students of philosophy, and to that end I have tried to cut out digression and to restrain technicality and exuberance of style. But I hope that it will also prove useful to linguists or psycholinguists, for example, who want to find out, without exorbitant expenditure of time and patience in reading, what philosophers have to say about language. And of course I hope that other philosophers will find something of interest in it.

It is only fair to such readers to let them know at what points my own ideas have crept into the discussion. The main areas of originality – or idiosyncrasy – in the book are: the discussion of the autonomy of language in chapter 1 and the use made of this in chapters 7 and 8 to construct a critique of Quine and Davidson; some parts of the discussion of Locke and Russell in chapters 2 and 3; the theory of promising as a contractual relationship, advanced in chapter 11; and to some extent, of course, the treatment of the development of Wittgenstein's thought in chapters 13 and 14. The general argument, or drift, of the book also represents my own opinion, but that can relatively easily be disentangled from the discussions of particular writers and schools.

The bibliography is as full as I could make it within reasonable bounds of length, and I have added a select bibliography of further reading for each of the main divisions of the text.

Sections of the book have been read to a variety of audiences over the past few years, and I have profited a good deal from the subsequent discussion as well as from numerous discussions with individual colleagues and students. Those friends and colleagues who have

*My treatment of naming and 'objects' in the *Tractatus*, for example, owes a great deal to Hidé Ishiguro's excellent paper 'Use and Reference of Names', in Winch (1969).

helped to save me from error include Roy Edgley, Timothy Sprigge, Benjamin Gibbs, Barbara Lloyd and Aaron Sloman at Sussex; Julius Kovesi, Stewart Candlish, Graham Priest, Hartley Slater and Richard Borthwick at the University of Western Australia; Tony Coady and Brenda Judge at the University of Melbourne; Peter Herbst, Michael Stocker, Stanley Benn, Genevieve Lloyd, William Godfrey Smith and Maurita Harney at the Australian National University; David Angluin at the North London Polytechnic; in Oxford, Jerome Bruner; at the University of Lille III, Noël Mouloud and Charles Galperin. Such errors as remain are no fault of theirs.

Parts of the book were conceived or written during periods when I was, successively, a Leverhulme Research Fellow, a fellow of the Humanities Research Centre at the Australian National University and a visitor at the University of Western Australia. I wish to express my gratitude to all these institutions, and to the University of Sussex, which generously granted me leave on each occasion.

I owe a special debt of gratitude to Lee Carter of the University of Western Australia, the best secretary I have ever had, who typed the manuscript in record time, with flawless accuracy and efficiency.

Finally, the book would not have been completed without the love and support of my wife, who with unfailing generosity forgave all that the wives of writers have to put up with.

Falmer, Sussex   B. H.
January 1979

I
Names

The Autonomy of the Linguistic Sign

1. Utterance and sign row

Suppose that, in a prehistoric burial chamber in south-west Cornwall, I discover the following marks carved on one of the granite slabs which hold up the roof:

I ask myself: are they merely marks made at random by a stonemason testing a chisel, or do they collectively make up an utterance in a language whose script this is? To ask this is to ask a question about history. But it is a question which implicitly suggests a prior question of a different and philosophically puzzling sort. What is it for a sequence of marks, or for that matter a sequence of vocal noises, to 'be' or to 'constitute' an utterance in a language?

This, it seems to me, is the central question of the philosophy of language. On the face of it it may not appear a very 'philosophical' question. Indeed, to anyone with an ordinary capacity to smell a rat, it may seem that such a question demands to be answered not by a philosopher but by some species of natural scientist; by a linguist, perhaps, or a psychologist. There are two reasons why this apparently sound and progressive proposal ought to be resisted. The first is that our question is a *very* abstract and general one: so abstract and general, in fact, that linguists and psychologists, who must, understandably enough, conduct themselves as practical people responsible for the advancement of reasonably well defined bodies of concrete and detailed knowledge, spend very little time discussing it. (It may occur to an especially perspicacious critic that this may be because they know the answer to it. It would be nice if this were so, but it is not.) This leaves it by default to the philosopher, in his hereditary role of Curator of the Department of Foolish (but also, sometimes, fundamental) Questions. The second, and better, reason is that it is a question of fundamental interest and importance for philosophy itself, and one upon which very little *direct* light can be obtained from linguistics or psychology as they are at present constituted – which is not, of course, to say that linguistics and psychology may not provide, incidentally, a good deal of information which needs to be taken into account in philosophical discussion. English-language philosophy since the turn of the century has been quite largely a meditation upon the nature of language, so there is a sense in which all other philosophical questions have become or been made secondary to this fundamental question. I shall try to sketch in some, at least, of these connections as we go along.

2. The autonomy of language

Recent, and for that matter traditional, philosophy offers us a number of direct and fairly elaborately worked-out answers to our primary question. I shall go on to consider some of these in the next few chapters. Before doing so it will be worth spending a little time on a possible answer which will no doubt seem so trivial as scarcely to count as philosophy, although it has the advantage of being true, or, rather, truistic. It is not as trivial as it seems, however, and in discussing it we can uncover some important conditions which must be met by any proposed solution to our central problem, if it is to stand any chance of being a successful solution.

The answer I have in mind is this. The marks (or any subset of them) constitute an utterance in a language just in case some person or other, if he were now living and were to be presented with the marks, would recognise them as constituting an utterance in his language.

The merit of this answer, truistic though it is, is that it invites us to consider carefully what is involved in *recognising* some set of marks as constituting an utterance in a language. I think it is at once evident that certain things could be ruled out immediately as possible cases of such recognition. Thus, it would not suffice to show that the marks made up an utterance in a language if I myself, for example, were to impose an arbitrary and fanciful interpretation upon them, thus:

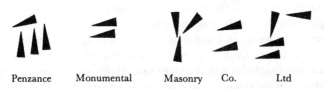

Penzance   Monumental   Masonry   Co.   Ltd

What makes this interpretation 'arbitrary' and 'fanciful'? Pretty clearly, I think, the fact that it is not imposed by the marks on me, but imposed by me on the marks. I am not 'reading off from' the marks the meaning and the grammatical structure which I attribute to them, but simply attributing to them meaning and grammar in any way I please. If I *really* know a language I cannot 'make what I please' of strings of signs which constitute utterances in it: the signs themselves *dictate* the interpretation I place upon them.

This feeling, that the signs of a language dictate the interpretation which a speaker of the language places upon them, is indeed, I think, what ultimately leads us to draw the distinction between an utterance and a row of marks or signs, or a string of vocal noises. A row of marks *qua* row of marks is, as it were, *lifeless*. A mark which serves as the physical vehicle of an utterance, on the other hand, has a life of its own, independent of the will of speaker or hearer. When a fluent speaker of a language understands a sentence, when he assigns a grammatical structure to it, or expresses its meaning in a paraphrase or a piece of *oratio obliqua*, or when he merely takes note of the meaning in the course of reading or listening, he is, so far as he is really using language and not merely playing at using it as a child may play at reading before he can read, guided and directed by the signs themselves: for him they bear their meanings and their grammatical structure upon their face.

So far as I know, the commonplace terminology of philosophy includes no general term for this feature of language. I shall call it *autonomy*.

3. Linguistic autonomy and communication

The autonomy of language is pretty clearly closely connected with the utility of language as a system of communication. Autonomy as we have defined it excludes the assignment of private and personal meanings or grammatical interpretations to utterances in a natural language. The utterance itself dictates its meaning, not the speaker or hearer. This should not surprise us. A system of communication is necessarily 'public' in the sense that it excludes private and personal interpretations of the symbols used in it. The reason for this is simply that whatever meaning I *impose* upon a string of signs presented to me is, obviously and by that very fact, not meaning which has been *communicated* to me through the medium of those signs. And, conversely, unless a given string of signs possesses a grammar and a meaning independently of any mere arbitrary imposition of them by me as speaker, I shall be unable, by uttering that string of signs, to communicate anything to anybody.

Thus, if I utter a nonsense syllable such as *bip*, I have in so doing *said*, and hence communicated, nothing at all. It is worth noticing that this remains true even if I 'meant by' *bip* in that context, 'Please shut the door', for example. We can see that this is so if we simply ask ourselves what somebody who claimed to have 'meant by' *bip*, when he said it, 'Please shut the door' could conceivably mean by such a claim.

It seems to me that all he could mean is that when he said *bip* he made a sort of private, internal note or memorandum to some such effect as this:

(a) What I mean by *bip* on this occasion is 'Please shut the door.'

But I think it is intuitively obvious that internal-memorandum making of this sort is, from a linguistic point of view, idle. It has no effect: it does not instantly turn *bip* from a nonsense syllable into an expression in a language. But the reasons why this is so are perhaps not altogether obvious.

The first reason is, of course, that a private memorandum such as (a) is, because it is made silently and internally by the speaker, inaccessible to the hearer, and hence cannot help him to assign a meaning to *bip*. But this does not seem to be a very conclusive reason. For suppose we abandon the idea that (a) is uttered silently and internally by the speaker: suppose he says it out loud? In that case would not the speaker's mere *intention to confer a meaning* (in the linguistic sense of 'meaning') on *bip* after all suffice actually to confer a meaning on *bip*?

I think the answer is no; and the reason for this is simply that in such a case the hearer's capacity to assign a meaning to *bip* would depend entirely on his or her possessing a capacity to assign a meaning to certain sentences in a natural language (we shall suppose the language to be English): namely, (a) and the sentence 'Please shut the door', which forms part of (a). The speaker's ability to make *bip* communicate something to his hearers thus seems wholly dependent on his possessing an antecedent ability to communicate with them in a natural language; and hence reference to the former ability will not suffice to explain what is involved in the latter.

We seem, then, to be forced to conceive of 'a language' rather along the lines of Saussure's distinction between *langue* and *parole*.[1] Language (*langue*) exists independently of particular speakers or hearers; has, as it were, a life of its own, and this life is *essentially* public, in the sense of being accessible in common to all speakers of the language.

The existence of *ambiguity* does not, I think, alter the fundamental publicity of meaning and syntactic structure. Sometimes a sentence may be grammatically or semantically ambiguous, or both, as for example is (if you know that in England a down is a special sort of hill):

(b) From the steep down fell the impetuous youth.

Here the words leave me free to place one or other of two possible interpretations upon them. But that is all the freedom they leave me, and it amounts merely to the freedom to treat 'steep' as a noun or as an adjective. The meaning and syntactic structure of the sentence, although different in either case, remains perfectly clear and well defined in either case. We can take account of ambiguity simply by restating the principle of the autonomy of meaning and syntactic structure as follows. Any well constructed sentence in a natural language has one or more possible syntactic structures (parsings) and one or more possible meanings. Any fluent speaker of the language can in principle read off all the possibilities from the physical sign row which constitutes the written or spoken representation of the sentence (I say 'in principle' for one thing because a particular speaker may not see all the possible interpretations at first sight: it may not occur to him for some time, for example, that (b) may be construed as conveying information about what kind of down it was from which the impetuous youth fell). And it is just the fact that meaning can be 'read off' in this way by speakers and hearers alike that makes a language an instrument of communication: what we impose on or read into the sign row is neither communicated nor communicable. Words mean what they mean: we cannot make them mean something else by merely wishing it; and the idea that we might (in some happier world perhaps) accomplish this feat is not a wistful adumbration of a more perfect form of human communication, but the denial of a condition which is fundamental to the possibility of any communication whatsoever.

4. The constitution of language

Looking at matters in this way makes it difficult to deny that *something* differentiates someone who knows a language from someone who does not. And this something, to put it in the most cautious and general terms possible, must consist in access to some set of publicly accessible procedures or criteria for determining the grammar and meaning of utterances in that language. We can perhaps use *constitutive mechanisms* as a sufficiently neutral and colourless phrase with which to refer to the criteria in question.

It seems, again, obvious that what transforms a mark or a vocal noise into an utterance in a language is that the mark or noise in question is, somehow or other, connected with, or enmeshed in, the constitutive mechanisms of the language.

Such a claim is controversial in contemporary philosophy, however. Many philosophers would deny that we need bring in any reference to rules, or procedures, or criteria, in order to give an account of meaning in natural languages. Some, such as H. P. Grice, or Jonathan Bennett or David Lewis, would want to argue that the concept of a rule or convention can be analysed in terms of the intentions, goals and beliefs of the parties to the convention. Others, such as W. V. Quine or Donald Davidson, would want to argue that the root notion of meaning itself simply evaporates once we form a clear conception of the relationship between sentences and the conditions for their truth and falsity. And, even if these views are all false, it is not at all clear how we might go about stating the constitutive conventions of a language. The notion of a 'rule' or 'criterion' of meaning is most at home in the work of Wittgenstein. But, as we shall see, Wittgenstein offers powerful reasons for thinking that a *criterion*, in his sense, cannot be *stated* at all.

Let us leave these complexities on one side for the moment however, and continue for a little longer to develop the discussion intuitively.

5. *Linguistic creativity*

Someone who understands a language can grasp the grammatical structure of sentences which he has never in his life heard before, and which could not, therefore, have had any response conditioned to them. Similarly, someone who is fluent in a language can construct sentences which he has never before uttered or heard uttered, and which may indeed never have been uttered by any other speaker in the history of the world, in complete confidence both that they are grammatical and that their grammatical structure will be evident to other speakers. This feature of natural languages is often called *linguistic creativity*. It has recently been made the basis of a whole linguistic methodology – 'transformational generative grammar', or 'TG grammar' – by Zellig Harris and Noam Chomsky, and this in turn has been extended still more recently into what is known as 'generative semantics'.

The idea of linguistic creativity is sometimes explained by saying that a fluent speaker of a language can assign one or more possible grammatical descriptions (phrase structural descriptions, parsings) and one or more possible senses to *any* well constructed sentence in the language which he may encounter. Put this way the claim seems empirically false. There are probably plenty of native speakers of English who would find it difficult to attach any clear meaning to: 'Terminalisation of chiasmata in bivalents with quasi-terminal centromeres is comparatively well understood', and some who would have no clear grasp even of its grammatical structure, while many would be unable to say whether 'Oogonia detach serially' is a sentence or a list of unrelated words.

On the other hand, any fluent speaker can understand and attach possible structural descriptions to some, indeed to many, sentences which he has never before encountered; while any possible sentence in a language must, it would seem, be capable of being semantically and syntactically interpreted by some possible speaker. It is therefore possible to envisage an ideal speaker who can semantically and syntactically interpret any English sentence. Having envisaged him we have a problem. The ideal speaker, like the real speaker, can attach grammatical descriptions to sentences which he has never before encountered. How does he do it?

The answer which TG grammarians give is that he can do it because he has access to the rules of a transformational grammar. These rules are essentially *recursive*: that is, they allow complex syntactic structures to be interpreted as formed from simpler syntactic structures through the application of precisely specified rules of replacement and transformation in specified sequences. These rules are clearly, in the sense we defined in section 4, *constitutive mechanisms* of language: the distinction between grammatical and ungrammatical strings exists only because the rules of the TG grammar exist.

Most philosophers, including Quine, who scout the idea of accounting for meaning in terms of rules, or constitutive conventions, of language, would be prepared to admit that a natural language certainly has rules in the sense of grammatical rules of the sort defined by a TG grammar. But the ground for postulating such rules in the first place is that the use of language is *creative*; and the notion of linguistic creativity can, I think, be extended far beyond its application to the study of syntax. It is, in fact, a simple consequence of the autonomy of the linguistic sign.

As we argued in section 2, we should not want to ascribe meaning to the marks in the burial chamber unless there were at least one person, living or dead, who could 'read off' a meaning from the signs, as distinct from reading one into them. But, suppose we found some self-proclaimed philologist prepared to interpret the marks as, say, 'Eru raised these stones': we should not feel all that much confidence in his judgement (remember the Piltdown fakes!) unless we could discover another philologist who, *quite independently of the first*, proved capable of reading off exactly the same sense, or an equivalent one. There seems to me to be implicit here a quite general criterion for saying of anyone that he understands a language. He must be able to read off from the marks or noises which constitute the sign vehicles of the language exactly the same sense which any other competent speaker independently reads off from them. And he must be able to do this even when the sentence is one which he has never encountered before.

Put in this way it looks, even so, as if the concept of linguistic creativity is applicable only to the understanding of sentences. For it is only in the case of sentences, it seems, that a speaker can come across a linguistic unity which he has never encountered before, and understand it. Words are not like that. Either a speaker has encountered a word before or he does not understand it, at least until he looks up its meaning in the dictionary or has it explained to him.

Contrary to appearances, however, linguistic creativity is just as much a feature of the use of general names as it is of sentences. We can think of the business of using a general name as equivalent to making an indefinite series of applications of it to objects in, or aspects of, the world: 'There's a tree', 'There's another tree', and so on. As well as applying it, we deny its application. 'That's not actually a dwarf tree', we say to someone who thinks he is looking at an example of the art of *bonsai*; 'It's just a shrub.' And sometimes we feel dubious. A holly bush is a holly *bush*, but sometimes, if it is well grown and has a well marked division of trunk and branches we feel inclined to call it a tree. In such cases, 'You can call it a tree or not, as you please: it's a bit big for a bush', we say, or something to that effect.

Each of us makes these judgements all the time, often of objects which are unfamiliar to him, and quite dissimilar, perceptually speaking, to other, more familiar objects which fall under the same general name, as 'bean-bag' chairs are perceptually dissimilar to 'standard' armchairs. And the judgements we make about the applicability of general names, broadly speaking, match those which other competent speakers are also making, quite independently of us. That is to say, in each case where one competent speaker applies a general name, denies its application or is dubious about its applicability, any other competent speaker will also apply it, deny its applicability, or feel a similar dubiety. Moreover, competent speakers achieve and sustain agreement in the application of general names without consultation: each knows simply by virtue of his own competence as a speaker of the language 'what any other speaker would have to say'. That this is in fact the criterion we use in deciding whether someone understands a general name is evident, I think, from a moment's consideration of what we should say in a case where the criterion was not met. We need only imagine a sarcastic schoolmaster, suspicious that a schoolboy does not understand the meaning of the French word *plume*, holding up one or another object – a piece of chalk, a pencil, the board rubber – and asking the boy whether *this* is a *plume*; and the laughter of the class at the boy's ever-repeated and quite sincere uncertainty. Unless different speakers apply a general name in the same way, independently of one another, there is simply no point in saying that the expression in question is a general name: it is a nonsense syllable of some kind. But the general applicability of the notion of linguistic creativity to naming, and to the understanding of the sense, and not just the grammatical structure, of a sentence, raises with new urgency the question of how such creativity is to be explained; and makes it hard to see what answer could suffice, except common access by all speakers of the language to a set of constitutive mechanisms of some sort.

6. Dialect and metaphor

At first sight, however, these criteria for saying of someone that he understands a sentence or a general name may seem altogether too strong. The range of application of a term does vary from speaker to speaker. What one person will call, with fair certainty, 'blue', another will, with equal certainty, call 'green'; what one calls a 'bowl' another will call a 'dish'; and so on. Such examples, however, concern at most a few borderline instances of the application of names. The point at which real doubt sets in over the application of 'green' or 'blue' in a sequence of greenish blues and bluish greens, or over the application of 'bowl' and 'cup' in a series of cuplike bowls and bowl-like cups, may vary somewhat from speaker to speaker but remains for all within the same narrow zone of dubious exemplars. If the differences in use are discontinuous, in the sense of characterising large groups of speakers, we may feel inclined to speak of differences of dialect. If the differences are scattered evenly over the whole array of speakers, it simply means that the criteria which enable speakers to match each other's independent linguistic performances are not powerful enough to generate an exact, or sharp-edged, match. But a blurred edge is still an edge. What communication requires is that speakers exhibit, independently of one another, broad conformity in what they group, for any general name *N*, into the categories *N*, non-*N*, dubious *N*. The contents of these categories may overlap a little when we compare different speakers' versions of them, but if they overlap too much we shall be forced to say that the speakers in question are not speaking the same language, or at best are speaking different dialects of the same language.

Another reason why the ability to match the linguistic performances of individual speakers may seem too strong as a criterion of understanding is that it seems to make language altogether too rigid and formal a structure. Surely words cannot mean *exactly* the same thing for every speaker, otherwise how would poetry or literature in general be possible? Is not the meaning of a word something essentially evasive, fragile and imponderable: infinitely variable from context to context and from one speaker's mouth to another? Does 'time' mean the same thing in the *Four Quartets* as in a work on physics? And so on.

'Defences' of literature of this kind are not uncommon, and they strike me as more in the nature of betrayals. If the meanings of words were as unstable as the objection suggests, there could be no poetry, only pleasing jingles. Serious literature, like serious science, depends upon the exact and scrupulous use of words. Such scrupulousness precisely implies the existence of precise and public criteria of meaning. Even in the most apparently loose and 'imagist' writing this is true: indeed, it is perhaps most true there, where only the meanings of words, which includes the limits of ambiguity of words, hold the poem together. When Auden, in a well known early poem, writes, for example,

> The glacier knocks in the cupboard,
> The desert sighs in the bed,
> And the crack in the tea-cup opens
> A lane to the land of the dead.

what is it that enables us to make sense of this sequence of surrealist images embedded in little gnomic assertions? Its sense is perfectly clear, after all. Auden is saying that death and time attack us not only from without, but also from within, from the most private refuges of our lives, from the seats of our loves and our small pleasures, such as tea-drinking. But this clarity of sense springs from the fact that we know what 'glacier', 'cupboard', 'sandstorm', 'teacup' *mean* in the most flatly literal sense. It is the *poem* that creates a new linguistic object, not any essential evasiveness or waveringness in the meanings of the words which compose it; and, indeed, if those meanings were not fixed and solid points upon which the poem could erect its structure of metaphor and image, the poem would not be possible.

There is a real problem about metaphor: namely, the problem of how, as speakers of a language, we can grasp the sense of a metaphor given that a metaphor necessarily involves the application of words to an unfamiliar and apparently unrelated subject matter. But that problem is simply a special case of the problem of linguistic creativity itself, and therefore cannot be solved but can only be evaded by denying that linguistic creativity exists.

7. Perceptual discrimination and linguistic discrimination

The problem of creativity is often thought to be solved out of hand merely by the existence of the capacity to recognise recurrent patterns of stimulation and to discriminate between one such pattern and another. Once we have learned, for example, that red apples are ripe, we are able to pick out ripe apples even though not all ripe apples are the same shade of red. The ability to group our perceptual experience into natural categories of this kind is fundamental to learning in all organisms, after all. Cats can recognise birds as a category of edible prey, requiring certain patterns of hunting and stalking behaviour, even though different kinds of birds are perceptually dissimilar to one another in many ways. That is to say, the category 'bird' has a certain perceptual reality for the cat: a reality which is manifestly rooted in perception and has nothing to do with language at all.

Why should not the most basic terms in a language simply be defined in terms of categories which have this sort of perceptual reality for each speaker of the language? Then perhaps other, less basic terms could be defined using these basic ones.

Talk of 'the most basic terms in a language' suggests, if it suggests anything, the language of immediate sensory description: colour names, names for qualities of sound, tactile sensations and so forth.

It is not at all clear, however, what it would mean to say that animals have a *natural capacity* to recognise things called 'red' in English when they see them. Certainly a human being, or a monkey, can recognise two objects as being *of the same colour*: the same shade of red, for example. And certainly, too, human beings and animals can recognise different shades of colour as being relatively more or less similar to one another. Monkeys which have been conditioned to expect to find food behind a red trap-door will respond positively to a trap coloured in a different shade of red. In this sense animals and men do have access to a 'quality space' of colour which is 'natural' in the sense that it can in principle be specified in terms of differential dispositions to respond behaviourally to stimuli: to coloured patches, coloured trap-doors, and so forth.

But, if we are interested, as we are, in understanding the *linguistic* capacity to use colour *names*, what is at issue is not simply the capacity to respond behaviourally in the same way to qualitatively similar stimuli. What is at issue is the capacity of each competent speaker to predict what colour name another speaker will apply to a shade of colour which neither speaker may have encountered before; to predict whether he will use, of a particular shade, a compound colour name such as 'aφ-ishψ'; to predict what grammatically possible colour designations (such as 'a greenish red') he will find unintelligible, in what circumstances he will find them unintelligible (for example, some leaves in which a green pigment is marked by a red one look 'greenish red' to most people, but only the colourblind are prepared to use the expression 'greenish red' of homogeneous coloured surfaces), and much else besides.

Let us take the simplest of these capacities, predicting what colour name a speaker will apply to a shade of colour which neither he nor the speaker who makes the prediction has seen before. It is not, I take it, conceivable that each of the 7×10^6 shades of colour discriminable by the human eye could be expressly tagged with a colour name in the process of teaching a child its native language. We might, however, be able to explain the capacity as 'natural' if it turned out to be the case that the human perceptual system encoded a behaviourally specifiable 'quality space' which exactly mirrored the capacities of speakers of English to apply English colour names. We can perhaps imagine what that would be like by analogy with the familiar experiment in animal learning in which a monkey is trained to seek food behind trap-doors coded in various colours. We might begin by training the monkey to seek food behind trap-doors painted pure blue, but give it an electric shock if it enters a trap coloured pure green. And then we might find that the monkey willingly enters trap-doors coloured in any shade of blue, but begins to show hesitation with bluish greens. To apply this to the case of colour *language* all we have to do is to suppose that the human speaker possesses a neurologically encoded colour space exactly like that of the monkey, but that in the human case the monkey's behavioural response is replaced by a verbal one:

saying 'blue' or 'bluish green'. Then, if this story is true, the reason why all English-speakers apply colour words within the same limits of application is that the same quality-space – the same set of tendencies to associate qualitatively related stimuli together relative to specific responses – is neurologically encoded in the central nervous system of each speaker.

But if this story *were* true, and colour-naming followed boundaries marked out 'naturally' in a neurologically-encoded quality space, then the limits of application of colour names in all languages would presumably be the same. But in fact the limits of application of colour names differ a great deal from language to language. There are languages, for example, whose speakers would, if asked for 'pure' or 'focal' cases of colours falling under a particular colour name in their language, give samples which English speakers would regard as, say, pure reds; but who would also associate under that colour name samples which English-speakers would call browns, pinks, oranges and yellows.[2] The point is that any speaker of *that* language will also be able to predict the linguistic behaviour of other speakers of *his* language in applying colour names to shades of colour which he or they may not have encountered before. But we cannot now explain this capacity by appeal to the nature of a postulated quality space of colour supposed to be neurologically encoded in the central nervous systems of the speakers in question, unless we are prepared to say that differences in colour language correspond to quite radical differences in neurophysiology, so far as colour perception is concerned. And in fact there seems to be no evidence for the radical differences which would be required for such an argument to succeed. The psychologist M. H. Bornstein[3] has recently argued for a systematic yellowing of various anatomical structures in the eye, which he suggests may account for the fact that some languages employ a single colour term for all shades of green and blue; but Bornstein's hypothesis, if true, would explain only a minute fraction of the observed differences between the colour vocabularies of different languages.[4] And there seems otherwise to be much positive evidence that the perceptual and discriminatory capacities of human beings as regards colour perception are more or less constant across the whole species.[5]

We must conclude then, it seems, that, even in the case of the vocabulary of immediate sensory description which includes colour names, problems arise, about how one speaker is enabled to predict the linguistic performances of another speaker, that cannot be settled out of hand by appeal to psychology or neurology, and that therefore require an explanation in terms of some shared system of conventions or procedures, the description of which would form part of the description of the constitutive mechanisms of the natural language in question.

A far more general reason can be given, however, for why linguistic discrimination is not to be identified with perceptual discrimination. Perceptual recognition is always, and inherently, recognition of the recurrence of a complex which can be characterised in many different ways. When I recognise a blackbird I am recognising something black, a bird, something which flutters, something bipedal, something feathered, and so on. These multiple patterns of similarity can be extended in any direction. Suppose *per impossibile*, that the cat can speak, but only to itself, and that it mutters words to itself as it hunts. As it hunts blackbirds it mutters 'blackbird, . . . blackbird'. For a long time we conjecture that the cat's word 'blackbird' means the same as 'blackbird' in English, but one morning a strange bird, a hoopoe, enters the garden. The cat hunts it, saying 'blackbird'. We then see that there is a *recherché* similarity between the hoopoe's legs and the blackbird's legs, and we conjecture that *that*, after all, was what the cat meant by 'blackbird'. But this time we make the translation cautiously: perhaps there is some still more *recherché* similarity, yet to be revealed, and *that* is what the cat's word 'blackbird' really refers to.

Now, obviously, if I had to use this kind of caution in interpreting my neighbour's use of the word 'blackbird', either he or I would not really be a competent speaker of English. And, equally obviously, I do not *have* to use that kind of caution in interpreting what my neighbour says. I know that for him, as for me, 'blackbird' is the name of a species of bird, and not the name of a *recherché* property which happens to characterise the legs of birds of that (and other, rarer) species, because I know that that is what the word means *in English*. To put it another way, I know with absolute certainty that no natural event however improbable, such as the incursion of a hoopoe into the garden, could ever put such a complexion upon my neighbour's use of the word 'blackbird' (as it does in the case of the cat's use of it in my example) as to make me conclude that I have always been mistaken, hitherto, about what the word *meant*. I *know*, knowing English, what my neighbour would say if a hoopoe did appear in the garden: he would say, *inter alia*, 'That's not a blackbird!'

Such certainty is conferred upon me just by knowing English. The difficulty is to understand just *what it is I know* in knowing English. But what I know cannot be a set of correlations between general names and complex patterns of stimulation the recurrence of which I am able, psychologically, to recognise. I possess that much in the case of my imaginary cat, but possessing it manifestly does not enable me to predict the cat's future use of 'blackbird' as knowing English enables me to predict my neighbour's future use of 'blackbird'. Perceptual similarity is simply too weak and ubiquitous a relationship to bear the weight of explaining the capacity of one speaker of a language to predict the independent linguistic responses of another. In the case of the cat I can, of course, recognise *those black birds the cat says 'blackbird' to,* as well as the cat can; but all that *that* enables me to do is to say, 'Ah, there is another of those birds the cat says "blackbird" to!' It does not enable me to say, *speaking the same language as the cat,* 'Ah, there is a *blackbird*!' Possession of what H. H. Price[6] called a 'recognitional capacity' in common with the cat, in other words, does not make me a member of the cat's linguistic community; and therefore appeal to recognitional capacities cannot explain what is involved in membership of a human linguistic community.

Nor, evidently, does it make much difference if we allow the cat the capacity to indicate negative instances, to say 'not blackbird' to thrushes, tits or rabbits, for example. Such feline mutterings go to show only that the feature, F, of blackbirds which the cat's utterance 'blackbird' picks out is not a feature which blackbirds share with thrushes, tits or rabbits. But it does not at all tend to show that F is exemplified by no non-blackbird. In modern logical terminology, what we need is some means of predicting in advance how the cat would apply 'blackbird' in other *possible worlds* – for example, one which contains hoopoes. That seems to be something which one speaker of English is able to do with respect to other speakers of English. But what enables him to do it is a harder question.

8. Ostensive definition

The impossibility of accounting for the capacity to use general names in terms of perceptual discrimination is also fatal to the theory of ostensive definition. The theory of ostensive definition is the theory that it is possible to give a meaning to a name, independently of appeal to any prior linguistic capacity, by pointing to an object and saying its name. Thus, it is said, we teach a child the meaning of 'cow' by pointing at cows and saying 'cow'.

But what is the teacher pointing at? Or, to put the objection more precisely: under what exemplary aspect is he pointing at the cows? Is he pointing at them as examples of a certain *shape*; as examples of animals; as examples of beasts permitted to be eaten by a certain dietary code; as examples of members of a certain *species*, as exhibiting a certain pattern of colours? Or what? The list of possibilities is endless. The learner can answer this question only when he knows the logical category of 'cow': whether it is a species name, or a name for some less exactly specified category of true-breeding animals, or a colour name, or a shape name, or whatnot. And so he needs to know already how the word is to function in language. Wittgenstein makes this point in the *Philosophical Investigations* (1. 29–30):

> Perhaps you say: two can only be ostensively defined in *this* way: 'This *number* is called "two".' For the word 'number' here shows what place in language, in grammar, we assign to the word. . . . So one might say: the ostensive definition explains the use – the meaning – of the word when the overall role of the word in language is clear.

9. Causal theories of meaning

The same difficulties which beset the theory of ostensive definition, and theories which attempt to explicate linguistic discrimination in terms of perceptual discrimination, also beset what are known as 'causal' theories of meaning.

A causal theory of meaning is one which attempts to explain the meanings of utterances, and what it is for an utterance to *have* a meaning, in terms of the causal processes which govern the production of utterances by speakers.

Most causal theories of meaning, from Ogden and Richards[7] to Skinner[8] have interpreted the causal processes in question in terms of associationist or stimulus-response psychology – although a rather different kind of causal theory, which we shall discuss in chapter 9, has recently been put forward by Saul Kripke and Hilary Putnam, among others.

Skinner's theory will serve as an example of the *genre*. Skinner accounts for linguistic behaviour in terms of the concept of *operant conditioning*, developed in connection with his studies of animal learning. *Operant* behaviour is behaviour which an organism produces spontaneously. It can be shaped, in experimental conditions, by reward and punishment (*positive* and *negative reinforcement*). Thus, Skinner has been able to train pigeons to walk in circles or figures of eight by differentially rewarding the natural side-to-side movements which the pigeon makes as it searches for food.

The application of such processes to language is exemplified in Skinner's treatment of simple declarative sentences such as 'It's raining', or 'Here is a red ball', which he calls *tacts*. The child's babbling is gradually shaped by differential reinforcement until the production of a given tact is conditioned to the occurrence of recurrent patterns of stimulation in the child's environment: rain, or red balls. At this point the child's utterance of the tact in question is said to be under the *stimulus control* of the patterns of stimulation in question.

Noam Chomsky[9] has argued very persuasively that the theory is vacuous – that is, without explanatory force – because Skinner gives us no means of identifying a *controlling stimulus* without reference to the meaning of the verbal string the utterance of which it is supposed to control. If a man standing in front of a picture utters the verbal string *ab*, we may conjecture that the controlling stimulus is a certain harmonious arrangement of the elements of the picture: that is, that *ab* means 'beautiful!' But it may just as well mean 'hideous', 'his early period' or 'fake'. We have no means of knowing without appeal to our own, or someone else's, linguistic intuition; and hence talk of 'controlling stimuli' throws no light whatsoever upon the nature of the capacity which we exercise in making such linguistic judgements.

Skinner's theory would be non-vacuous, of course, if, by comparing the stimulus circumstances in which an utterer produces the string *ab*, we could isolate a 'controlling stimulus' by reference to which we could always predict accurately whether or not a speaker would utter the string *ab* in any future circumstances.

But the problem we face in doing this is precisely the problem which we encountered in the case of the talkative cat: the problem, also, which Wittgenstein raises in connection with the theory of ostensive definition. That problem is that we cannot, it seems, merely by comparing the stimulus conditions under which a speaker produces an utterance, arrive at the point of being able to predict with certainty what the same or another speaker will say in some new and unforeseen set of stimulus conditions. But that very ability, it seems, is one which we possess, and exercise effortlessly, as speakers of natural languages. There is thus a gulf between the explanatory machinery which causal theories bring to the explanation of linguistic capacities, and the capacities to be explained. The gulf is one which Chomsky and Wittgenstein have both, from very different points of view, pointed out. It is difficult to see how any causal theory could contrive to bridge it.

2

Reference and Generality

1. Meaning and reference

If we are asked what, in general, it is that someone knows when he knows the meaning of a word, it seems natural enough to reply: what that word *stands for*. 'Stands for' is of course a metaphor. The phrase suggests a model or picture, of what happens when a language is instituted. The picture it suggests is this. There is an object in the world, and the word serves as a substitute for that object; as, that is, a kind of proxy: something that *does duty for*, or *stands in place of*, the object.

The picture is seductive because it seems to make the nature of meaning transparently clear and simple. On the one hand we have objects of various sorts, which together make up our world: colours, perhaps; houses, trees, animals, pains, emotions, moods, chairs, tables, and so on. These objects exist quite independently of our talk about them, and certainly they exist independently of linguistic convention of any sort. They provide a background against which the business of setting up a natural language can be imagined as proceeding. And thus the constitutive mechanisms which define and establish a natural language can be seen as exceedingly simple conventions. They can be seen, in short, as involving nothing more than – and nothing more mysterious than – the following two steps.

(1) Placing strings of sounds – phonemic strings, to use a technical term of linguistics – in one-to-one association with objects.
(2) Adopting a convention that each word is to stand proxy for the object with which it has been associated.

We thus have an elegantly parsimonious theory which seems to solve our problem about the nature of the constitutive mechanisms of language almost before we have managed to formulate it. Versions of this theory, which we shall call the referential theory of language, have been influential in the philosophical discussion of language since Plato. But will it do?

As we have stated it, the theory requires that the world as human beings experience it should be divided up, independently of any linguistic conventions human beings may institute, into an array of objects with which phonemic strings may be placed in one-to-one correspondence. The theory achieves its aim of making the mechanism of meaning limpidly clear only if we can say what these objects are. That is, we need to be able to go on from the general statement of the theory to identify, for each word of a natural language, the object for which it stands proxy. And we need, of course, to be able to perform this identification without reference to the meanings of words, and in general without presupposing any linguistic concept.

A philosopher reading this, though, might well enter a *caveat*. Surely we are being too hard on the theory, and hard on it in a naïve and simpleminded way. We have been talking as though the objects in question could be identified with 'objects' in the ordinary physical sense, objects such as trees or houses or people. No serious proponent of the theory has ever imagined such a thing: the 'objects' which such philosophers have had in mind have always been things of a much more rarefied kind.

It is quite true that no defender of the theory has ever stated it in the simpleminded way in which we have just stated it. On the other hand, I think it is equally true that the attractiveness of the theory stems from the fact that it offers a picture – a way of conceiving the fundamental nature of meaning – which seems to make the nature of meaning transparently clear. If you take that picture literally, it turns out, as we shall see, to be quite untenable. What people have hoped, however, is that the clarity and explanatory force of the original simpleminded picture may be retained if the theory is reformulated in some less prosaically concrete, and so more plausible way. I think this is in the end a vain hope. But we cannot see why it is a hope – why people should have devoted so much time and energy to the elaboration of successively more sophisticated variants of this type of theory – unless we first formulate the theory in its crudest form. In that form it does indeed seem to embody a major insight about meaning, in the shape of a rough but easily understood theory which looks as though it might well be made wholly acceptable by further refinement. It is the fortunes of this programme of theoretical refinement which we are to trace in this and the following chapter. We shall therefore continue for a little while yet to maintain a stance of resolute simplemindedness. It will prove to have been worthwhile in the end, for, though it is true that one aim of philosophy is intellectual sophistication, it is also true that nothing strangles the subject faster than premature cleverness.

2. *Universals as referents*

It seems at first sight relatively easy to say, without circularity, what object a proper name stands for. It stands for its bearer. 'Richard Nixon' stands for Richard Nixon. 'Mummy', as used by a small child, stands for the child's mother. I do not have to appeal to the *meaning* of 'Richard Nixon' in order to identify him, any more than the baby has to appeal to the *meaning* of 'Mummy' in order to tell its mother from other adults. If I can tell Nixon from, say, Kissinger, Sadat or Charlie Chaplin, it is because I know him by sight, having seen him on television, and not because I have a sound grasp of the English language. In the same way I do not have to know Chinese in order to know who Chou En-Lai is, and the baby does not have to know any language at all to recognise his mother and greet her with the cry 'Ma-ma'. And, of course, this is as it must be. I could not identify Nixon by appeal to the meaning of his name, because 'Richard Nixon' has, in that sense, no meaning. It is simply a semantically arbitrary label attached by convention to the individual Nixon, whom, as a matter of psychological, and not at all of linguistic fact, some of us happen to know how to identify. With proper names, or some proper names, in short, there seems to be a clear and satisfying partitioning between psychological and linguistic questions about meaning. As a psychological matter of fact we can identify individual men: as a linguistic matter of fact we label such individuals with arbitrarily chosen phonemic strings, which in consequence of being assigned to this function become proper names. It is here that the conception of meaning as an associative relationship between expressions in a language and objects in the world finds its easiest and most secure footing in our minds.

But even with proper names all is not quite such plain sailing. Frege, and numerous other writers, would not be content with the view of ordinary proper names as purely denotative or designating expressions which I have just outlined. They would argue that the meaning of a proper name must be a definite description which uniquely identifies, at least from the point of view of a particular speaker, the individual intended.

These are disputes which, despite their importance, we must leave on one side. But other difficulties arise. What is the individual picked out by 'Moscow', for example? Is it a certain collection of buildings? Suppose they are demolished and replaced? Is it a site? Suppose, through the growth of some quarters and the decay of others, the city moves over the centuries three miles to the east? These examples raise no very troublesome metaphysical questions (no doubt the identity of the city, as Hume suggested in another context, consists in a continuous web of spatial relationships uniting the changing physical components of the city). But they do make it difficult to regard the proper name 'Moscow' as an arbitrary noise associated, by linguistic fiat, with an object, Moscow, which exists in the world and can be individuated without the exercise of any linguistic capacity (as Nixon and the child's mother can). For surely a Martian, or even a forest Indian from Brazil, if he had never before encountered or heard tell of civilised men, would have to have a great deal explained to him before he could grasp the significance of a proper name such as 'Moscow'. He would have to grasp, for example, that 'Moscow' is not just the name always assigned to the chief place where the wandering tribe of Muscovites happens to have settled for the moment and where its leaders are to be found by traders, emissaries or marauding enemies. He would have to grasp that the area within which a man may say 'I am in Moscow' includes the areas of application of subordinate place names: that a person does not cease to be in Moscow because he or she is in Red Square or in the Cathedral of St Basil. All such distinctions are in a commonplace sense 'conventional': it is hard to see why we should not regard them as representing *linguistic* conventions. But now the meaning of 'Moscow' ceases to look like an arbitrary association between a noise and an object; it begins to look as though its meaning could be fully grasped only by someone who understood how to use it in sentences (we have come back in other words to the gravamen of Wittgenstein's objection to defining meaning by appeal to ostensive definition). Indeed, it looks as though only someone who knew how to use the word in sentences could have any idea of what sort of 'object' could be named by 'Moscow'.

Matters become more puzzling still if we turn to general names. 'Horse' clearly cannot stand for Arkle or Dobbin, or even for each and every horse, for in the first case it would then be merely a proper name, and in the second place merely a ludicrously common proper name. (A common noun, in other words, is not the same thing as a common proper noun.) What, then, can it stand for?

Answers of a sort to this question are given by the classical 'theories of universals': realism, nominalism and conceptualism. Nominalism holds that everything in the world is a particular thing. Conceptualism holds that the world contains 'general natures', or universals, as well, but that they are to be found only 'in the mind'. Sometimes this is put, as for example by Locke, by saying that universals are made by the mind; are 'the work of the mind'. And, finally, realism holds that universals as well as particulars exist, and that they exist 'outside', and independently of, the mind.

Little can be grasped from these bald conventional summaries, however. We shall do better to pursue the problem of what a general term stands for as it arises in the work of an actual philosopher. And here the obvious choice is Locke, not only because Locke more than any philosopher, grappling manfully with problems somewhat beyond him, reveals innumerable pitfalls by falling into them, but because in spite of, perhaps even because of this, he remains a very great philosopher whose thought on these topics continues to influence contemporary thought about language more than some of its authors may be aware.

3. Locke on words and ideas

'The use then of words', says Locke, 'is to be sensible marks of *ideas*, and the *ideas* they stand for are their proper and immediate signification.'[1] For, 'the comfort and advantage of society not being to be had without communication of thoughts, it was necessary that man should find out some external sensible signs, whereby those invisible *ideas*, which his thoughts are made up of, might be made known to others'.[2]

If 'the proper and immediate signification' of a word is an idea, then we must have some clear and unambiguous account of the nature of ideas before we can assess the value of Locke's theory of language. Unhappily, Locke is at his least luminous on this point. Ideas are the objects of thought.

Every man being conscious to himself that he thinks, and that
which his mind is applied about whilst thinking being the ideas that
are there, it is past doubt that men have in their minds several *ideas*,
such as are expressed by the words *whiteness, hardness, sweetness,
thinking, motion, man, elephant, army, drunkenness* and others . . .[3]

This does not get us very far. It suggests that thinking is not just a
conscious process, but a process *of which we can be conscious*, as I am
conscious, for example, of the separate notes in the song of the bird
singing just outside my window, and that ideas are the elements
which make up the perceived thread of thought, just as the separate
notes make up the perceived thread of song. Other things that Locke
says connect the having of ideas so closely with the having of
perceptions that it looks as though the *idea* of the bird's song must be
some shadowy image of the actual heard notes.

. . . our *senses*, conversant about particular sensible objects, do *convey
into the mind* several distinct *perceptions* of things, according to those
various ways wherein those objects do affect them. And thus we
come by those *ideas* we have of *yellow, white, heat, cold, soft, hard, bitter,
sweet,* and all those we call sensible qualities.[4]

But equally, according to Locke, ideas are what is 'expressed by the
words *whiteness, sweetness,* [etc.]'. What is expressed by a word is a
meaning, or a concept, and it is not obvious that the concept of
sweetness is at all the same thing as some shadowy recollection of the
taste of sugar which might pass through my mind when I was
thinking about going to make a cup of coffee, and so might reasonably
be thought to be one of the mental states which go to make up the
thread of my thoughts on that subject. One reason is that I can use
words intelligently without any images at all passing through my
mind. On such occasions my thought simply *is* the words I utter; what
makes them an 'expression of thought' (unlike words uttered by a
parrot, for example) being their coherence, originality and approp-
riateness to the matter under discussion, and not the fact that they
occur in temporal conjunction with some sequence of mental states
distinct from them.

A second, and from our point of view more fundamental, problem is
that, if ideas are 'distinct perceptions of things', or more likely some
kind of mental representations or images of such perceptions, they are
presumably perceptions, or representations of perceptions, of *particu-*

lar things. But, if so, they can hardly be identified with what is 'expressed by the words *whiteness*' and the rest, for what is expressed by such names is a general notion. A good deal of ingenuity since Locke's time has gone into elaborating 'image theories of meaning' which endeavour to show how entertaining a general notion might come to the same thing as having one or more mental images,[5] but our present business is with Locke, who is in any case the author of the fundamental ideas on which all this modern work builds.

4. Abstraction

Locke saw clearly enough that there was a problem about generality: 'since all things that exist are only particulars, how come we by general terms, or where find we those general natures they are supposed to stand for?'[6]

It is worth noticing, moreover, that the way in which he states the question commits him to answering it in accordance with the referential theory of meaning. Locke assumes, in effect, that a word acquires meaning by standing as a token or substitute for a thing. That assumption made, the problem of generality presents itself as the problem of finding a class of suitably 'general' things ('general natures', in Locke's phrase) for general names to go proxy for, since clearly they cannot stand for particular things.

Locke's thought from this point onwards can be roughly summarised as follows. When I characterise something by predicating a general term of it I do not, obviously, characterise it in detail. If I say of someone merely that he is a man, then so far I have not said what sort of man he is: whether he is fat or thin, sanctimonious or sardonic, red- or brown-haired, sick or well. What I have said about him is merely what could be said with equal truth of any man whatsoever. Locke's doctrine of abstraction and abstract ideas builds upon this obvious and indeed platitudinous thought. It needs only a little further development to extract from it the idea that what a general term such as 'man' stands for is what all men have in common; in other words that set of properties or predicates which we arrive at by deleting from ('abstracting' from) the descriptions of individual, particular men all those features which serve to distinguish individual men from one another. This residue of properties common to all men Locke calls the 'abstract idea' of a man. His theory of generality is that general terms acquire meaning by standing as tokens or substitutes for such abstract ideas.

> Words become general by being made the signs of general *ideas*; and *ideas* become general by separating from them the circumstances of time and place and any other *ideas* that may determine them to this or that particular existence. By this way of abstraction they are made capable of representing more individuals than one; each of which, having in it a conformity to that abstract *idea* is (as we call it) of that sort.[7]

In some places Locke is resolutely nominalist: 'All things that exist [are] particulars.'[8] Elsewhere he leans towards conceptualism: there *are* general natures, but they are somehow illusory or at least conventional in nature; they belong only to the human mind.

> ... it is plain, by what has been said, that *general* and *universal* belong not to the real essence of things, but *are the inventions and creatures of the understanding*, made by it for its own use, *and concern only signs*, whether words or *ideas*.[9]

Since Locke holds that ideas become general by being formed through the mechanism of abstraction, he must, if his conceptualism is to stand, hold that abstraction is a process operating upon collections of ideas of particular things. And this is what he does hold.

> For let anyone reflect and then tell me wherein does his *idea* of *man* differ from that of *Peter* and *Paul*, or his *idea* of *horse* from that of *Bucephalus*, but in the leaving out something that is peculiar to each individual, and retaining so much of those particular complex *ideas* of several particular existences as they are found to agree in.[10]

On this account of abstraction we begin with particular things – Peter, Paul, Bucephalus – and we likewise end, when abstraction is complete, with particular things: with those 'particular existences' that Peter, Paul and the rest have been 'found to agree in'. Indeed, in Locke's chapter 'Of General Terms', the word 'particular' recurs like a litany, or a talisman.

But the hypnotic repetition of the word 'particular' cannot disguise the essential incoherence of Locke's position. For how can two particulars 'agree in' respect of other *particulars*? If two particular things 'agree in' respect of something – or, to use a modern terminology, are similar in respect of something – then the something in respect of which they resemble each other must by that very fact be a property or feature which has more than one instance.

But the distinction between universals and particulars which Locke is here trying to explain away is, precisely, the distinction between things which have only one instance (are unique, or particular, or individual – things such as Winston Churchill, or Snowdon, or the Empire State Building) and things which can in principle recur and be manifested in many instances (things such as redness, or triangularity, or the property of being a man, or a horse).

Locke at bottom wishes to talk as if individual things such as 'Peter', 'Paul' or 'Bucephalus' were complex particulars constituted by, or made up of, collections of simpler particulars. Now, there is indeed some sense to be made of this, but not, unfortunately, the kind of sense which Locke needs. Peter is indeed in one sense a composite of particular things: namely, Peter's spatial parts – his arms, legs, head, hands and so on. But manifestly Peter cannot share components of *this* sort with Paul: science fiction or surgical miracles apart, Peter and Paul cannot 'agree in' possessing, for example, the same particular pair of legs. The kind of thing that they might, logically speaking 'agree in' is bowleggedness or blondness. But 'bowleggedness' and 'blondness' are names of properties and not names of individual things. That is, they exhibit precisely the puzzling characteristic of generality which Locke is trying to explain away.

5. Abstraction and simple ideas

Locke distinguishes between *simple* and *complex* ideas. He introduces the distinction as if it were a piece of descriptive introspective psychology:

> As simple *ideas* are observed to exist in several combinations united together, so the mind has a power to consider several of them united together in one *idea*, and that not only as they are united in external objects, but as itself has joined them. *Ideas* thus made up of several simple ones put together, I call *complex*; such as are *beauty, gratitude, a man, an army, the universe*; which, though complicated of various simple *ideas*, or complex *ideas* made up of simple ones, yet are, when

the mind pleases, considered each by itself as one entire thing, and signified by one name.[11]

Locke clearly intends this passage and others like it in Book II of the *Essay* as definitions, but all that they really accomplish is to offer examples of simple and complex ideas and to explain, trivially, that complex ideas are composed of simple ones while simple ideas are not, in that sense, composite. What is Locke's *criterion* of simplicity?

To discover this we have to turn to Book III of the *Essay*, which deals with language, where we find that 'The *names of simple* ideas *are not capable of any definitions*; the names of all complex *ideas* are';[12] and, later:

I think it is agreed that a definition is nothing else but the showing the *meaning of one word by several other not synonymous terms.* The meaning of words being only the *ideas* they are made to stand for by him that uses them, the meaning of any term is then shown or the word is defined when, by other words, the *idea* it is made the sign of and annexed to, in the mind of the speaker, is as it were represented or set before the view of another and thus its signification ascertained. . . .

. . . This being premised, I say that *the names of simple ideas*, and those only, *are incapable of being defined.* The reason whereof is this, that the several terms of a definition signifying several *ideas*, they can all together by no means represent an *idea* which has no composition at all; and therefore a definition which is properly nothing but the showing the meaning of one word by several others not signifying each the same thing, can in the names of simple *ideas* have no place.[13]

This gives us a clear enough criterion of simplicity and complexity for ideas: a complex idea is one, such as 'horse', the name of which can be verbally defined; a simple idea is one, such as 'blue', the name of which can not. It is, however, a linguistic, and not a psychological, criterion, and this, we shall see in a moment, is important.

Let us return to abstract ideas. The idea of Peter is presumably a complex one. I should therefore be able to describe Peter more and more minutely in terms of less complex ideas until I arrive at a description, no doubt a very long and complex one, couched entirely in terms of simple ideas. The same goes for Paul, so that the abstract idea corresponding to 'man' will presumably consist of just those simple ideas which recur in the description of Peter, Paul and every other man. If abstraction is a process operating upon ideas of particular things, simple ideas must all be ideas of particular things. And yet how could they be? Redness is presumably a simple idea on Locke's criterion of simplicity, for no verbal definition of redness can be given. And yet redness is not a *particular*. 'Red' is a general term and not a proper name.

A new problem now arises for Locke. If 'red' is a general term, as it clearly is, it must on Locke's account stand for an abstract idea. But how can there be an abstract idea of redness? An abstract idea is formed by omitting from the ideas of different particular things those features in which they differ. If we omit from the ideas of particular shades of red the features in which they differ, we shall be left with nothing: crimson and scarlet are simply themselves and simply different from one another; hence their status as shades of red cannot depend upon the possession of any abstractable common property.[14]

But there is more, and worse, wrong with the theory than this. Simple ideas are, for Locke, mainly sensory qualities: particular colours, tastes, sounds, smells, and so forth. But, if we simply try to list all the distinct kinds of basic sensation available to us, we find that the resulting lists are not unstructured lists. Simple sensations seem to divide up into general sorts, or categories of sensations. At the highest level of the resulting hierarchy are what are sometimes called the sensory modalities: colour, taste, sound, smell, touch.

The problem for a Lockian theory of generality[15] is that 'colour' is, just as much as 'red' or 'horse', a general term. According to Locke, therefore, 'colour' must correspond to an abstract idea, formed by omitting from the ideas of particular colours everything not common to them all. But think of the red, yellow and green of a traffic signal. All are colours, all are different. But there is no way of separating, even in thought, some 'feature' which makes each a colour from the 'features' which make each the particular colour – red, yellow or green – that it is. In this sense – that they defy abstractive analysis – colours are indeed simple.

6. Generality and resemblance

It seemed to Hume that Locke's nominalism could be saved provided we allow that particular things can *resemble* each other. On this view, as Russell pointed out in *The Problems of Philosophy*, resemblance becomes in effect the only universal. General ideas need now no longer be regarded as formed by 'abstracting' from the descriptions of a set of particulars all that is not common to them. Hume's own account of generality is that

> all general ideas are nothing but particular ones, annexed to a certain term, which gives them a more extensive signification, and makes them recall upon occasion other individuals, which are similar to them. . . .

> When we have found a resemblance among several objects, that often occur to us, we apply the same name to all of them, whatever differences we may observe in the degree of their quantity and quality, and whatever other differences may appear among them.[16]

In the second of these two passages Hume in effect drops the notion that a general name gets its meaning by standing for an idea, and explains meaning by simply describing how we attach a general name to all those particular things to which it applies: by noticing resemblances. This resolves Locke's difficulties over simple ideas. Two things, x and y, can resemble one another without their possessing any common feature or characteristic which can be clearly distinguished and separated by 'abstraction' from other features of x and y. Hence, scarlet and crimson count as varieties of red, and red and blue count as colours, not because they possess some abstractable common property, but because they resemble one another.

Seen from this point of view Hume's theory of generality can be taken as a theory about the constitutive mechanisms of language. Its thesis is that general names are essentially conventional labels for patterns of resemblance. 'When we have found a resemblance among several objects . . . we apply the same name to all of them . . . whatever other differences may appear among them.'

Will the theory do? One problem, obviously enough, is that many things which resemble men are not things which in ordinary English one would call 'men', but gorillas, squirrels, dogs walking on their hind legs, women,[17] children, mandrake roots, statues, cloud formations, queer outcroppings of rock, and so on. Of course, the resemblance theorist can retort that the resemblances which link *these* things to the sort of things we ordinarily call men are not at all the sort of resemblances he had in mind. They are not *essential* resemblances but accidental ones. Quite so, we reply, but which *are* the resemblances he had in mind? How do we tell resemblances which are essential from the point of view of determining the application of a general term from those which are not?

The resemblance theorist could answer – and it would be a very Humian answer – that at this point philosophy must stop. We all know how to apply the general word 'man', and so *a fortiori* we all know which resemblances to pay attention to when applying it and which to discount. It is the former set that he has in mind, and for us to claim that we do not know which set this is ('know', at least, in the half-conscious way characteristic of linguistic intuition, which makes its possessors sure-footed in actually *using* language, but tongue-tied when it comes to saying how they achieve such sure-footedness) is merely to score a debating point.

This answer is in itself no more than a bald request to stop asking awkward questions. Certainly we know in practice how to apply a general name such as 'man'. Two competent speakers of English, acting independently of one another, will generally agree in applying the term to some things, denying it to others, and in identifying a third class of objects (for example, human bodies with robot brains installed by the sinister Dr No; members of lost tribes of Australopithecines or Neanderthalers) as dubious or uncertain cases for the application of the term. But how do they do it? What shared system of rules or criteria guides each competent speaker in making judgements about the applicability of general terms in his language?

The theory before us is that the competent speaker does it by noticing resemblances between things, and the objection to this is simply that this answer is insufficient as it stands to account for the capacity to apply general names. At the very least it requires some supplementary account of the difference between essential and accidental resemblances.

The idea that the meaning of a general term corresponds to an essence, or a set of essential attributes, is, of course, a very ancient one. It is one that we can neither quite dispense with nor accept at face value. And, once again, the simplest way of approaching the difficulties which it raises is by way of Locke's discussion of the topic.

7. Locke on essences

'*Essence*', says Locke, 'may be taken for the being of anything whereby it is what it is.'[18] The idea behind this definition is that, whereas some

of the properties of a thing are properties which it could lose without
ceasing to be a thing of that sort, others – the essential ones – are not.
A man may cease to be ignorant without ceasing to be a man, but he
cannot metamorphose into a pig, say, without ceasing to be a man.
Locke elswhere speaks of knowing the essences of things as knowing,
for example, 'what are the alterations which may or may not be in a
horse or *lead*, without making either of them to be of another species.'[19]

The phrases 'making . . . to be of another species' and, 'whereby it
is what it is' are of course ambiguous. Locke may be taken as meaning
that the essence of a thing of a given sort is literally what *makes* it a
thing of that sort, as the structure of the atoms in a sample of gold
makes them atoms of gold and not copper. Or he may be taken as
meaning that the essence of a thing is what enables us to recognise or
to classify it as a thing of that sort. In practice he wavers between
these two senses, a fact which accounts for a good deal of the difficulty
of grasping what exactly his doctrine of essence is.

At certain points Locke is ready to equate essences with the
contents of abstract ideas:

> it being evident that things are ranked under names into sorts or
> *species,* only as they agree to certain abstract *ideas* to which we have
> annexed those names, the *essence* of each *genus* or sort comes to be
> nothing but that abstract *idea* which the general or *sortal* (if I may
> have leave to call it from sort as I do *general* from *genus*) name stands
> for.[20]

Abstract ideas, as we know, are formed by removing (abstracting) all
those properties of a set of particular things which merely concern and
define their concrete particularity. But it is we – human beings – who
in the first place assemble the collection of particulars upon which this
operation is performed. Presumably we shall normally assemble such
collections with regard to our own convenience and not with regard to
the 'essences' of things in the metaphysical sense: those mysterious
and largely unknown inner virtues which, according to Locke, *really*
'make things what they are'. And so, just as the collections of
individuals upon which abstraction is performed will reflect human
convenience and convention rather than the nature of reality, so will
the contents of the complex ideas (abstract ideas) which the process of
abstraction yields.

Locke has here hit upon a version of nominalism which is all his
own. Nominalism in the ordinary sense is simply the view that there

are no universals, only particulars. If this is right then the only thing which unites the particulars to which men choose to apply a general term is the fact that men choose to apply that general term to them. If we chose to call mountains, milk vans and bicameral legislatures 'horses', then horses they would be, along with Arkle and Dobbin. Although some nominalists, including Hobbes, have explicitly maintained this view, I think it is obviously absurd. The view towards which Locke's theory of essences seems to be carrying us is more complex and subtler. It is that the application of a general term to a particular is not itself arbitrary. It depends whether that particular exhibits the properties essential to a given genus or sort, which is to say whether the particular corresponds to a given abstract idea. But the question of whether a given property forms part of the essence of a sort (whether a given idea enters into the corresponding abstract idea) *is* settled by pure, arbitrary convention: it depends upon how we selected the particulars upon which the abstractive process which yielded the abstract idea in question was performed.

It is this tendency in Locke which is often identified as conceptualism.[21] And certainly it would give a clear sense in which universals could be regarded as 'the work of the mind' or as 'existing only in the mind', if it were not for the difficulties about giving accounts of concepts in terms of abstraction, of which the ones concerning simple ideas which we canvassed earlier are a sample.

Locke, however, was not himself wholly happy with this position, for reasons which we shall find it worthwhile to examine. He thought it worked well enough for a class of general names which he called, for reasons which need not detain us, 'names of fixed modes'. The complex ideas corresponding to such general names '*are* not only *made* by the mind, but made *very arbitrarily*, made without patterns, or reference to any real existence'.[22] One of Locke's examples is 'murder': 'For what greater connexion in nature has the *idea* of a man, than the *idea* of a sheep, with killing, that this is made a particular species of action, signified by the word *murder* and the other not?'[23] No connection at all, Locke wants his readers to say: the only thing which links the idea of a man and the idea of killing under a simple general term, 'murder', is the term itself; or, to put it another way, the arbitrary linguistic convention that that term shall stand for that combination of ideas. An equally arbitrary connection might yield, say, 'ovicide' for the killing of sheep.

And yet, Locke thought, not all general names are like this: arbitrarily chosen noises standing for arbitrarily chosen combinations of ideas. The names of substances, such as 'gold', for example, 'carry with them the supposition of some real being, from which they are taken, and to which they are conformable'.[24] Whereas the linking of the ideas of man and of killing under the general name 'murder' is arbitrary, Locke thinks, the linking of the ideas of yellowness, ductility, malleability, metallic lustre, solubility in *aqua regia*, and so on, under the general name 'gold' is not: these ideas 'have an union in nature'.[25]

The notion of 'having an union in nature' is, like so much else in Locke, ambiguous as it stands. It can be taken, epistemologically or ontologically. Epistemologically speaking, what 'natural union' amounts to is the fact that the characteristic properties of a substance such as gold are observed in nature (that is to say, quite independently of human wishes or conventions) 'always joined and existing together'.[26] In other words, whenever we find, in nature, a piece of heavy, yellow, lustrous metal of a certain characteristic appearance, we invariably find that it also turns out on investigation to be malleable, ductile, soluble in *aqua regia*, and so on.

But from an ontological point of view the existence of an epistemological union of properties implies, in Locke's view, a deeper union. It implies the existence of a hidden occult essence which *accounts for* the observed or epistemological union. This occult essence Locke refers to as the *real essence* of gold. The collection of characteristic properties by which we recognise gold and which, although they have 'an union in nature' have only an epistemological union in nature, Locke calls the *nominal essence* of gold.

We know, Locke thinks, few real essences. The geometrical specification of a triangle as a three-sided plane figure is a real essence, because it can be shown to entail all the properties of such figures. And, almost paradoxically, we can know the real essences of mixed modes, simply because there is nothing beyond the artificial and conventional union of ideas in them to be known about such abstract ideas as that of murder. But in general, throughout the entire field of our empirical knowledge, we know nominal and not real essences; and, although Locke toys with the idea that the advance of physical knowledge — knowledge of the 'minute constitutions' of things — may bring some change in our fortunes on this point, he does not toy with it to any great purpose, since it is clear that a real essence, to satisfy his demands, would have to offer a logically exhaustive and rigorously deductive explanation of the 'natural union' of the characteristic properties of a substance.

3

General Names and Particulars

1. Sortal hierarchies

I shall disregard the metaphysical implications of Locke's theory of essences, historically interesting though these are, and consider it simply as a theory of language. Locke's view is that an essence, whether or not the properties which compose it have 'an union in nature', is a simple, unstructured list of properties. This is most certainly not a view of merely historical interest: indeed, it all but exhausts presently available wisdom on the subject. Very many contemporary philosophers write and talk as if to know the meaning of a general name (to possess a sortal concept in Locke's sense of 'sortal') were to know a list of characteristic properties which things of that sort possess. The main difference between Locke's account and present-day discussion is that most contemporary philosophers following – or, rather, assigning – a certain interpretation to Wittgenstein's remarks on 'family resemblances' would deny that a thing need exhibit *all* of the properties corresponding to the name of a given sort, in order to be a thing of that sort. The concept of a game, for example, it is commonly said, covers a very large number of different sorts of activity. There need be no common property which *all* these activities possess and in virtue of possessing which they are all games, provided that there is a list of properties some large *selection* of which a thing must possess to be a game. The selections will overlap, of course, and no doubt by tracing out these overlaps anything which we call a game can be connected *via* other sorts of game with anything else that we call a game. But there need be no one property common to all.

There is indeed a sense in which this Wittgensteinian[1] position does evade both realism and nominalism. It is anti-realist because it holds that there is no *one* property or relationship linking all the particulars which fall under a given universal. It is anti-nominalist because it denies that there is *nothing* which connects the particulars in question but the fact that the same general name is applied to each and every one of them. Nominalism of this extreme sort makes the use of a general name seem quite arbitrary, which it clearly is not. But, although the application of a general name is not arbitrary, it is not possible to identify the rule according to which it is applied by reference to a common property. In fact, it is not possible to identify the rule according to which it is applied otherwise than simply by showing how the word is actually used. We can give examples of games, and show in detail how they resemble other examples of games; and children by attending to such explanations come in fact to use the word 'game' much as their parents do. But here we must repose all explanation, as Wittgenstein somewhere remarks, upon 'a shared response'. We know that a child has understood the word 'game'' because it uses it, and goes on using it, as we do. And if we want to know what relates examples of games to other examples of games we can look at the detail of concrete cases. And that is the end of the matter.[2]

Perhaps philosophy does stop here. But an obstinate worry remains, connected with the problem about linguistic creativity which we canvassed in chapter 1. Granted that different speakers manage to achieve 'a shared response', *how* – by reference to what criteria – do they achieve it? And here we must ask ourselves whether a sortal concept can really be equated with an unstructured list of properties. I think it cannot, for a quite simple reason. Even if we knew of a list of properties which contains only the properties common to each and every thing to which a given general name N applies, we still should not know enough to enable us to set about actually applying N to anything, for we should still now know of what *sort* of thing the listed properties were supposed to *be* the characteristic properties.

An example will make clear what I mean. Imagine a Martian, who, being a philosophical Martian with an affection for the eighteenth century, has set out to learn English on strictly Lockian principles. In his notebook opposite the word 'gold' he has scribbled down a list of properties: yellowness, metallic lustre, malleability. He has also noted that these have 'an union in nature', and that what this means is that they occur frequently conjoined in our experience. He now sets out to look for samples of gold, and enters a valley where, over a space of an hour, he very frequently encounters metallic lustre (in the iron pyrites staining the rocks of the valley wall), yellowness (in the shape of the buttercups on the valley floor) and malleability (the resin on the boles of the pine trees). He writes in his diary, 'The valley contains gold.' Where has he gone wrong? The three properties were repeatedly conjoined in his experience in the valley, at least in the sense that they recurred in exactly the same set of relationships to each other and to other things; and that is all that Locke's account requires.

What is missing is an account of the *sort* of 'union in nature' which the properties in the list must exhibit if they are to be taken as jointly characterising a sample of gold. There is nothing occult or arcane about such an account: we can give it simply by saying that in English 'gold' is the name of a *kind of stuff* and not, as the Martian supposed, the name of a combination of environmental circumstances.

It is worth noticing carefully what we have done in thus supplementing Locke's account. We have specified a class of objects, *kinds of stuff*, which can be regarded, logically and grammatically, as particular things. We can speak, for example, of '*a* kind of stuff', 'the kind of stuff you mentioned this morning', '*the particular* kind of stuff in question', and so on.

Many logicians and philosophers have noticed that the relationship between universals and other universals is analogous to the relationship between particulars and universals. Thus Strawson:

> thinking of different hues or colours as bright or sombre, thinking of different human qualities as amiable or unamiable, is analogous to thinking of different particulars as characterized in such-and-such ways. In all these cases we think of universals collecting other universals in ways analogous to the ways in which universals collect those particulars which are instances of them or are characterized by them.[3]

But the analogy is no more than an analogy. Gold, we feel like saying, can be *thought of as* a particular, but it is not a real particular, such as *this lump of gold*. Perhaps, following a long logical tradition, we can locate real particulars as things which do, or might, bear proper names. I can call my sword Excalibur, or nine standing stones the

Nine Maidens, or a hurricane Enid, but it would be very odd to call gold Arthur on the ground that it is a particular (viz. a particular kind of stuff). Perhaps we can call such particulars *quasi-particulars*. It is not easy to see what exactly makes the difference between a real particular and a quasi-particular, but it has something to do, I think, with the fact that a quasi-particular is a particular not *in its own right*, as it were, but only by courtesy of a higher sortal. We can grasp the sense in which gold can be regarded as a quasi-particular only by reference to a further sortal concept of higher generality than *gold*: to wit, *kind of stuff*.

With respect to the identification of quasi-particulars, sortal concepts rank themselves into hierarchies. Thus, pink is a *shade* of a particular colour (red). Red is a particular *colour*. Colour is a particular *sensory modality*. Now, if there is any sense to be made at all in ordinary English of the claim that words acquire meaning by standing for objects 'in the world', then the 'objects' for which general names stand are quasi-particulars. Red is the name of a colour; gold is the name of a kind of stuff; *Rumex sativa* is the name of a species, and so on.

But this creates difficulties for Locke's whole conception of philosophical analysis. Locke held that the meanings of general terms could ultimately be explicated by reference to particulars in the ordinary sense of 'particular'. There is, he thought, no problem about identifying particulars: we are simply directly acquainted with them: 'All things that exist [are] particulars'. The problem is to find a *perspicuous* way of relating the meanings of general terms to the knowledge of particular things which is fundamental in Locke's epistemology; a way, that is, which enables us to show clearly that, and why, sortal concepts have no real existence but are simply 'the work of the mind'. This is the problem which the doctrine of abstraction is supposed to solve.

But, if general names name quasi-particulars, and if we can identify a quasi-particular only by appeal to the meaning of another general name of higher generality, then Locke's programme of explicating the general in terms of the (genuinely, i.e., proper-namable) particular falls to the ground. The direction of analysis of the meanings of general names is not, it seems, from the general to the particular, but from the general to the still more general.

The reasons why Locke failed to see this are interesting. First of all, he confuses the linguistic and the metaphysical senses of 'essence'. He confuses the 'essence' of gold in the sense of what really accounts for the 'natural union' of its properties, with the 'essence' of gold in the sense of what criteria enable us to distinguish things to which the word 'gold' applies from things to which it does not apply. Thus, if it occurs to him that to give a list of characteristic properties is not an adequate way of specifying the essence of gold, he locates the inadequacy in the fact that such a list does not give the *real* – the metaphysical – essence of gold, and not in the fact that such a list is in itself inadequate to determine the reference of 'gold'. And, secondly, he confuses questions of meaning with questions of epistemology. Because he supposes that the meaning of a word is the idea for which it stands, he supposes than an inquiry into the nature and content of meanings is a psychological and epistemological inquiry into the causal origins of ideas. The empirical process of discovering the properties of gold is indeed a process of discovering first one property and then another, as our experience of working with metals advances. Without benefit of a developed science of physical chemistry, what is produced by this process is simply a disorganised heap, or list, of empirically discovered properties. But that does not mean that our *concept* of gold is, or could be, a list of properties.

2. Natural kinds

If Locke's position seems incoherent, however, the position from which we have just been attacking it seems at first sight no less so; for what we seem to be saying is that in order to understand any general name we have to understand a further general name of higher generality. In order to understand what 'red' means we have to understand that 'red' is a colour name, and so we have to have grasped the meaning of 'colour'; in order to understand the meaning of 'colour' we have to have grasped the meaning of 'sensory modality', and so on. This is surely absurd, because it, just like radical nominal- ism, though in a different way, makes language unlearnable. There must be some point at which language is put into relationship with the world: at which the meanings of words are explained not by reference to other words but by reference to reality; and at that point it must be possible to define at least some general terms simply by indicating those features of the world for which they stand.

The implication of this argument is that some features of the world are general features; that we are simply acquainted in our experience with universals, or, as an old-fashioned but graphic terminology would put it, with *natural kinds.* Thus, we find Russell in 1912 defending this sort of realism about universals on grounds very similar to those we have just raised.

> It is obvious ... that we are acquainted with such universals as white, red, black, sweet, sour, loud, hard, etc., i.e. with qualities which are exemplified in sense-data. When we see a white patch, we are acquainted, in the first instance, with the particular patch; but by seeing many white patches, we easily learn to abstract the whiteness which they all have in common, and in learning to do this we are learning to be acquainted with whiteness.... Universals of this sort may be called 'sensible qualities'. They can be apprehended with less effort of abstraction than any other, *and they seem less removed from particulars than other universals are.*[4]

3. Logically proper names

Names for natural kinds can be learned before we learn any other names, or any other language at all. (They possess this property *ex hypothesi*, of course; we postulate the existence of natural kinds simply in order to have a way of explaining how language-learning could get started.) It follows that it is not necessary, in order to know the meaning of such a name N, that the natural kind which N designates should be characterisable or describable by means of language; except, of course, by means of such sentences as 'This is an N', and so on.

But now names for natural kinds begin to look suspiciously like proper names (the italicised passage in the above quotation shows that Russell entertained the same suspicion). In section 1 we suggested that the difference between the quasi-particulars which general names stand for and genuine particulars (particulars which can be the bearers of proper names) is that a quasi-particular can be identified only by appeal to the meaning of a general name other than the one which stands for the quasi-particular in question. But of course it might be objected that there is a sense in which I can only identify the particular which bears a given proper name provided I know that that particular is characterisable by one or more general names. Before I can identify the bearer of the name 'Nixon' I have to know that 'Nixon' is the name of a man; before I can identify the bearer of the proper name 'Enid', I have to know that Enid is the name of a hurricane; and so on.

What is correct about this objection, I think, is that, even to learn the meaning of a proper name, I have to know something about the role which names of that kind play in language. I have to know that it can only be used again to designate the numerically identical object which it was introduced to designate; that mere similarity to that object is not a sufficient condition for its application. And I have to know what kind of object a given proper name is intended to designate. But at least the object which a proper name designates is not *completely* identified by appeal to the meaning of general names. Once I know that Enid is the name of a hurricane, I want to know *which* hurricane, and this is not a question which can be settled by appeal to the meanings of general names. It is a question of empirical fact that Enid is the name given to the hurricane which formed on or about 26 July 1954 off the Bahamas and struck the coast of Panama on the night of 28 July.[5] On the other hand, once I have identified the object (the quasi-particular) which 'gold' designates as a kind of stuff (which involves appeal to the concept *kind of stuff*), all I can do in answer to a demand to know *which* kind of stuff, is to refer the inquirer to the meaning of 'gold'. Quasi-particulars seem to have their whole being situated within the corpus of human linguistic convention.

General names, proper names and names of natural kinds seem, in fact, to rank themselves in descending order from the point of view of the degree to which we must appeal to the meanings of terms and to linguistic convention in general in assigning them a meaning. The name of a natural kind can be regarded as a pure proper name. Before I can identify the bearer of the proper name 'Nixon' I need to know that 'Nixon' *is* a proper name and that the object which it designates is an object of a certain sort. This is stage 1 in the identification of the bearer of a proper name. Once I have settled the linguistic questions which arise at stage 1, I can proceed to stage 2, at which no linguistic questions arise. At stage 2, identifying the bearer of the name 'Nixon' is simply a matter of being able, most of the time at least (we can all be fooled some of the time by CIA men in disguise), to tell him from other men.

The name of a natural kind, now, resembles a proper name which has managed to slough off stage 1 in the identification of its bearer. To locate the object, O, which a natural kind name, N, designates, I do not have to know that any general term ('man', 'colour', 'kind of stuff') other than N applies to O; I do not even – and this makes the learning of natural-kind names even more mysterious than the account which the theory of natural kinds was designed to replace – have to have any grasp of the way in which N is or may be used in the construction of sentences. I just have to be able, most or all of the time, as a matter of empirical fact, to distinguish O from other natural kinds.

Someone who arrives at the idea of a natural kind, as we have just done, as a way of explaining how it is possible for language learning to get started, need not suppose that a natural kind *cannot* be characterised by any general term other than its name. All that is needed to satisfy his theoretical requirements is that some general names should have objects of reference which can be specified without appeal to the meaning of any other general name.

However, philosophers have had other reasons for postulating the existence of natural kinds. Locke, for example, in order to demonstrate that the mind is a passive recipient of information from the senses, wished to show that the meanings of all names of complex ideas can be exhaustively explained in terms of the meanings of simple ideas, and that names of simple ideas can be given no verbal definition or explication at all, but can be defined only by indicating the simple sensory ideas for which they stand. On this view a simple idea cannot be described, it can only be named. It cannot be described, because *ex hypothesi* it is one of the ultimate, simple objects by reference to which all complex ideas are specified: if it could be specified in its turn by a description, it would not be simple in this sense.

The idea that there are simples – objects which can be named but not described – has a long subsequent history in philosophy. Russell, for example, is committed to assuming the existence of simples by his distinction between knowledge by acquaintance and knowledge by description. He argues (1946, ch. 5) that 'we have *acquaintance* with anything of which we are directly aware, without the intermediary of any process of inference or any knowledge of truths',[6] and that I can acquire knowledge of something by description only if the description in question can ultimately be rephrased in terms which refer to objects with which I am acquainted. 'Every proposition which we can understand must be composed wholly of constituents with which we are acquainted.'[7] Objects of acquaintance must thus be simples, things capable of being named, but not in themselves describable.

This implication becomes manifest in the account of proper names and 'logically proper names' which Russell gave at this period. Ordinary proper names, he thought, are disguised descriptions. When I refer in a sentence to Bismarck, I am ordinarily not referring to a particular with which I am acquainted. In such a case, Bismarck is known to me by description and not by acquaintance, and hence the name 'Bismarck' could be replaced in the sentence with a definite description: 'The late German Chancellor', or something of the sort. Real proper names must denote particulars with which I am directly acquainted. The only words which Russell is prepared to admit as meeting this exacting requirement are the demonstratives 'this' and 'that', when they are used under very special circumstances. They must be being used to denote a simple sensation, say a white patch, which I am actually apprehending at the moment when I use the demonstrative expression. If the white patch is a piece of chalk which I am holding, then, if I use 'this' to mean 'this piece of chalk', I am still not using 'this' as a real proper name (logically proper name) for in that case 'this' does not stand for an object of acquaintance, it does duty for a description: 'the piece of chalk I am holding'. But, if 'this' is used to denote the bare experience of the whiteness of the chalk, it is being used as a genuinely, or logically, proper name.[8]

Logically proper names are, according to Russell, names of particulars. It is not altogether clear whether Russell thought that names of simple sensible qualities such as whiteness or redness are also logically proper names. Certainly he wished to say that 'red' is a predicate name, and that understanding the name of a predicate, even a simple predicate name such as 'red', is not the same thing as understanding a proper name, for Fregian reasons having to do with the conception of predicate names as incomplete symbols.[9] But Russell certainly thought, as we saw earlier, that 'simple sensible qualities' are objects of acquaintance, and that seems to entail that they are simples in the sense of things namable but not describable. Indeed, the view that qualities such as redness are *ineffable* – that we can convey the nature of redness not by any verbal description or characterisation, but only by showing samples of redness – goes back to Locke, and seems, indeed, to be trivially true.

Epistemological theories which postulate the existence of simples and philosophies of language which postulate the existence of natural kinds are often combined in the thought of particular writers. Indeed, the idea that natural kinds must exist in order to explain how language learning can get started has often seemed to provide a powerful additional (i.e. non-epistemological) argument for the existence of simples.

But the theory of natural kinds, far from saving the possibility of language learning, makes it harder than ever to understand. Natural kinds were introduced as putative denotata for general terms. But in fact a natural-kind name, if such a thing were possible, would be analogous not to a general name but to a proper name. Locating the reference of even a proper name, in the ordinary sense, however, involves, as Russell correctly saw, an element of description. I cannot identify the bearer of the name 'Nixon' unless I know that 'Nixon' is the proper name of a man. With names of natural kinds, as with Russellian logically proper names, all description is ruled out. Names of natural kinds exhibit, in short, *only* those features of proper names which discriminate proper names from general names. That in itself is enough to show that the referent of a general name cannot be a natural kind. Indeed, it is difficult to see how one could introduce names for simples or natural kinds into a natural language, simply because the theoretical specification of such entities seems to rule out the possibility of identifying them for purposes of communication. We cannot make it clear to each other which entity a word picks out unless we can in some way or other describe the entity in question. All naming implies description.

II

Meaning and Truth

4

Sense, Reference and Truth

1. Word meaning and sentence meaning

The meaning of a sentence depends, obviously enough, on the meanings of its component expressions. It is natural enough, therefore, to suppose that words are the primary bearers of meaning.

Few contemporary philosophers, with the recent exception of Professor Hilary Putnam,[1] would accept such a view. Conventional wisdom is that the sentence is the primary bearer of meaning. This view is not entirely without its own brand of intuitive appeal, of course. Even if we suppose a sentence to be a combination of independently meaningful expressions, it is clear that the mode of combination at stake cannot be mere aggregation. A string of names – for example, 'John James Peter' – *asserts* nothing, communicates nothing, *about* the persons named. What a sentence *means* is, intuitively, what it affirms *about* whatever it is about: there thus seems to be at least one sense of 'meaning' which attaches peculiarly to sentences and not to names, or to any other of the various classes of expressions which enter into sentences. But why should we regard this sense of 'means' as the primary sense?

2. Frege on number

The best answer is an historical one. The ultimate source of the idea that the sentence is the primary bearer of meaning is the work of Gottlob Frege (1848–1925), a mathematician and philosopher of logic whose work received very little recognition during his lifetime, but who was *inter alia* the creator of much of modern formal logic.

Frege's work in philosophy and the foundations of mathematics had two main goals: first, to construct a 'conceptual notation', or *Begriffsschrift*, which would serve to clarify the notion of logical consequence in such a way that mathematical proofs could be expressed in an absolutely rigorous and consequential way, without suppressed tacit assumptions; and, secondly, to apply the language so constructed to a rigorous formalisation of number theory and arithmetic. The former enterprise produced the profound discoveries in formal logic upon which Frege's posthumous fame ultimately rests: the theory of quantifiers and variables and the modern theory of propositional operators. The latter produced, among other things, Frege's celebrated analysis of the concept of number in terms of classes and the notion of one-to-one correlation, and, consequentially, the logicist programme for the reduction of the axioms of arithmetic to truths of logic. Frege's philosophy of logic is a by-product of these investigations.

Frege's analysis of the concept of number is presented in his first major work, *The Foundations of Arithmetic* (*Die Grundlagen der Arithmetik*, 1884, English trans. 1953).[2] The argument of the *Foundations* falls roughly into two parts. The first half of the book, up to about section 45, attacks various views on the nature of number and the nature of arithmetical propositions. The second half, from section 45 to the end, develops Frege's own theory.

The theories of the nature of number which Frege attacks (and demolishes, at least in the form in which he attacks them) include the theory that number is 'a property of external things' and the theory that it is 'an object for psychology'. Number is not a property of things 'on a level with colour and shape', for, among other reasons, whereas I can choose how to divide up an object for the purpose of numbering its parts or aspects, I cannot choose whether to regard it as blue or square. But, on the other hand, number is not something merely ideal, something, in Berkeley's phrase, 'entirely the creature of the mind'. For, once we have decided under what aspect we wish to number something, we are no longer free to determine what number we shall give it. Hence 'The botanist means to assert something just as factual when he gives the number of a flower's petals as when he gives their colour.' Number is objective in a sense in which what is objective can be distinguished from 'what is handlable or spatial or real'. The axis of the earth, the equator and the centre of gravity of the solar system are objective in this sense, although, says Frege, we 'should not call them real in the way the earth is real'.[3] A concept is in one sense a mental construction, but once we have constructed it – if the work of construction has been properly done – questions about the objects which fall under it are nevertheless factual questions. 'We often speak of the equator as an *imaginary* line; but it would be wrong to call it an imaginary line in the dyslogistic sense; it is not a creature of thought, the product of a psychological process, but is only recognised or apprehended by thought'.[4] The equator, in other words, may be an imaginary line, but we cannot determine *by imagination*, for instance, whether the ship we are travelling on has crossed it or not.

One can see from this that for Frege the process of constructing a symbol is not, as it is for the Lockian abstractionist, merely a matter of assembling together elements already given in experience. For Frege, symbolic construction is an active and creative process. In 'On the Scientific Justification of a Conceptual Notation', one of his essays in defence of the *Begriffsschrift*, he maintains, rather obscurely, that the formation of symbols frees us from our dependence upon sense impressions and memory images, and concludes, 'Symbols have the same importance for thought that discovering how to use the wind to sail against the wind had for navigation'.[5]

The obscurity of this, however, is sufficiently dispelled, to my mind, by the detail of Frege's own conceptual constructions. One can see what he has in mind by looking, for example, at the analysis of the concept of number given in the *Foundations*. Frege begins with the idea that number is a property not of objects, nor even of groups, but of concepts:

> If I say 'Venus has o moons', there simply does not exist any moon or agglomeration of moons for anything to be asserted of; but what happens is that a property is assigned to the *concept* 'moon of Venus', namely that of including nothing under it. If I say 'the King's carriage is drawn by four horses', then I assign the number four to the concept 'horse that draws the King's carriage'.[6]

We now have the notion of a number as an object of a particular sort: namely, a property of a concept. What remains is to specify criteria of individuation for objects of this sort; as Frege says, to 'fix the sense [*Sinn*] of a numerical identity'. We need, in other words, a criterion for deciding when two concepts have the same number. This Frege constructs, following a suggestion of Hume's, by appeal to the procedure of one-to-one correlation: 'When two numbers are so combined as that the one has always a unit answering to every unit of the other, we pronounce them equal.'

Frege's actual development of the criterion is complex and elegant, and involves a theory of relational predicates in logic and the consequent reduction of one-to-one correlation to a set of purely logical relationships. It need not concern us here. For the moment, we need only notice a certain feature of the general strategy of the definition: namely, that Frege has not addressed himself directly to the definition of the term 'number' at all. What he has done is, in his own terms, to 'fix the sense' of propositions of the form 'The number which belongs to the concept F is the same as that which belongs to the concept G.'

The sense of such propositions is 'fixed', in essence, by giving a procedure – one-to-one correlation – which defines the conditions under which such propositions are true and false.

Quite early on in the *Foundations* Frege delivers himself of a pronouncement which has become a *locus classicus*, perhaps even the *locus classicus*, for the idea that sentences, not words, are the primary bearers of meaning. He gives a list of three fundamental methodological principles to which he promises to adhere throughout the ensuing discussion. The second of these 'fundamental principles' reads, 'Never ask the meaning of a word in isolation, but only in the context of a proposition.'

Why, exactly, is this such a fundamental principle? Wittgenstein considered it so important that he gives it a prominent position both in the *Tractatus* and in the *Philosophical Investigations*. And yet the grounds for its importance are not all evident or immediately obvious. Much clearly depends upon what Frege means, or is to be taken as meaning, at this point by 'the meaning of a word'. The German reads, 'der Bedeutung der Wörter'. *Bedeutung*, in terms of Frege's later distinction between *sense* and *reference*, is the term usually translated as 'reference'. But when Frege was writing the *Foundations* the distinction between sense and reference still lay in the future. For that reason it has been suggested by Michael Dummett[7] that *Bedeutung* in the *Foundations* could be taken as bearing the wider interpretation 'meaning'; so that Frege's dictum comes out as 'Never to ask the *sense* of a word in isolation, but only to ask it in the context of a sentence.'

But there are difficulties about this interpretation, which Dummett himself notices. A word must have a *sense* independently of any sentence in which it occurs, since otherwise how could we understand the thought expressed by some sentence we have never before encountered? Frege himself held, though admittedly not explicitly at the period occupied by the *Foundations*, that the sense of a sentence is the resultant of the sense of its component expressions, which must, therefore, be independent of their inclusion in any particular sentence. We are likely to gain a better insight into the importance of Frege's dictum, I think, if we take *Bedeutung* as bearing the meaning which it bears in Frege's later work: namely, the 'meaning' of an expression in the sense of what it *denotes* – what it refers to, or picks out, in the world. After all, the terms *Sinn* and *Bedeutung* both occur in the German text of the *Foundations*, and in clearly separated uses. We must turn, then, to Frege's explicit formulation of the sense–reference distinction in his celebrated paper 'Über Sinn und Bedeutung'.[8]

3. Sense and reference

Frege introduces the notions of sense and reference by considering pairs of descriptive expressions which uniquely specify the same object. The examples he gives are 'The Evening Star' and 'The Morning Star', and 'The point of intersection of *a* and *b*' and 'The point of intersection of *b* and *c*' where *a*, *b* and *c* are the lines connecting the vertices of a triangle with the midpoints of the opposite sides. The members of each pair of propositions denote, or refer to, the same *object*: respectively, a certain planet (Venus) and a certain geometrical point. The object in question is the *reference* of the expression. However, we must also take account, Frege says, of the 'mode of presentation' of an object by a given expression. The 'mode of presentation' is 'contained in' the *sense* of a sign. In Frege's four examples we have two distinct references, but four separate senses.

What is the connection between sense and reference, or, to put it another way, how can a sense 'present' an object to us? Each of Frege's examples is, or corresponds to, a uniquely identifying *description* of some object. The reference of the sign, therefore, is whatever object falls under that description. A sign picks out an object as its reference just in case some proposition which expresses the sense of the sign is true of that object. It is now clear why sentences have to be regarded as the primary bearers of meaning. Grasping the reference of a name or descriptive expression involves, for Frege, assenting to the truth of a proposition to the effect that a certain object falls under a certain description. Unless, therefore, we allow ourselves the prior possibility of formulating propositions, we cannot specify the 'meanings' of terms in the sense of specifying the objects for which they stand.

We can now see the force of Frege's overall strategy in the *Foundations*. Numbers, as one category of objects, constitute the referents of such expressions as 'nine', 'The number of the planets', and so on. Once we have some settled, public procedure for deciding the truth or falsity of propositions asserting numerical identities, and only then, we can attach a precise reference to each such expression: we can say, for example, that the expression 'The number of the planets' picks out the number nine as its referent. Frege's criterion, constructed in terms of the notion of one-to-one correlation, gives us such a procedure. We can thus define the expression 'Number', and the names of individual numbers, not by relating them directly to our experience of external things or to 'ideas' or other mental contents, but by giving a public criterion by means of which we can determine the truth or falsity of sentences in which such terms occur.

4. The objectivity of sense

It is important to Frege's position that the procedures by which we pass from apprehending the sense of an expression to apprehending its reference should be *public* in the sense of being common to all speakers of a language. He distinguishes the 'idea' which a painter, a horseman or a zoologist may connect with the sign 'Bucephalus', and which will be different in each case, from the sense of the sign, which 'may be the common property of many [persons] and therefore is not a part or mode of the individual mind'. And a page later he says,

> The reference of a proper name is the object itself which we designate by its means; the idea, which we have in that case, is wholly subjective; in between lies the sense, which is indeed no longer subjective like the idea, but is yet not the object itself.

The reason he gives in 'On Sense and Reference' for requiring that senses be public and common to all speakers of a language is, however, obscure. It consists solely in the laconic remark that 'one can hardly deny that mankind has a common store of thoughts which is transmitted from one generation to another'.

Fortunately we can obtain further light on the force of this gnomic aphorism if we turn to Frege's theory of 'thoughts' and 'incomplete symbols', in, for example, the essays 'What is a Function?'[9] and 'Thoughts'.[10]

An important plank of Frege's philosophy of mathematics, and his philosophy of language, is his account of functional expressions as 'incomplete' or 'unsaturated' signs. A functional expression such as 'X^2', for example, designates nothing until we 'complete' it by replacing the symbol X with a numeral, which we call the argument sign. If, for example, we choose '2' as the argument, we complete, or saturate, the function sign and obtain the expression, '2^2', which designates a number, 4. Frege's theory of logical generality rests upon the insight that we can treat predication as essentially functional in this sense, and as involving saturated and unsaturated signs. In the sentence 'Socrates is bald', we can distinguish an unsaturated predicate expression '—— is bald' and a proper name, 'Socrates', which saturates, or completes, the predicate expression to give a *complete thought*: the thought that Socrates is bald.

Only a thought – the sense of a completed predicative function expression – can have a truth value. 'Socrates' clearly cannot be either true or false, and neither can '—— is bald', as long as it remains a mere unsaturated function sign. And, conversely, only the senses of sentences which can be true or false are thoughts. Sentences which express commands, questions, 'exclamations in which one vents one's feelings' have senses, but these senses are not thoughts. A thought is the sense of a sentence 'in which we communicate or assert something'.[11]

The connection which Frege here sketches between the concept of a thought and the notion of communication is, I think, something more than a mere turn of phrase. Thoughts – the senses of sentences – are what we affirm and deny in argument. It is essential that different speakers attach the same thought to the same sentential sign, otherwise they will not be disputing about the truth or falsity of the same propositions, and neither argument nor the common pursuit of truth will be possible.[12] A thought is not, unlike trees, stones and houses, part of the material furniture of the world. But nevertheless it must, like a tree, be capable of 'being presented to people as identical'.

The publicity of sense – the status of senses as public objects accessible in common to all the speakers of a given language – is thus, for Frege, a necessary precondition of the possibility of argument and the common pursuit of truth. For, if we must ascribe such a status to the special category of senses which Frege calls thoughts, clearly we must assign it to all senses, since the sense of a sentence – the thought – is the resultant of the senses of the subordinate expressions which make up the sentence.

We can now grasp the full force of Frege's maxim, 'Never to ask the reference [*Bedeutung*] of a word in isolation, but to ask it only in the context of a sentence.' The only way of specifying the reference of a word 'in isolation' is to associate it with some object of immediate sensory acquaintance, in the manner of a Russellian logically proper name. But any such specification will be private, and accessible only to the person who makes the association, unless he can find some way of identifying the object of acquaintance in question in such a way that it can be unambiguously located by other speakers. But how can he do that unless he can describe the object of acquaintance, by availing himself of some sentence the sense of which is clear to, and the same for, each of them? In Frege's thought, in other words, the primacy of the sentence as the fundamental bearer of meaning and the publicity of sense are intrinsically connected as preconditions for the common pursuit of truth.

5. Meaning and truth

The effect of these arguments is to forge a strong connection between the concept of meaning and the concept of truth. A speaker grasps the sense of a sentence when he grasps what must be the case if the sentence is true. Any feature of the meaning of a sentence which does not affect its truth or falsity is assigned by Frege not to its sense but to its *Beleuchtung* ('illumination', 'shading', 'tone').

Nevertheless, Frege was not a verificationist. He does not, that is, hold that we grasp the sense of a sentence when we see *how to establish* its truth or falsity. The meaning of a sentence is not, for him, defined relative to any particular procedure of investigation; rather, the relevance of a particular procedure of investigation to the truth or falsity of a particular sentence is established by appeal to the truth conditions of the sentence. He distinguishes 'the grasp of a thought – thinking' from 'the acknowledgement of the truth of a thought', and says, 'An advance in science usually takes place in this way: first a thought is grasped, and thus may perhaps be expressed in a propositional question; after appropriate investigation, this thought is finally recognised to be true.'

Let us review Frege's doctrine on sense and reference as we have stated it so far. A complex name, or denoting expression, such as 'Plato's teacher', has a sense and picks out a reference. Its reference is an *object*, in this case a particular man, Socrates. Likewise, predicate expressions – incomplete or unsaturated symbols – and complete sentences have senses. The sense of a descriptive sentence is a thought. But do incomplete symbols and sentences have reference? On both these points Frege has an opinion which is clear enough in itself, but which in each case leads to difficulties over which an enormous amount of ink has subsequently been spilt.

6. Concept and object

Frege says that the reference of an incomplete symbol is a *concept*, and that the reference of a sentence – or at least, of a sentence which expresses a thought – is a truth value, either truth or falsehood (Frege says, 'The True' and 'The False').

Because of the part which the notion of a concept plays in the *Foundations*, it is essential to Frege to maintain a radical distinction between concepts and objects. Objects are the referents of proper names. Only one object can be designated by each such name. More than one object can fall under a concept, however; that is why a concept such as '*moon of Venus*' or '*horse drawing the King's carriage*' can have a number: the number is the number of objects forming the extension of the concept.

Concept signs, Frege holds, can become names of objects by being conjoined with a deictic expression or the definite article: 'This horse . . .', 'The horse that carried Napoleon at Austerlitz . . .', and so on. But in that case they are no longer functioning as concept signs. Moreover, a concept sign does not become a proper name merely because its extension happens to comprise exactly one object. 'Moon of earth', for example, is a concept sign and not a proper name.

What are we to say, however, about counter-examples such as the one raised against Frege's thesis by the mathematician Benno Kerry: 'The concept *horse* is a concept easily attained'?

What Frege actually says in discussing this example is that the expression 'The concept *horse*', because it contains the definite article, refers not to a concept but to an object: is, in short, logically speaking a proper name. But this, while it is in itself a move consistent with Frege's general position, forces him to maintain the apparent (and perhaps real) paradox that 'the concept *horse* is not a concept, whereas, e.g., the city of Berlin is a city, and the volcano Vesuvius is a volcano'.[13]

One paradoxical consequence of saying this is that when we try to state the reference of expressions such as 'The referent of *horse*' we find ourselves baffled by an apparent unwillingness on the part of the words we use – the only words we *can* use – to say what we intended them to say. In this respect there is a radical asymmetry between proper names and concept signs. It makes perfectly good sense to say, for example, '"The referent of *Socrates' teacher*" stands for an object', but not, it seems, to say '"The referent of *horse*" stands for a concept'; for, on Frege's view, the expression 'The referent of *horse*' must stand not for a concept but for an object.

These difficulties might seem to suggest strongly that we should simply abandon as unworkable the Fregian distinction between complete and incomplete symbols. But matters are not as simple as that. Frege gives the following reason for maintaining the distinction: 'not all the parts of a thought can be complete; at least one must be "unsaturated" or predicative; otherwise they would not hold together'.[14] If we take two names for objects, in other words, and put them side by side, thus,

$$a\ b$$

nothing is asserted; moreover there is not even any reason why we should suppose that the two signs belong together as forming part of a single complex sign. They are not, therefore, elements of a single thought, and there is no sense in which we could be justified in attaching either the value 'true' or the value 'false' to their conjunction. The possibility of attaching truth values to linguistic expressions, in other words, depends on the maintenance of the concept–object distinction in some form or other; any adequate theory of language must, therefore, embody some form of the distinction, and preferably explain how such a distinction is possible.

Gilbert Ryle put his finger on the essence and the importance of this insight in speaking (1971, p. 58) of

Frege's difficult but crucial point that the unitary something that is *said* in a sentence or the unitary sense that it expresses is not an assemblage of detachable sense atoms, that is, of parts enjoying separate existence and separate thinkability, and yet that one truth or falsehood may have discernable, countable and classifiable similarities to and dissimilarities from other truths and falsehoods. Word meanings and concepts are not proposition components but propositional differences.[15]

And yet, although keeping hold of this insight seems to require us to make a radical distinction between names and sentences, Frege treats sentences as names. 'Every declarative sentence concerned with the reference of its words is . . . to be regarded as a proper name, and its reference, if it has one, is either the True or the False.'[16]

7. Truth values as referents

The reasons Frege gives for making this move are not in themselves particularly hard to follow. He considers the alternative possibilities[17] (1) that the thought is the reference of a sentence, and (2) that a sentence has no reference, but only a sense. Proposal (1) is defective, because the replacement of one expression in a sentence by another expression having the same reference but a different sense clearly ought to have no effect on the reference of the sentence, for we shall still, presumably, be talking about the same object, only now presented under a different concept. And yet, clearly, if the reference of a sentence is the thought it expresses, such a move would change the reference of the sentence, since it would change its sense.

Proposal (2) likewise collapses. It is clear, Frege says, that there are some sentences which have sense but no reference. 'Odysseus was set ashore at Ithaca while sound asleep' is one such. The sentence has no reference because :'Odysseus' has no reference. Because 'Odysseus' lacks a reference, Frege thinks, we cannot 'seriously' raise the question whether the sentence is true or false. We can 'neither apply nor withhold the predicate' to an object which does not exist. But that shows that what interests us about the sentence is not merely the thought which it expresses: *that* remains the same whether Odysseus exists or not. If we are concerned with the truth or falsity of the sentence, however, we have to 'advance from the sense to a reference':

in this case the reference of the sentence. But, since this drive towards the identification of a reference for the sentence, as well as a sense, arises only when we raise the question of the truth or falsity of the sentence, it is clear that the reference which the sense of a sentence 'picks out' or 'presents' can be nothing other than a truth value.

This curious and rather tormented argument does, if we accept it, make it very hard to understand the relationship between the component expressions of a sentence. How can a name for an object and a name for a concept possibly join hands to yield a complex proper name for a truth value? And what becomes of the insight that a sentence cannot be an aggregation of names?

Conditions On the other hand, Frege's account of the sentence does give added force to the claim that the meaning of a sentence is its truth value. On Frege's view, a sentence expresses a complete thought, which picks out a definite truth value as its reference when we have grasped the sense and the reference of each of the component expressions of the sentence. The sense and reference of component expressions are thus both to be grasped in terms of the difference they make to the truth values of the sentences in which they occur. And it is because what we say must ultimately be brought before the bar of truth and falsehood that the words we utter have a publicly ascertainable meaning, the same for all speakers of the language.

Frege's general account of sense and reference as public requires that a given expression possess the sense and reference which it possesses independently of who utters it, and of the particular context in which it is uttered. If the sense and reference of a sentence depended upon the identity, the intentions or the circumstances of a particular speaker, both sense and reference would have to be explained afresh upon each new occasion of utterance (and how could they possibly be explained, if the speaker could not rely upon any sentence having a publicly accessible sense and reference?). If the meaning of a sentence is to be identified with its truth conditions, therefore, it must be possible to state those truth conditions in a fully general way which makes no reference to particular speakers or to particular contexts of use.

8. Proper names

This requirement leads to a number of familiar difficulties (see chapter 7, section 1) when we attempt to apply it to natural languages, which we shall have occasion to consider in a subsequent chapter. One of them involves the reference of ordinary proper names: for example, proper names for persons. Knowing the reference of a proper name does involve knowing to whom a particular speaker intends to refer by that name. Different speakers may even refer to the same person under the same proper name, and not know that they are referring to the same person, because they each identify the person in question by appeal to different descriptions. If Leo Peter knows a good deal about Dr Gustav Lauben, but does not know that he was born on 13 September 1875 in N. N., while Herbert Garner knows nothing about Dr Lauben *except* that fact, then, Frege is prepared to say (1977, p. 12), 'as far as the proper name "Dr Gustav Lauben" is concerned, Herbert Garner and Leo Peter *do not speak the same language*' [my italics].[18] This, I think, shows clearly how closely, for Frege, the requirement that the sense and reference of sentences be determinable independently of context is bound up with the concepts of communication and truth, and these latter two concepts with each other.

9. *Truth and communication*

Recent philosophy of language has witnessed a fundamental cleavage of opinion between those who think, with Frege, that meaning is to be understood in terms of truth conditions, and those who do not. The two sides are generally held to divide over the question of whether language is to be regarded primarily as an instrument for expressing truths or as a medium of social interaction. Chomsky, although he has argued in recent controversy against the idea that these alternatives are exclusive, or that there is no common ground between their supporters, acknowledges the existence and the *prima facie* force of the division in the following terms (1976, pp. 56–7):

> [Searle] claims that language has an 'essential purpose', communication, and regards my denial of this claim as counter to commonsense and implausible. It is difficult to argue about common-sense. There is, in fact, a very respectable tradition . . . that regards as a vulgar distortion the 'instrumental view' of language as 'essentially' a means of communication, or a means to achieve given ends. Language, it is argued, is 'essentially a system for expression of thought'. I basically agree with this view.[19]

Strawson has put the division in stronger and more explicit terms.

> I want . . . to discuss a certain conflict, or apparent conflict, more or less dimly discernable in current approaches to these questions. For the sake of a label, we might call it the conflict between the theorists of communication-intention and the theorists of formal semantics. According to the former, it is impossible to give an adequate account of the concept of meaning without reference to the possession by speakers of audience-directed intentions of a certain complex kind. . . . The opposed view, at least in its negative aspect, is that this doctrine simply gets things the wrong way round or the wrong way up, or mistakes the contingent for the essential. Of course we may expect a certain regularity of relationship between what people intend to communicate by uttering certain sentences and what those sentences conventionally mean. But the system of semantic and syntactical rules, in the mastery of which knowledge of a language consists – the rules which determine the meanings of sentences – is not a system of rules *for* communicating at all. . . . It would be perfectly possible for someone to understand a language completely . . . without having even the implicit thought of the function of communication. . . .
>
> A struggle on what seems to be such a central issue in philosophy should have something of a Homeric quality; and a Homeric struggle calls for Gods and heroes. I can at least, though tentatively, name some living captains and benevolent shades: on the one side, say, Grice, Austin and the later Wittgenstein; on the other, Chomsky, Frege, and the earlier Wittgenstein.[20]

Later Strawson adds,

> It seems to me that there is only one type of answer that has ever been seriously advanced or developed, or needs to be seriously considered, as providing a possible alternative to the thesis of the communication-theorist. This is an answer which rests on the notion of truth-conditions.[21]

One ought to pause, I think, before accepting Strawson's conscription of Frege to the camp of the 'theorists of formal semantics'. Of course, in a sense he obviously belongs there. Who else, after all, invented the idea that the meaning of a sentence is to be identified with its truth conditions? But does he not also belong, with equal right, in the opposing camp? Frege's account of the relationships between sense, reference and truth is essentially and inextricably bound up, as we have seen, with his belief that argument and the common pursuit of truth are possible only if a given linguistic expression has the same sense and reference for every speaker of the language: in short, only if genuine communication is possible.

As I have tried to show in chapter 1, this founding principle of Frege's philosophy of language has considerable intrinsic force. The possibility of communication does seem to require that there should be some sense of 'meaning' in which any competent speaker of a language is able to read off the same meaning as any other speaker from any well formed sequence of signs constituting an utterance in that language: idiosyncratic readings are not *read off from* but *read into* the linguistic sign, and what is read into a sign is not something communicated by that sign.

It is the work of Frege's genius to connect this insight with the concept of truth: to see that the possibility of rational debate about truth and falsehood requires the objectivity and publicity of sense.

But, if we also make that Fregian connection, what becomes of Strawson's 'Homeric struggle'? Perhaps, indeed, a way lies open by which the opposition between theorists of communication-intention and theorists of formal semantics may be transcended.

In Part IV I shall try to show that this' is indeed the case. Meanwhile, we must address ourselves in the next six chapters to the large and substantial body of work which falls into one or other of Strawson's opposing camps. Part of what we have to see is how and why the partitioning of theoretical alternatives which Strawson records has come to seem both exhaustive and inevitable.

5

Meaning and Verification

1. Truth and knowledge

Frege, as we have seen, held a realist theory of the relationships between truth and meaning. He held, that is, that the truth conditions of a sentence are to be understood as the conditions which obtain *in the world* if, and only if, the sentence is true.

To some philosophers, this view has seemed altogether too realistic for its subject matter. Sentences have meaning, after all, not absolutely and in themselves, but *for speakers*. Frege's realism appears to leave open the possibility that we, as speakers, may simply be unable to determine whether the conditions which justify the assertion of a certain sentence obtain or not. But then, if knowing the meaning of a sentence involves knowing its truth conditions, how could we ever come to know, by studying the use made of it by our fellow speakers, the meaning of the sentence in question? In short, as Michael Dummett has recently observed (1976), Frege's realism about truth conditions seems to be inherently at odds with his belief in the objectivity of sense:

> On a realist theory ... we must say ... that a grasp of the sense of a name consists in a knowledge of what has to be true of a given object for it to be the bearer of the name; and, since the condition to be satisfied by the object may be one our apprehension of which will transcend our capacity to recognise, in special cases, whether or not it obtains, an understanding of the name, as so conceived, will not, in general, be something that can be fully manifested by the use of a name.[1]

SIC

Dummett argues, on these grounds, for the revival of a theory of meaning embodying some version of verificationism. Whatever we may think of the prospects for such a revival, I think Dummett has here put his finger upon a potent reason for the perennial attractiveness of verificationism. For what more natural way of evading the dilemma which Dummett sketches than by dropping Frege's realism about truth conditions while keeping to an objective conception of sense? The shift simply involves reinterpreting the phrase 'the truth conditions of *p*' so that we take it to mean, not 'What conditions must obtain in the world if, and only if, *p is true*', but 'What conditions must be met, if, and only if, we are to be *justified in asserting p.*'

2. The verifiability criterion

Such arguments seem to offer strong *prima facie* support for the Verifiability Criterion – advanced in the 1930s, with revolutionary enthusiasm, as the key to all philosophical problems, by Schlick, Ayer, von Mises and other members of the Vienna Circle, and often expressed as the slogan 'The meaning of a statement is its method of verification.' Nevertheless, verificationism is not an easy theory to defend.

The Verifiability Criterion can function either as a theory of meaning, or as a criterion of meaningfulness (or, as its supporters often put it, of 'empirical meaningfulness', or 'cognitive content').

If we are to take it as a theory of meaning, we must take the slogan 'The meaning of a statement is its method of verification' at its literal face value. Sentence meanings just *are* verification procedures. To explain the meaning of a sentence just *is* to give an account of some appropriate verification procedure, and *vice versa*.

It is in this version, however, that the theory of verifiability seems most easily refutable. It does not seem to be the case either that in explaining how to verify a statement I necessarily explain the meaning of any corresponding sentence, or that in order to explain the meaning of a sentence I need explain how to set about verifying any corresponding statement. For example, I may teach someone who knows no English, and no chemistry either, how to do qualitative chemical analyses. He is very quick and accurate, and he learns how to perform standard sequences of chemical procedures, and to write down in a notebook, depending on how the procedures turn out, English sentences such as 'The sample contains ferric oxide', 'The sample contains some aluminium salt', and so on. My pupil thus knows, and can even carry out with perfect accuracy, verification procedures appropriate to a large number of statements, and moreover knows, in the sense that he can write down, corresponding English sentences. But, knowing neither chemistry nor English, he does not know the meaning of what he writes, nor even that he is writing down sentences.

Conversely, the fact that we can give no empirical verification procedure for a sentence such as 'God loves the world' does not seem *prima facie* to offer any impediment to explaining its *meaning*. Theology offers us explanations in abundance. God is that being whose existence is prior to, and the ground of, all other existence; who is a person, but is nevertheless in a mysterious sense also three persons; who created the world *ex nihilo*; who loves it in a way analogous to human love, but not to be equated with any love of which human beings are capable; and so on.

It is open to toughminded people to object, of course, that such 'explanations' of meaning do not *explain*, but merely bandy words. There are, it seems to me, three ways of supporting such a claim, only one of which has a direct connection with the Verifiability Criterion, although all three are often taken for 'verificationist' arguments. Still, they will serve as an introduction to the discussion of the Verifiability Criterion in its second role, as criterion of meaningfulness.

The first argument is that theological explanations such as the above merely define one term of art – 'God' – by appeal to other terms of art, without ever showing how any of these terms are, to use William James's metaphor, to be cashed at the bank of experience. The argument clearly will not do as it stands. It fails to make explicit what sort of 'cashing' in terms of experience is demanded. Terms and phrases such as 'person', 'world', 'creation' – even 'ground of', or '*ex nihilo*' – clearly carry *some* reference to 'experience', in some sense of what is, after all, in itself a fairly nebulous term. Why is this degree of connection with experience insufficient to bear the weight of their present, theological use? The various formulations of the Verification Criterion in the 1930s and 1940s were in essence attempts to meet this objection to a more traditional, more vaguely formulated empiricism about meaning, by stating the precise nature of the connection between language and experience required in order for a statement to be 'literally' or 'cognitively' meaningful. But, as we shall see in a moment, these attempts met with no very striking success.

The second argument is that a description of God such as the one given above is meaningless because it is formally self-contradictory. And, indeed, one can derive a formal self-contradiction from, say, the doctrine of the Trinity, if one makes the assumption that the theologian is using the term 'person' in its ordinary sense. But of course he is not: he is using it in an 'analogical' sense, for he is speaking of what theologians call a 'mystery'.

The third argument attacks the notion of 'mystery' by appeal to which we have just dismissed the second. Surely, to say that a term of art has a 'mysterious' or 'analogical' meaning, distinct from that of the everyday term upon the ordinary use of which it is founded, but distinct from it in ways which are not precisely specifiable, is merely to choose a roundabout and obfuscatory way of saying that it has no meaning at all.

3. *The projection of meaning*

Attractive as this argument is, it is founded, I think, upon a misconception about language; but a profound misconception – one which goes to the heart of a perennial empiricism about meaning which has taken many forms in philosophy, and of which verificationism is only one modern expression. The theologian who believes in the possibility of 'analogical' senses of 'loves' or 'is a person', in which these predicates may be ascribed to God, believes, after all, only the following not very surprising or scandalous propositions.

(1) The same term may have different senses, which are related semantically to one another, even though they pick out different references or extensions (in the case of 'love', for example: fraternal love, parental love, erotic love, friendship, love of place, platonic friendship, courtly love, and so on).

(2) Someone who has once grasped the meaning of a term through acquaintance with its application in one or two of its possible senses can later recognise and assent to the propriety of its use in other senses (for example, someone who has encountered the concept 'love' only in connection with erotic love, platonic love and ordinary friendship can recognise courtly love, when he later encounters it, as a form of love), even though he could not have predicted beforehand that such an extension of the term would be possible.

(1) and (2) seem in fact, once stated, to be truisms. The meanings of most terms are, we might say, *projective*. That is, by applying the term in a new way to some set of phenomena quite distinct from the set in connection with which its meaning was first established, we can give it a new sense and reference which are distinct from, and yet related to, the original sense and reference; so that the new sense appears as an enriching of a concept which we already possessed, rather than as marking the introduction of a wholly new concept.

It is very hard to see how the meaning of a term *can* have this potential for new applications inherent in it. In fact, the existence of such projective potential constitutes one of the central problems of the theory of meaning (though it is seldom recognised as such) and we shall return to it in later chapters. But the phenomenon itself is too common and familiar for its existence to be denied.

It is to this essentially commonplace and familiar phenomenon of the projectivity of meaning that the theologian appeals in speaking of 'analogical' meanings. The orthodox theologian believes that God's love, if it were within our comprehension, would be recognisable to us as love; but that it is not within our comprehension, any more than courtly love was within the comprehension of a Greek of the fourth century BC. Thus, the belief that God loves the world, though it may be false, or rather vain (there may just be no God), is not *meaningless* or vacuous because 'love' is intended analogically.

4. Verifiability and nominalism

There are two philosophical doctrines which if they were true would each rule out the projectivity of meaning. Both, in various ways, contribute to the attraction which verificationism possesses for many minds despite repeated refutation.

The first is radical nominalism, the doctrine that the different particulars picked out by a general name have nothing in common beyond the use of that name to refer to them. The other is the notion that the 'content' of what we assert cannot possibly go beyond the 'content' of some suitably chosen set of statements expressing the evidence which entitles us to assert it.

One of the difficulties about attempting to criticise this second doctrine is that it is hard to find a clear and precise way of stating it (we need, for a start, clearer notions of 'content' and 'equivalence of content', and these may, if certain arguments of Quine's are correct, be unobtainable). However, it seems to presuppose an ideal picture, or model, of the workings of language, which can be fairly clearly stated. According to this ideal picture, a language contains words which express logical or syntactic relationships ('or', 'but' ,'if', and so on) and also 'content-bearing' expressions. Each of the latter is defined by reference to some simple feature of experience, and bears the meaning acquired in this way, and only that meaning, in all subsequent contexts of use.

Such a conception of language is not, of course, strictly speaking, nominalist. The features of experience which content-bearing expressions denote are no doubt recurrent features. Therefore, there must be something which entitles us to speak of such a feature, when it recurs, as *the same one* which figures in earlier recurrences. Whatever entitles us to speak in this way of *the same* feature also entitles us to use the same content-bearing expression to denote it in all its recurrences, and that content-bearing expression thus becomes a general name. But that is as far as generality goes. All that can ever license the application of a given general name is the recurrence of precisely that simple feature of experience by reference to which it was originally defined. There can be no question of extending the empire of generality by 'projecting' or extending the sense and reference of general names, and hence no possibility that a general name could have a meaning which could not be explained by direct reference to presently accessible experience of the user. The notion of 'transcendent' or 'analogical' meaning – the notion that it might be possible to refer to realities going beyond what we experience, or can envisage experiencing – simply collapses.

The doctrine that the content of what we say cannot exceed the content of the evidence we have for saying it is thus profoundly nominalist in spirit. It aims at restricting the scope of generality in language, and in the formation of concepts, to the greatest extent consistent with avoiding the absurdities of radical nominalism itself.

5. Meaninglessness and cognitive content

Bearing this in mind, let us return to the Verifiability Criterion in its role as criterion of empirical meaningfulness, and let us assume for the moment that the notion of a statement's having a verification procedure is intuitively clear. If we apply the criterion rigorously, now, the proportion of ordinary discourse which must be dismissed as strictly meaningless becomes so great as to strain credulity. If we are sufficiently toughminded, and if we possess the good debater's blessed insensibility to the inwardness of an opponent's position, we may be able to sleep easy with the proposition that everything that metaphysicians and theologians have ever said has been strictly senseless; but can this really be so of all moral judgements, all novels and all poetry, with the possible exception of those footnotes of Wordsworth's which deal with such matters as water levels in the River Wye?

Again, as we noticed earlier, there are the propositions of logic and mathematics, which can in a sense be 'empirically verified', but which do not derive their truth from empirical verification, and thus, presumably, do not derive their meaning from it either.

Verificationists have generally not chosen to grasp these nettles, preferring to restrict the scope of the Verifiability Criterion once more, from a criterion of meaningfulness in the strict sense to a test of 'whether a sentence expresses a genuine empirical hypothesis'.[2] Logical and mathematical statements, on such a view, are 'analytic' or 'tautologous', which means, according to the account Ayer gave in 1936, that 'they do not make any assertion about the empirical world, but simply record our determination to use symbols in a certain fashion'. Poetry and moral discourse, similarly, can be admitted to the category of meaningful discourse, but denied 'empirical meaning' if we take their function to be that of expressing, say, 'feelings', or prescriptions or injunctions, or persuading, rather than that of describing what, as William P. Alston drily remarks, 'in this connection is quaintly called "the world"'.[3]

Summary divisions of linguistic labour of this sort abound in positivist writings. Many philosophers, and non-philosophers, have found them implausible, without always being able to say clearly why they are inadequate. It makes a good debating point to apply the conventional positivist trichotomy to the Verifiability Criterion itself. Is it an empirical assertion or an analytic one? Either choice seems beset with difficulties for the verificationist.

The fundamental defect of the Verifiability Criterion is not, however, to my mind either that it can give no adequate account of its own logical status, or that it commits us to inadequate accounts of literary or moral discourse, or of necessary truth. The real difficulty is that it offers an inadequate account of ordinary descriptive and scientific discourse.

There are clearly some statements which are immediately verifiable in the sense that their truth can (at least *in principle*: no verificationist wishes to dismiss as meaningless statements which are only *in practice* unverifiable) be ascertained by direct observation. Let us call these *observation statements*. In this rough and intuitive sense, 'The Albert Memorial is a Gothic edifice' is an observation statement, while 'An electron carries a negative charge' is not. It is tempting, now, to suppose that we can proceed to define verifiability for any statement in terms of some logical relationship between that statement and one or more observation statements.

In the event, however, the exact nature of the required relationship has proved very difficult, if not impossible, to specify.

One's first impulse is to say that a statement, S, is verifiable if, and only if, its truth can be conclusively established by observation; that is, if and only if there exists some finite set of observation statements, $O_1, O_2, O_3, \ldots O_n$, the joint truth of which logically entails the truth of S.

But, formulated in this way, the criterion proves too strong. It excludes, for example, all statements expressing general laws, and statements employing both universal and existential quantifiers, such as, 'For every poison there exists some antidote', since no statement of either kind can be deduced from any finite set of observation statements. For similar reasons it will not work, either, to formulate the criterion in terms of the notion of complete falsifiability in principle. Such a criterion would exclude such perfectly sensible, if probably false, existential hypotheses as 'There still exists at least one dodo in Madagascar'.

It seems natural to turn from this attempt to a weaker version of the criterion; one which requires, not that observation should be sufficient to *conclusively* establish the truth or falsity of S, but only that some observation should be *relevant* to the truth of S'. It will not do, however, to stipulate simply that a statement is verifiable if and only if it implies some observation statement. We want statements about the theoretical entities of physics – for example, 'An electron carries a negative charge' – to emerge as empirically meaningful, but such statements entail observation statements only when taken in conjunction with a great many other statements.

Intuition thus suggests some such formulation as the following one of A. J. Ayer's (1946, p. 38):

It is the mark of a genuinely empirical proposition, not that it should be equivalent to an experiential proposition, or any finite number of experiential propositions, but simply that some experiential propositions can be deduced from it in conjunction with certain other premises without being deducible from those other premises alone.[4]

But in this version the criterion is far too liberal. It admits any statement at all, by some variation on the following argument:

(a)   If monads possess no spatial extension, then the Albert Memorial is a Gothic edifice.
Monads possess no spatial extension.
Therefore, the Albert Memorial is a Gothic edifice.

In the Introduction to the second edition of *Language, Truth and Logic*, Ayer admits the force of this objection, and proposes a further modification to the criterion, which consists, in effect, in restricting the range of permissible supplementary premises to statements which are either analytic or can be shown independently to be verifiable in the sense of the modified criterion.

This, indeed, excludes supplementary premises such as the one in (a), but the stable turns out to have many other doors. The revised criterion admits any conjunction of the form $S \cdot N$, where S satisfies Ayer's criterion and N is a sentence which the criterion is supposed to exclude. And Alonzo Church, in a brief review of *Language, Truth and Logic*,[5] provides an elegant demonstration that, given three observation statements such that no one of the three, taken alone, entails any of the others, it can be shown that any statement whatsoever, or its negation, is verifiable.

6. The phenomenalist turn

These arguments are, historically, the ones which made verificationism unfashionable. But they strike one nevertheless, I think, as curiously *technical* objections. They leave intact, of course, the equation of knowledge of sentence meanings with knowledge of truth conditions upon which the appeal of verificationism is partly based. But, even discounting that, they do not seem to diminish much the intuitive plausibility of equating knowledge of truth conditions with knowledge of verification procedures. There remains, even after one has fully understood the conventional counter-arguments, a satisfying clarity and simplicity about the idea that to know the meaning of a sentence is to know how to *operate* with respect to it, and with respect to things in the world, in determining the truth or falsehood of the corresponding statement.

Besides, it seems arguable, at least, that the conventional criticisms bear as much on a truth-functional conception of logical consequence as on the verificationist account of meaning. Has the absurd argument (a), licensed by the truth-functional rule of inference $p \supset q \cdot p : \supset q$, any more significance, in short, than the equally absurd arguments licensed by the so-called 'paradoxes of material implication'?

What these doubts offer us, however, is not a way out for the verificationist, so much as a clearer view of the real nature of his predicament.

The theory of verifiability was originally intended as a way of specifying the *content* of a statement, and secondarily of distinguishing sentences with content from sentences with none (sentences which 'say something about the world', and so correspond to statements) from sentences which do not. If this is the verificationist's aim, then the relationship between observation statements and verifiable statements which are not, on the face of it at least, observation statements cannot indeed be a truth-functional one. It must be a very much stronger relationship: namely, equivalence of meaning, synonymy.

Such a requirement imposes, in its turn, severe restraints on what can be allowed to count as an observation statement. We cannot treat a sentence such as 'The Albert Memorial is a Gothic edifice' as an observation statement, that is, even though it satisfies the common-sense requirement that the truth or falsity of an observation statement should be ascertainable by direct observation, because it contains terms such as 'Gothic' and 'edifice' the content of which – the content they contribute to the statement, that is – needs to be specified in observational terms. Verificationism as a programme of specifying the *content* of statements develops ineluctably, in short, into a programme of phenomenalist reduction. Such a programme requires the notion of what Ayer (who saw more clearly than some other members of the Vienna Circle the phenomenalist implications of logical empiricism, construed as a theory of meaning) called 'basic propositions'. Basic propositions, in Ayer's words (1946, p. 10), 'refer solely to the content of a single experience . . . [so that] what may be said to verify them conclusively is the occurrence of the experience to which they uniquely refer'.[6] They are also incorrigible, in the sense that 'it is

impossible to be mistaken about them except in a verbal sense'
(ibid.).[7] The connection of these ideas with the quasi-
nominalist model of language mentioned in section (4) of this chapter,
and with the underlying intuition that the content of a statement
cannot exceed the content of the evidence for asserting it, is, I think,
clear enough.

Now, the difficulty with 'basic propositions' is that of formulating
them in a natural language.[8] Nothing that we can *say* about the world
is incorrigible in the required sense. Even if I try to confine myself to
describing the immediate character of my experience, I find that the
English words I am constrained to use possess a certain autonomy
which makes them more than arbitrary tags attached by convention
to recurrent stimuli. As cautious an assertion as 'This is red' may be
mistaken: the thing may only *look* and not *be* red; or I may mistake for
redness what most speakers of my language, and I myself under less
confusing circumstances, would call a shade of brown. It scarcely
seems possible to analyse 'red' in terms of still more 'observational' or
'basic' predicates; and the only remaining alternative is to attempt a
yet more cautious style of assertion: 'What I am now seeing (never
mind what it is) is what I choose at the moment to call 'red' (never
mind what colour it really is).' But this, far from giving us a sentence
the informational content of which is hard, basic and observational,
gives us a sentence with no content at all: a joke, or a logical parody of
informative discourse, though one not without the philosophical
interest which such parodies often have. To inform I must identify
what I observe; to do that I must use a language, and in committing
myself to the use of a natural language I take for granted the
possibility of grasping the meaning of well formed sentences in that
language, and hence *a fortiori* the meaningfulness of such sentences.
But then I also admit the possibility that a sentence which lacks, even
in principle, a verification procedure, may nevertheless possess a
meaning.

6

Logic and Ordinary Language

1. Formal semantics

By the early 1950s, the supporters of the Verification Criterion had for the most part transferred their attention to what has come to be known as 'formal semantics'. There is a sense in which formal semantics can be seen as representing a continuation of the thought of the Vienna Circle positivists. But this relationship is generally obscured because, naturally enough, the approach to the problem of meaning through the construction of formal, set-theoretic languages is very often presented as a way of avoiding the errors of verificationism.

Let us return again to Frege's dictum: knowing the meaning of a sentence is knowing what is the case if it is true. Verificationism is, in effect, an attempt to apply Frege's insight on a sentence-by-sentence basis. For each different (meaningful) sentence which can be formulated in a language, there will be, verificationists hope, a distinct verification procedure which will account for the meaning of that particular sentence.

Thus, even if verificationism were in other respects an adequate theory, it would give us no account of the semantic relationships between propositions. For instance, it would not explain, to borrow an example from Davidson,[1] why 'Grundy was a short basketball player' implies, 'Grundy was a basketball-playing man', but not 'Grundy was a short man'.

The attempt to account for semantic relations of this sort, while maintaining the Fregian doctrine that the meaning of a statement is to be equated with its truth conditions, yields the programme of formal semantics. The object of formal semantics is to understand relationships of truth and reference in natural languages by constructing formal languages which offer rigorously defined formal analogues of such relationships.

In setting up a formal language, it is customary to give precise definitions of the following elements.

(1) An array of primitive expressions, falling into one or more syntactic categories (for example, names, predicates).
(2) A set of formation or concatenation rules which allow us to combine the primitive expressions to form complex expressions, including sentences.
(3) A 'theory of truth' for the language. This tells us how to determine the truth conditions of any sentence which can be formulated in the language. Normally such a theory is formulated in terms of Tarski's notion of *satisfaction*;[2] that is, a functional expression such as 'x is white' is satisfied by a given object just in case the function becomes a true sentence when we replace the free variables in it by the name of that object. Thus, snow satisfies the sentential function 'x is white', because, as Tarski puts it, 'the sentence "snow is white" is true'. Further recursive procedures then allow us to specify the truth conditions of complex sentential functions, including sentences (in Tarski's terminology a 'sentence' is a sentential function without free variables), in terms of the satisfaction of simple sentential functions.

2. Formal and natural languages

Why, now, should it be supposed that the study of formal languages constructed in this way should, even in principle, throw any light upon the nature of meaning in natural languages? There are several reasons.

First, and most obviously, logic quite often does appear to explicate the meaning of expressions in natural language. The Frege–Tarski analysis of quantification in terms of individual variables and constants, for example, does seem to make clear what is implicit in the use of quantified sentences in ordinary language; and the same can be said, with certain well known reservations, of the truth-functional treatment of the logical connectives. To choose a more recent example, Donald Davidson's account of the logic of action sentences[3] seems, if it is correct, to throw light on the meaning of such sentences. Davidson's problem is in part to account for the inference from 'John walks in the rain' to 'John walks'. His solution involves the assumption that such sentences involve disguised quantification over events. Thus 'John walks' becomes '$(\exists x)$ (John walks x)', and 'John walks in the rain' becomes '$(\exists x)$ (John walks x and x is in the rain)', so that the inference from one to the other becomes a straightforward exercise in quantificational logic. The suggestion has elegance and a strong intuitive plausibility in its favour: logical ingenuity has here operated to make semantic intuition more precise, and in a sense also explain it.

In short, it seems as if logic in general can be regarded as formalising and making explicit certain features of ordinary language, and it can be argued that, so far as the use of language to make true statements is concerned, the features which can in this way be taken up into logic are the important ones. The aim of understanding meaning can thus seem best served by the effort to bring language piecemeal under the sway of logic.

Secondly, the idea that by giving a formal theory of truth for a language we thereby, and in so doing, give an account of meaning for that language is intuitively plausible in its own right. It is perhaps evident that the ability of native speakers of a language to interpret sentences which they have never encountered before must depend upon the application of some system of recursion rules or other. But it is not at all clear what sort of recursion rules these are, and how, and upon what, they operate.

The formal semanticist has an answer to these questions which has at least the merits of clarity and straightforwardness. His suggestion is that the recursion rules in question are of the relatively familiar kind employed in formal theories of truth. That is, they permit the truth conditions of complex sentences to be specified in terms of the truth and falsehood of simpler sentences, and ultimately in terms of truth and falsehood as applied to some set of basic sentences formulated in terms of the primitive expressions of the language, with or without some minimal use of logical operators.

A formal theory of truth thus looks as though it might well tell us what a speaker of a language needs to know if he is to be able to interpret any well formed sentence of his language; and that, as we have seen, is one way of formulating the central problem facing any theory of meaning.

There are two other major grounds for the *prima facie* attractiveness of such an approach. First, the alternative to a theory of meaning couched in terms of truth conditions and truth relationships seems to be a theory couched in terms of the notions of 'use' and 'rule of use', and these notions seem to many philosophers to be incurably vague and metaphorical, and to allow of explanation only in intuitive terms, which presuppose the ability to use a language, without throwing much light on the nature or foundations of such an ability. A formal theory of truth proceeds without appeal to such notions. At the most fundamental level the connection between the language and the world is made by assigning a denotation to each of its basic expressions. But such an assignment involves no appeal to 'rules of use', unless we regard the denotation of such an expression as itself a rule of use; and, once denotations have been assigned to the basic expressions, all other questions of meaning in the language are settled in principle by the recursive rules which assign truth conditions to its sentences.

3. Formal semantics and verificationism

Secondly, and perhaps most importantly, such an account of meaning seems to offer us a way of construing natural languages, particularly the language of science, which allows us to retain many of the insights of logical empiricism otherwise expressible only in terms of a verificationist theory of meaning, while apparently avoiding most of the errors of verificationism.[4] It allows us, for example, to single out the class of sentences which possess genuine empirical content as the class of sentences the truth conditions of which can be specified by means of a formal theory of truth adequate to some appropriate, and suitably formalised, fragment of a natural language; and it ensures the empirical status of such sentences by the manner in which denotations are assigned to the basic expressions of the formal language in question. At the same time, logical empiricism so formulated can get along without the dubious informal notions of a verification procedure, of analyticity, and of synonymy, not to mention the underlying commitment to a phenomenalist treatment of observation sentences: all of which, for the reasons we have examined, contributed to the downfall of the earlier, verificationist versions of logical empiricism. As a further bonus, it avoids the *a priori* rejection, so characteristic of 1930s logical positivism, of whole categories of sentences as meaningless or nonsensical. This it does by making the inquiry into the logical

structure and the empirical credentials of judgements a more modest
and piecemeal undertaking than it seemed to many of the writers of
the Vienna Circle. 'You will not find in semantics', says Tarski (1944,
p. 235), 'any remedy for decayed teeth or illusions of grandeur or class
conflicts. Nor is semantics a device for establishing that everyone
except the speaker and his friends is speaking nonsense.'[5]

It is perhaps hardly surprising that logical empiricism as a
philosophical outlook should turn out to be reformulable in this way.
One of its most fundamental features – more fundamental, I am
inclined to think, than the reductionism founded upon the twin pillars
of synonymy and analyticity stigmatised by Quine as dogmas of
empiricism – is, as we saw in a previous section, a commitment to
nominalism, or rather to what one might call *nominalising*: the endeavour to reduce as far as possible the range of operation of
generality in language. Formal semantics offers us the possibility of
realising this commitment in a new form. It is to be hoped we can
assign a single, constant and unchanging denotation to each of the
basic expressions of a language (perhaps in terms of recurrent
features of our perceptual experience: Quine's discussion of stimulus
meaning in *Word and Object* shows us how this might go). In so doing
we supply an interpretation for the basic sentences of the language.
Any resulting set of truth values for such sentences can now be
projected throughout the entire array of well formed sentences of the
language *via* the recursive criteria of satisfaction embodied in the
appropriate theory of truth. The result will be a language in which the
meanings of sentences stand in perfectly clear and perspicuous
relationships to truth conditions. And perhaps, once we have
achieved the required clarity in the artificial medium of a formal
language, a certain amount of luck and ingenuity will enable us to
bring at any rate the more cognitively important parts of ordinary
language into the plain daylight of logical rigour through the application of quite ordinary and well understood processes of logical
interpretation and regimentation.

4. Obstacles to regimentation

Ordinary language, complained Frege, is inherently vague and im-
precise, as contrasted with the clarity and precision of a formal
language. That may mean merely that it is not obvious at first sight
how we are to extract and formalise those features of language which

account for the validity of a given type of argument; that it requires, for example, great effort and a kind of genius to see that such sentences as 'Every man has some cause for rejoicing' can be represented logically in terms of the machinery of quantifiers and variables which Frege largely invented. Then, again, there are a wide variety of problems which arise when we try to equate the operators and sentence patterns of a formal calculus with propositions and arguments in ordinary language – the sort of problems ably dealt with in P. F. Strawson's *Introduction to Logical Theory*.

Besides these problems about the relationship of formal systems to ordinary language, however, there are certain specific obstacles which ordinary language opposes to the process of logical regimentation which arise in connection with Frege's doctrine of sense and reference, and which have exercised a very great influence upon the directions which the philosophy of language has subsequently taken. Frege held, as we have seen, that a sentence (a sentence expressing a Thought, that is) denotes, or picks out, a truth value, and that the truth value which it picks out is determined by its sense, which in turn depends upon the sense and reference of its component, or sub-sentential, parts.

Suppose that a sentence contains an expression which is apparently a proper name or a denoting expression (a compound expression containing the definite article or a deictic term such as 'this' or 'that') but which does not, in fact, pick out a specific, actually existing object in the real world. In this case we cannot assign any truth value to the sentence, neither the value 'true' nor the value 'false'. We seem, in these circumstances, to have the option of saying one or another of the following things:

(1) that the sentence has a clear sense but lacks a reference (a truth value);
(2) that there is a third truth value, distinct from the true and the false, which we might call the 'undecided'; or
(3) that the sentence has no clear sense.

To which we might also add as a further possibility:

(4) that some sentences have a notional, or conventional, truth value, depending upon the arbitrary assignment of a notional referent to any proper names which happen to lack a natural referent.

Option (1) seems to sever the connection between the meaning of a sentence and its truth conditions, or at least to make it much harder to state in what the connection consists. Option (2) is unappetising, because it carries us into the cloudy waters of three-valued logics, and again obscures the relationship between meaning and truth. Frege sometimes chose option (3) and sometimes option (4), but Russell found neither choice very satisfactory, as we shall see in the next section. In 'On Referring', Strawson (1971b) argues persuasively in favour of option (1), but his arguments depend upon detaching the notion of meaning from that of truth, and explicating it instead in terms of the notions of 'role', or 'use', and in the end, on giving up the idea that meaning in ordinary language can be definitively explicated through the construction of formal languages.[6]

Nor do the problems presented by the expressions which Frege lumped under the heading 'proper names' end here. Although two denoting expressions with different senses can, in Frege's system, have one and the same object as their reference ('The Evening Star' and 'The Morning Star' are examples), it seems clear that two denoting expressions which pick out different objects as their referents cannot have one and the same sense. It follows that two sentences which have different objects (different truth values, that is) as their referents cannot have one and the same sense. But, if the sentence contains, say, a proper name which happens to be borne by more than one person, the sentence may have a different truth value, and thus on Frege's account a different sense, depending upon which person is intended by a given speaker. Furthermore, even though each of two speakers may intend one and the same person in saying,

(a)   Dr Gustav Lauben was wounded

the descriptions under which they identify the bearer of the proper name 'Dr Gustav Lauben' may be such as to make each speaker think that he intends a different person from the person intended by the other speaker. Here Frege is prepared to say that (a) as uttered by the first speaker expresses a different thought from (a) as uttered by the other speaker – possesses a different sense, that is.[7]

Hence, it can seem as if in 'ordinary language' the sense of a sentence can vary from speaker to speaker, depending upon the context, and we clearly cannot allow *that* if we want to give a precise definition of meaning in terms of truth conditions; for the very concept of the truth conditions of a sentence is the concept of the conditions which make it true or false irrespective of who utters it, or the specific context in which it is uttered. The difficulty, however, is not one that affects only formal, as distinct from natural, languages; nor is it one which would disappear if one were to abandon a specifically Fregian point of view. To say that the truth of a sentence, even in ordinary language, can vary according to the identity of the speaker and the context seems tantamount to saying that there is no one single thought (sense) which the sentence expresses and which is common to all speakers of the language, and that in turn seems to come to much the same thing as saying that the supposed 'sentence' is not really a *sentence* at all, but a mere noise: a vocal reaction, perhaps, to some specific occurrence, which has no more to do with *language* than the inarticulate bellow of an angry man or the cry of a gull.

False

Hence, it seems that, if we wish to incorporate proper names into a logical reconstruction of ordinary language, or even if we wish to understand how communication is possible in a natural language, we must somehow make logically explicit the mechanisms which, in everyday discourse, keep the reference of proper names stable from speaker to speaker. Frege's, and Russell's, solution was to treat the sense of a proper name as equivalent to a uniquely identifying description, and this solution, or some version of it, has been very widely accepted; but it is, as we shall see in chapter 9, a far less innocent and acceptable move than it appears at first sight.

And, of course, proper names are not the only sort of expression which make the reference of denoting expressions, and hence the truth values of sentences, in which they occur dependent upon considerations of context and the identity of speakers. Other examples include pronouns, deictic items such as 'this', 'that', 'hers', 'now', 'then', and tenses. It is general usage to refer to all such cases as *indexical* expressions, a terminology stemming from Yehoshua Bar-Hillel.[8]

So far we have been considering problems which arise over particular categories of denoting expressions in ordinary language – over names for objects, as Frege would say. A quite different, though related, category of difficulties arises over the way in which ordinary language handles reference to the senses of sentences and sub-sentential expressions. The truth of the sentence

(b) Leo Peter believes that Dr Gustav Lauben was wounded

for example, clearly does not depend in any way upon the truth or falsity of (a). If, as Frege thought, the reference of a sentence is a truth value, a sentence presumably must carry that reference with it into any context in which it occurs. Since the truth of (b) does not depend upon the truth of (a), we have, Frege thinks,[9] to say that the reference of what follows the word 'that' in (b) must be to the *thought expressed by* (a): that is, to the *sense* of (a). Such a reference Frege calls *indirect* (*ungerade*).

The logical structure of (b) is thus, on Frege's view quite different from that of , say,

(c)   Dr Gustav Lauben was wounded, and Leo Peter was wounded too.

Here all the expressions making up the sentence have exactly the same sense and reference they would have if they occurred separately, and the truth or falsity of the whole sentence depends in a straightforward way on the truth or falsity of the contained sentences.

The whole interest of a formal semantic theory of truth, from a philosophical point of view, lies in its recursiveness. That is, we want a formal theory of truth to provide rigorous definitions of the truth conditions of all complex sentences in terms of the truth conditions of the simpler sentences of which they are composed, and ultimately in terms of the truth conditions of some set of basic sentences, to be defined, one hopes, in purely observational terms. The existence in a natural language, such as English, of sentential contexts which function as (b) does obstructs the application to everyday usage of any such limpidly recursive model.

Quine calls such contexts *referentially opaque*, distinguishing them from *referentially transparent* contexts such as (c). The mark of a referentially opaque construction is that we cannot replace any singular term which it contains by a different term having the same reference (a *codesignative* term); or a general term by a different one which happens to be true of the same objects (a *coextensive* term); or a component sentence by a different sentence having the same truth value, without altering the truth value of the sentence which contains the construction.[10] It does not follow from the truth of (b) that, for instance,

(d)   Leo Peter believes that the doctor who lives at Bismarckstrasse 142 was wounded is true, even if that description uniquely identifies Dr Lauben.

All three types of failure, Quine says, are failures of *extensionality*. It is worth pausing for a moment to consider the implications of this term and its opposite, *intensionality*. (Contexts such as (b) and (d) are often called 'intensional' contexts, and formal languages in which the recursive definition of the truth conditions of complex sentences in terms of those of simpler sentences proceeds straightforwardly are often called 'extensional' languages.)

The *extension* of a term is the set of objects to which it refers. In this sense the extension of 'Socrates' contains a single object, Socrates, while the extension of the term 'planet of the solar system' comprises nine objects. An *intension* is, roughly speaking, the concept or description under which a given extension is located on a given occasion of discourse: clearly, different intensions can correspond to the same extension.

The term 'intension' corresponds more or less to Frege's 'sense' (*Sinn*), but 'extension' does not correspond to Frege's 'reference' (*Bedeutung*). For Frege, the *Bedeutung* of a predicative expression such as 'horse' is a concept. For most modern logicians the *extension* of 'horse' is a set, or class, of objects, the class of horses.

A natural language such as English allows reference to intensions; and it is this which creates the second category of obstacles to logical regimentation which we have been discussing. Intensions are the objects of the *propositional attitudes* (Quine's term) of belief, wishing, and so forth, which correspond to the so-called 'intensional verbs' 'to believe', 'to doubt', 'to wish', and so on. It is for this reason that referentially opaque contexts such as (b) or (d) are sometimes referred to as 'intensional' or 'epistemic' contexts.

Suppose now that we could find a way of saying everything which English allows us to say by means of the device of reference to intensions in a language which lacked that device. Such a (fully extensional) language would allow only reference to extensions, and hence the recursive specification of truth conditions in such a language could proceed without the hindrance of referentially opaque constructions. Hence, the relationships between complex sentences and their component sentences would be 'extensional' in the sense that the truth conditions of the former would be fully specifiable in terms of the truth conditions of the latter.

5. *Regimentation and ontology*

Talk of reference leads naturally to talk of the objects to which reference is made, and thus to talk of ontology: that is, to talk about what kinds of object the world 'ultimately' or 'fundamentally' contains.

In an obvious way, such questions arise as soon as we attempt to pursue, say, the problems about the reference of proper names or denoting expressions which we raised in the last section. Frege's dictum that a proper name denotes an object issues in a harmless enough ontology as long as we restrict it to the case of proper names for actually existing persons or features of the landscape. We can feel, perhaps, happy enough to say with Frege, for example, that the reference of 'Mont Blanc' is the actual mountain, Mont Blanc. (In this, as in other respects, Frege was a resolute realist.) But what of names which appear to designate fictional entities, such as 'Pegasus' or 'Uriah Heep', or non-existent ones, such as 'The (present) King of France'? Are we to say, with Meinong, that such entities in some sense exist? One solution which Frege adopted to this problem is the one we listed in the last section as option (4). The solution is to regard names which have no natural referents as having some arbitrarily postulated referent, symbolised '*', specified as belonging to a given domain of discourse. On this view the truth value of, say, 'Pegasus is a horse' will be 'true' just in case * is conventionally regarded as belonging to the extension of '. . . is a horse'.

This device gives a reference to every proper name even in the absence of a 'natural' reference, and there are reasons for thinking that it is a device to which Frege was committed by other elements of his theory of meaning.[11] But it is, in itself, no more than a convenient logical device. Its philosophical limitations are obvious at once, the moment we connect, as Russell did in 'On Denoting',[12] logical questions about reference with epistemological questions. If we are to attach a definite truth value to a sentence containing a proper name or denoting phrase, we must know what the name or denoting phrase denotes, and hence we must know that it 'denotes unambiguously'. Russell points out that we know, for example, that the phrase 'The point occupied by the centre of mass of the solar system at a definite instant' denotes unambiguously, even though we have no immediate *acquaintance* with the object which it denotes. Russel held, as we saw earlier, that acquaintance is logically prior to description, in the sense that we can know what a term means only if there are some terms with the objects of which we are directly acquainted. By defining a term by reference to some object of direct acquaintance, I give it a meaning which does not depend upon the *description* – that is to say, the verbal specification – of the objects to which it refers; and, Russell argues, it is only if we can in some way define the meanings of the terms employed in descriptions by appeal to the meanings of terms defined by reference to the objects of direct acquaintance that any description can be understood.

It is therefore a problem for Russell – something that has to be explained – that we can 'think about', and refer to, objects such as the present centre of mass of the solar system, which are not for us objects of acquaintance. It is because Russell holds that direct acquaintance is the source of meaning – the point at which language is connected with the world – that Russell is prepared to affirm with such confidence that, because 'The King of France' lacks a reference, '"The King of France is bald"' ought to be nonsense'.[13] Frege held that a referring expression in a natural language can possess a clear sense but lack a referent, and although he held the opposite to be true of a properly constructed conceptual notation, his reasons have to do with his conception of what a properly constructed conceptual notation ought to be like. According to this conception, the sense of a well formed denoting expression should uniquely identify an object and the sense of a well formed sentence ought uniquely to identify a truth value: any sentence or denoting expression that fails this test is hence *a fortiori* not well formed.

Russell's reasons for holding that a denoting expression without a referent 'ought to be nonsense' are, on the contrary, epistemological ones. A description which cannot be grounded in acquaintance ought in general 'to be nonsense', because acquaintance is the *source* of meaning: unless we can give some terms a meaning by referring them directly to objects of acquaintance, no terms would be anything but empty symbols or tokens.

However, Russell did not think that 'The King of France is bald' was nonsense. He opted for the intuitively plausible claim that it has a clear meaning, and the somewhat less intuitively plausible claim that it is false. And he explains the fact that the sentence is not nonsense by denying that the expression 'The King of France' is a genuine constituent of the sentence. The machinery which Russell advances to justify this denial is, of course, the celebrated Theory of Descriptions, which transforms 'The King of France is bald' into, roughly speaking, the conjunction of three propositions, the first asserting that a King of France exists, the second that he is bald, and the third that, if any entity possesses exactly this combination of predicates, no other entity possesses it.

This analysis solves Russell's problem to his satisfaction because it enables us to dispense definitionally with the denoting expression, 'The King of France', which caused all the trouble. 'The King of France is bald' has a meaning because the conjunction of three propositions into which the Theory of Descriptions transforms it has a meaning, and it is false because the first of the conjunct propositions which make up that conjunction is false.

Moreover, interestingly enough, it enables Russell to dispense with the Fregian idea that denoting expressions such as 'The King of France' or 'The Morning Star' possess both sense and reference.

Russell begins by observing that we often distinguish between the meaning of a denoting phrase and its denotation by putting the phrase in inverted commas, as in the following examples –

(e)   The first line of Grey's *Elegy* states a proposition
(f)   'The first line of Grey's *Elegy*' does not state a proposition

– adding that the distinction between meaning and denotation which we mark in this way is 'not merely linguistic . . . there must be a logical relation involved, which we express by saying that the meaning denotes the denotation'. We want to say, in short, that a given denoting phrase C has both meaning and denotation, and that the meaning *determines* or *picks out* the denotation.

If meanings and denotations are quite separate sorts of entity, related in the way described, then presumably it ought at least to be possible to refer to them. It turns out, however, Russell argues, to be quite extraordinarily difficult to construct a denoting phrase which has a *meaning* as its denotation.

If our sample denoting phrase is 'The first line of Grey's *Elegy*', and we label it C for convenience, then a natural way of constructing a denoting phrase denoting the meaning of C is to insert C in the frame 'The meaning of . . .' But that gives us 'The meaning of the first line of Grey's *Elegy*', which does not denote the meaning of C. And, if we try 'The meaning of "C"', we get not a denoting phrase denoting the

Russell confuses quote-names with symbols for the meaning of an expression.

meaning of *C* but a phrase equivalent to '*C*' on its own. And '*C*' on its own stands not for the *meaning of C* but for *C* itself.

We are in a muddle, in short, from which the Theory of Descriptions extricates us at the cost of abandoning Frege's version of the distinction between sense and reference. According to the Theory of Descriptions, a denoting expression *C* has a reference just in case there happens to be an individual, *X*, of which the proposition '*X* is identical with *C*' is true (*C* being reinterpreted in the way proposed by the theory). In such a case, says Russell, the entity *X* is the denotation of the denoting phrase '*C*'. In saying that, of course, we put the denoting phrase in inverted commas. But that does not give us a denoting phrase the denotation of which is the *meaning of C*. 'The *C* in inverted commas will be merely the *phrase*, not anything that can be called the *meaning*.' The phrase *per se* has no meaning, because, in any proposition in which it occurs, the proposition fully expressed (i.e. as translated by the Theory of Descriptions) does not contain the phrase, which has been broken up.

Russell's Theory of Descriptions is generally regarded as an ontologically restrictive theory. It reduces the number of entities which we need postulate as forming part of the contents of the universe. It relieves us of the need to postulate the actual existence of the present King of France, round squares, flying mountains, unicorns, and so on, merely on the grounds that corresponding denoting expressions can be formulated in ordinary language. What is less often noticed is that the Theory of Descriptions offers, as we have just shown, the first beginnings of a suggestion as to how we might set about disposing of what one might call 'intensional entities', *meanings*, *propositions* and the like. Russell has, in fact, stumbled upon the short way with the theory of meaning which Quine has since developed into an elegant and powerful scientific naturalism.

6. *Intensions and modality*

Nor is this the only way in which formal semantics might set about dispensing with the embarrassment of intensions. There is a fairly obvious intuitive connection between the notion of intension and the logical modalities. One way of expressing the problem which intensions create for formal semantics would be to say that it consists in the fact that two or more intensions can correspond to one and the same extension. Thus, for example, the two intensions

(g)   Animal with a backbone
(h)   Animal with kidneys

correspond to one and the same extension: one and the same class of individual animals, that is.

Plainly, now, the extension of (g) *might* come to differ from the extension of (h) if certain logically possible changes were to take place in nature. It is possible, for example, that evolutionary change might bring it about that some vertebrates lacked kidneys, or that some degenerate vertebrate species lacking a backbone might nevertheless retain the vertebrate kidney. It is quite natural to express this possibility by saying that (g) and (h) would correspond to different extensions in a different *possible world.*

This notion of a *possible world*, in turn, is one which it is quite possible to represent formally. We need only stipulate a universe of discourse consisting of a set, possibly an infinite set, of individuals, together with a possibly infinite set of predicates. A *possible world* will then simply be an assignment of individuals to predicates. Each predicate will thus correspond to a determinate extension within a given possible world. A given extension can now be regarded as corresponding not to an extension in the sense of a set of individuals, but to a class of such sets, defined relative to the set of all possible worlds (all possible assignments of individuals to predicates). A formal reconstruction of a natural language, as Richard Montague puts it (1970, pp. 194–5), 'should assign to a basic expression not a denotation but a *denotation function*, that is, a function that maps each infinite sequence of individuals onto a possible denotation of the expression'.[14] Each intension can thus be thought of as corresponding to a single, unique extension, but an extension specified in modal terms 'across possible worlds'.

'Possible world semantics' can then, perhaps, be extended to give extensional analyses of the various kinds of intensional operators and constructions which obstruct the reinterpretation of ordinary language in terms of the recursive machinery of a formal language. Proper names, for example, will correspond to some set of predicates to the extension of which some appropriate denotation function assigns a single individual in any possible world. Similar manoeuvres might be expected to deal with epistemic contexts and tenses.

There are, it is true, some technical objections to this programme, which incidentally call into question the status of the quantified modal logics which the programme requires. Quine has argued, for example, that 'quantification into' a modal context is as illegitimate as 'quantification into' a context of quotation, or any other referentially opaque context: that, in fact, modal contexts are themselves opaque. When a variable x stands inside an opaque construction and $(\exists x)$ or (x) stands outside it, Quine argues, we cannot consider the variable to be bound by the quantifier. In non-opaque contexts we cannot change the truth conditions of a proposition by altering the variable symbols. Thus, in

(j) $(\exists x)$ (x is reading Catullus)

changing the variable to y throughout makes no difference to the truth of (j): it remains true just in case somebody is reading Catullus. The case is otherwise for an opaque context, such as

(k) $(\exists x)$ (x is writing 'Catullus is funnier than x').

Here we can replace the first two xs with ys, without altering the truth conditions of (k), which remains true just in case someone is writing 'Catullus is funnier than x'; but, if we replace the final x as well, then, of course, the truth conditions of the proposition do change. Clearly, the final x, inside the quotation marks, does not refer back to the existential quantifier and is not bound by it.

But in this respect modal contexts appear no different from contexts of quotation. From

(l)   Necessarily $9 > 4$

we can conclude, by substitution of a coextensive term, that

(m)   Necessarily the number of major planets > 4.

By Quine's criteria, then, modal contexts (similar arguments go through for the other modalities) are referentially opaque, so the same problems of 'quantifying in' arise for them as for other referentially opaque constructions.

Modal logicians have generally treated these Quinean strictures as founded at best upon a misunderstanding of modal logic. What seems most likely is that modal logics can indeed be constructed in ways which avoid Quine's objections, but at the cost of leaving open questions which, although they can perfectly well be taken by logicians as arising, and as being settled, outside logic, are certainly not questions which can be taken as settleable outside the philosophy of language: are, indeed, the crucial questions for the philosophy of language.

The difficulties which Quine discusses arise because it is possible, in everyday English, to specify objects uniquely in ways which are not necessarily equivalent to one another. They would disappear if it were the case that any two conditions uniquely determining an object x were, by that very fact, necessarily equivalent to one another. In that case, if it were true, for example, that the Evening Star is identical with the Morning Star, it would be necessarily true that the Evening Star is the Morning Star. Intuitively, this seems in some sense to be false: the Evening Star might not have been also the last star visible in the morning. Frege introduced his concept of sense, indeed, precisely to deal with this difficulty. Moreover, Quine shows in *Word and Object* that from the proposition that all identities are necessary,

(n) $(x) (y) [x = y \supset \Box (x = y)]$ _sic_

we can derive the consequence that all true statements are necessarily true,

(o) $p \supset \Box p$ _sic_

This appears to remove the very point of talking about the modalities in the first place, so that it is scarcely surprising that modal logicians have been inclined to regard Quine's arguments as ingenious paradoxes, rather than as serious objections (on the other hand, the history of paradox in logic is, as we know, a momentous one).

Church[15] and Carnap[16] have suggested ways of avoiding these difficulties. Church's suggestion is simply that we treat all variables as having referential position: that is, conduct modal logic in a formal language without opaque constructions. This solution simply expels opaque constructions and the problems which they create from the universe of discourse of the formal languages of modal logic, and thus excludes any possibility of arriving at an understanding of intensionality in modal terms. Carnap's solution is to treat the variables in his system (S_2) as ranging over intensions. It therefore follows, within the system, that, where two variables, a and b, refer to the same intension, they can be freely substituted for one another in all contexts. Again, this avoids Quine's objections by restricting the range of the variables in a formal language in a way which makes it hard to see how such a language could be used to throw light on the constructions of a natural language such as English.

Dagfinn Føllesdal,[17] upon whose discussion I have been drawing over the last two pages, argues that Quine's scepticism is 'too disastrous to be true', since it precludes any attempt to construct 'adequate theories of causation, counterfactuals, probability, preference' and a host of others. Føllesdal argues persuasively that a language which allows intelligible talk of modality must exhibit referential transparency and extensional opacity. That is,

(1) whatever is true of an object must be true of it regardless of how it is referred to (referential transparency); and
(2) among the predicates true of an object some are necessarily true of it, others only accidentally (extensional opacity).

It is strongly intuitively plausible, I think, that (1) and (2) are both properties of ordinary natural languages such as English, and some powerful arguments in support of intuition have recently been adduced by Saul Kripke and Hilary Putnam. But it is not at all easy to see how a natural language *can* have such properties: how, in Kantian terms, they are possible. Both (1) and (2) are certainly denied by Quine's philosophy of language, and it would be an understatement to say that at present it is quite unclear how Quine's philosophy might be shown to be mistaken as a description of the logical and semantic mechanisms of a natural language. Showing how it is possible for a natural language to be characterised by referential transparency and extensional opacity is a task for the philosophy of language. There would thus be some sense in saying that, far from modal logic offering a universal key to the problems of the philosophy of language, the philosophy of language is concerned, in part, with the foundations of modal logic.

If we return to the model-theoretic proposals of 'possible-world semantics', we do not find, I think, that they throw very much light on these fundamental questions of sense and reference. Montague speaks of the denotations of basic expressions as determined by 'denotation functions' but he does not explain what a denotation function is or how it functions. To give such explanations would, presumably, lead him outside the bounds of formal-language construction, but clearly some explanation is needed before we can interpret the notion of a denotation function in terms of the mechanisms – whatever they are – which determine the reference of expressions in a natural language.

For the theorist of possible-world semantics an intension is essentially a set-theoretic entity: a set of extensions defined across a range of possible worlds. As Putnam[18] observes in 'The Meaning of "Meaning"' (Putnam, 1975, pp. 263–4), it is not easy to connect this account with any account of what a speaker learns or grasps in learning or grasping the intension of a given term. Moreover, it does not look as though the problem here can be treated as one which arises from the vagueness of ordinary language. The possible-world semanticist tells us that an intension is a set of assignments of individuals to predicate symbols across possible worlds. This is, in itself, undeniable, but what we want to know, as philosophers of language, is how – by what mechanisms or criteria – the individuals would be assigned to the predicate terms by actual speakers of any natural language of which the formal system under discussion would provide a logical idealisation. Far from being settled within a formal system, in other words, the problem of the nature of intensions arises again, in a form in which it is not amenable to logical dissolution in terms of modality, when we come to interpret the formal system in terms of a natural language.

Further problems arise over what Kripke and Putnam call rigidity of designation, but we shall leave these to be dealt with in chapter 9. What seems sufficiently clear already is that intensionality creates problems which are not easily resolved in terms of modality. Perhaps the whole problem of intensions or meanings really *is* a pseudo-problem. Perhaps it *is* possible to dispense with such entities, and to do so without any trafficking with notions as vague as those of a 'rule of language' or of the 'use' of a term. But, if so, we need a more radical and caustic solvent for our perplexities than modal logic can provide. For that we must go to Quine.

7

Meaning, Translation and Ontology

1. Quine and verificationism

W. V. Quine's 'Two Dogmas of Empiricism'[1] is generally admitted to be one of the most important philosophical articles published this century. It is nominally, as the title suggests, an attack on empiricism. The 'two dogmas' which the paper attacks are, first, reductionism: 'the belief that each meaningful statement is equivalent to some logical construction upon terms which refer to immediate experience';[2] and, secondly the belief that there is a clear distinction to be drawn between analytic truths, which are true in virtue of the meanings of the expressions employed in stating them, and synthetic truths, which are true, if at all, because some matter of fact is the case.

But the hostility to empiricism is more apparent than real. Elsewhere Quine speaks of 'two cardinal tenets of empiricism' as remaining 'unassailable . . . to this day'.[3] The two cardinal tenets, as distinct from the two dogmas, are (1) that 'whatever evidence there *is* for science *is* sensory evidence',[4] and (2) that 'all inculcation of meanings of words must rest ultimately on sensory evidence'.[5]

We can easily recognise in these two propositions two of the fundamental intuitions, of nominalist (or, better, nominalising) tendency, underlying verificationism. And it will help us properly to understand the content and significance of Quine's work if we get the relationship of his thought to verificationism clear at the outset. As we saw in chapter 6, section 6, verificationism in its classical form

Peirce's Ven treatment + Duhemian holism ⇒
indeterminacy of trans latn of theoretical sentences
⇒ no propositional meanings.

MEANING AND TRUTH 97

requires (1) the possibility of a clear distinction between analytic and
synthetic truths, (2) a clearly formulable concept of synonymy, and
(3) the success of a programme of reductive analysis aimed at
demonstrating equivalence of meaning between each meaningful
statement and some longer statement couched entirely in terms of
what is immediately given in experience. Quine's 'Two Dogmas'
delivers, on all three counts, the *coup de grâce* to classical verificationism. But what goes, if Quine's arguments are sound, is the notion that
each separate meaningful sentence can be given a unique analysis in
sensory terms. If we abandon the belief in the possibility of a clear and
precise definition of synonymy, or of the difference between analytic
and synthetic truths, then, certainly, we must give up the programme
of sentence-by-sentence phenomenalist reduction. But we can still
hold that the *whole body* of sentences which embody a scientific theory
about the world (and for this purpose we can regard our common-
sense beliefs about the world as composing a primitive and immemor-
ial scientific theory) take their meaning *collectively* from their relationship to sensory experience, even though we cannot state, in terms of
'basic propositions' of the sort postulated by Ayer, say, what *the*
meaning of any *particular* theoretical statement is.

> The Vienna Circle espoused a verification theory of meaning but
> did not take it seriously enough. If we recognise with Peirce that the
> meaning of a sentence turns purely on what would count as
> evidence for its truth, and if we recognise with Duhem that
> theoretical sentences have their evidence not as single sentences
> but only as larger blocks of theory, then the indeterminacy of
> translation of theoretical sentences is the natural conclusion. . . .
> This conclusion, conversely, once it is embraced, seals the fate of
> any general notion of propositional meaning or, for that matter,
> state of affairs.
>   Should the unwelcomeness of the conclusion persuade us to
> abandon the verification theory of meaning? Certainly not. The
> sort of meaning that is basic to translation, and to the learning of
> one's own language, is necessarily empirical meaning and nothing
> more. . . . Surely one has no choice but to be an empiricist so
> far as one's theory of linguistic meaning is concerned.[6]   (Ibid.,
> pp. 80–1)

One aspect of Quine's achievement, then (we shall have occasion to
notice others, Quine's philosophy being notably many-sided in spite

of, or rather in proportion to, the clarity and simplicity of his fundamental insights), is his discovery of a way of rescuing the fundamental insights of verificationism by showing how they can be combined with linguistic holism or organicism: by exhibiting, as Michael Dummett puts it, 'the possibility of an organic verificationist theory'.[7]

2. Analyticity and synonymy

Kant held that an analytic statement attributes to its subject only what is already contained in the meaning of the subject term. Thus, according to the stock example, 'All bachelors are unmarried men', the concept *unmarried man* is contained in the meaning of 'bachelor'. But how can we tell when one meaning is contained in another? Quine argues with Frege that meaning (sense) and reference are quite distinct from one another. Two denoting expressions, such as 'The Evening Star' and 'The Morning Star', may denote the same object although differing in sense. Similarly, two general terms, such as 'creature with a heart' and 'creature with kidneys' may pick out the same extension, although clearly differing in meaning. Sameness of meaning, then, cannot be defined in terms of sameness of reference. Perhaps, though, we can define it in terms of definition. That is, perhaps we can say that 'bachelor' is simply *defined as* 'unmarried man', and leave it at that. But definitions do not, except occasionally, *create* synonymies: mostly, as in the case of dictionary definitions, they simply report them – the lexicographer relying partly upon his own linguistic intuition and partly upon textual evidence.

Perhaps, then, the synonymy of two linguistic expressions consists in the possibility of substituting them for one another in any sentential context without changing the truth value of the sentence: in what Leibniz called interchangeability *salva veritate*. Quine's argument at this point takes the form of a dilemma. If we are to extract a criterion of synonymy from Leibniz's criterion, we have to consider not merely the criterion itself, but also the language to which it is to be applied, and, in particular, whether the language in question is an extensional language, in the sense defined in chapter 7, section 1, or an intensional language.

In the former case, any two predicates which happen to be true of exactly the same objects will be interchangeable *salva veritate*. Thus, if all creatures with hearts, and only creatures with hearts, happen to have kidneys, then the general terms 'creature with a heart' and 'creature with kidneys' will, in an extensional language, be interchangeable *salva veritate*. But, clearly, 'creature with a heart' and 'creature with kidneys' are not, in the ordinary sense, *synonyms*: they merely, in Quine's phrase, *agree extensionally*. The trouble is, now, that it is merely a contingent matter of fact, if it is a fact at all, that all creatures with hearts have kidneys and *vice versa*. Synonymy requires not merely interchangeability *salva veritate*, but that the interchangeability in question should be not merely contingently feasible, but necessarily so. Now, provided we are working not with an extensional language, but with a language containing, as Quine says, 'an intensional adverb "necessarily"', we can easily build this requirement into the definition of synonymy: *a* and *b* will be synonymous just in case *necessarily* all *a*'s are *b*'s and all *b*'s are *a*'s. But it is only in so far as we already understand the notion of analyticity that we can make sense of the idea of an intensional language, and so of a language containing the adverb 'necessarily'.

In short, the attempt to define the notion of analyticity appears to lead into a closed circle. To explain analyticity in the obvious way, in terms of equivalence of meaning, we need the concept of synonymy. But, when we try to say what synonymy is, we are forced to rely upon an unanalysed concept of analyticity.

One way out of the impasse might be to retire once again from natural to formal languages, and to define analyticity for a given formal language *L* in terms of the Carnapian concept of a *semantical rule* of *L*. Now, an analytic statement is one which is not merely true but also true by virtue of a semantical rule. But what is a semantical rule? Unless we have some prior account of analyticity, a semantical rule is 'distinguishable . . . only by the fact of appearing on a page under the heading "Semantical Rules", and this heading is itself then meaningless'.[8]

Verificationism might offer a way out, if we could make sense of the idea that the meaning of a statement is its method of verification, for then we might define statement synonymy, at least, in terms of likeness of empirical confirmation or disconfirmation. That, of course, requires us to identify, for each individual statement, a unique range of sensory events which tend to confirm it, and a unique range which tend to disconfirm it. The doctrine that such ranges of sensory events are identifiable for individual statements Quine calls 'the dogma of reductionism'.

But the identification of sensory events required for reductionism can only proceed by way of language. Carnap's attempt, in *Der logische Aufbau der Welt*, to exhibit the physical world as a logical construction from sense data, begins ostensibly from a language consisting simply of names for sensory qualities together with the formal machinery of logic. But the most primitive statements about physical objects require the assignment of a sensory quality to a spatio-temporal point–instant specified as a quadruple of real numbers. This demands statements of the form 'Quality q is at point–instant x; y; z; t.' But even in this primitive type of proposition the connective '*is at*' remains undefined. It is neither a quality name nor a logical connective, and it is hard to see any way of definitionally eliminating it.

Unless a complete translation of ordinary language into a language consisting only of the ordinary symbolic machinery of formal logic supplemented by names for sensory qualities can be given, however, reductionism is merely a pious hope. The dogma of reductionism, and the dogma of a distinction between analytic and synthetic truths, in fact, are closely related, in that each helps to sustain the plausibility of the other. Both depend upon the conviction that it is possible to separate the *factual* or *empirical* considerations bearing upon the truth of a statement from the *semantic* or *linguistic* considerations bearing upon it. If such a separation were possible, then, on the one hand, reductionism would be a feasible philosophical programme – it would simply involve disentangling and exhibiting the factual component of the truth conditions of a statement – while, on the other hand, we could conceive of analytic truths as degenerate statements dependent for their truth or falsity solely upon linguistic considerations.

But the very difficulties which arise over the definition of synonymy and analyticity show that such a separation is impossible, and that the factual and linguistic components of the truth conditions of a statement are in the end inseparable. A convenient label for this conclusion has been coined by Michael Dummett,[9] who calls it the thesis of the inextricability of the linguistic and the empirical, or the Inextricability Thesis for short.

The Inextricability Thesis is the cornerstone of Quine's holism. Paul Gochet[10] draws a useful distinction between Quine's holism, which he calls *semantic holism*, and the *epistemological holism* of Pierre Duhem,[11] one of the major influences upon Quine's thought, along with Peirce, Dewey and Carnap. Duhem's holism consists in the thesis that scientific hypotheses are never verified in isolation, but only as part of a larger structure of theory. Quine's holism is the thesis that science as a whole – the entire body of our empirical knowledge of the world – is the unit of meaning. Gochet makes the shrewd point that this thesis flows logically from a combination of Duhem's epistemological holism with a verificationist theory of meaning such as that characteristic of Peirce or Schlick, according to which the meaning of a statement is the difference its truth or falsity makes to the empirical description of the world.

In 'Two Dogmas' it is as yet not entirely clear whether the holism Quine has in mind is epistemological – as appears very much more clearly in *Word and Object* – or semantic holism. He compares 'total science' with a net, or field of force, which 'impinges upon experience only along the edges'. Any conflict with experience will necessitate some readjustment to the field, but the conflict is with the field as a whole, and not with any particular sentence. Hence we have a great deal of leeway when it comes to deciding how – over which of the statements composing the net – to redistribute truth values. And hence there may be circumstances in which we are prepared to revise the truth values even of putatively analytic statements. The difference between analytic and synthetic statements, in short, is neither absolute nor a difference in kind. It is a difference of *degree of dispensability* only. Analytic truths are simply those statements the truth values of which we are, for the moment, least willing to alter, because the consequent redistributions of truth values to which such an alteration would commit us seem, for the moment, too radical and far-reaching to countenance. Analyticity is not an absolute property of statements: they possess it only relatively to a particular moment in the continuing process by which truth values are redistributed across the net, to take account of recalcitrant observations. Which brings Quine back to his starting point: the realisation that asserting the synonymy of two sentences comes to the same thing as asserting their agreement in extension.

3. Defending the dogmas

This conclusion is obviously paradoxical, at least in the sense that it seems flatly contrary to linguistic intuition, whether of philosophers or of ordinary people. When we say that two sentences are synonymous, we do not ordinarily suppose ourselves to be saying merely that they agree in extension. Moreover, the paradox can be sharpened. It looks, if Quine is right, as if any statement of the form 'Predicates *x* and *y* apply to the same objects but do not have the same meaning' must be senseless. Worse still, as H. P. Grice and P. F. Strawson have pointed out,[12] if it is meaningless to talk of synonymy, it must be meaningless also to talk about the meaning of a sentence. For, if we could specify the meaning of a sentence, we could then say that two sentences are synonymous if and only if any such specification which is true of either one of them is true of the other. If synonymy goes, then, meaning goes: the whole concept of a linguistic expression's having a sense, as distinct from a reference, collapses under us.

It is not at all easy to see, however, how the deliverances of linguistic intuition on these points can be made to yield a refutation of Quine. We want to say that the analytic–synthetic distinction does not concern *degrees* of dispensability at all; that the distinction follows precisely from the recognition that analytic truths cannot be dispensed with, while synthetic ones can. To this a Quinean can reply that sentences which have been regarded as analytically true do sometimes come to be treated as falsehoods. 'All married men have entered a church at least once in their lives' might be an example. It is tempting to reply to this that in every such case a shift of meaning has occurred. In one sense of 'married', 'All married men have entered a church at least once in their lives' is still (is timelessly) analytic; in another sense of 'married' it is not.

Taken in one sense, however, this reply can be turned very easily to Quine's purposes. We can interpret the alleged shift in the meaning of 'married' simply as a shift in its extension. On such an interpretation, the assertion that the proposition 'All married men have entered a church at least once in their lives' is analytic in one interpretation of the meaning of 'married' becomes equivalent to the assertion that the extension of 'married man' is included within the extension of 'man who has entered a church at least once in his life' on one (now outmoded) account of the extension of 'married man'.

Of course, the anti-Quinean will retort that this is not at all what he intended. What he had in mind is that there is a radical distinction to be drawn between relinquishing a proposition because of a change of opinion about matters of fact, and relinquishing it because of a conceptual change. The trouble is that it is not enough, as Strawson and Grice, for example, appear to suppose,[13] simply to say that this, or something like it, is the deliverance of linguistic intuition. Quine's point is indeed that factual revision and conceptual revision are indistinguishable: this is the force of the Inextricability Thesis. But to refute the Inextricability Thesis we need, surely, to show upon what grounds factual and conceptual revision can be distinguished; and to do that effectively we need some ground of distinction going beyond a mere appeal to linguistic intuition. Grice and Strawson make much of the fact that the distinction between analytic and synthetic truths can be defined informally, by appeal to such sentence pairs as 'My neighbour's three-year-old child understands Russell's Theory of Types' (contingently false) and 'My neighbour's three-year-old child is an adult' (analytically false); and they argue, as others of Quine's critics have done, that Quine's requirements for introducing a concept into a natural language are too strict: that informal elucidations are in general all that we require, and that, if these enable us, in practice, to use a term in discourse without misunderstanding, then they are sufficient, and all that we need, or can require. But this misses Quine's point. Of course, we can arrive at agreement with one another about how the words 'analytic' and 'synthetic' are to be used. But, in arriving at such an agreement, are we doing anything more than arriving at *extensional* conformity in our use of the terms? And is there not the possibility that different interpretations of the *meanings* of 'analytic' and 'synthetic' may correspond to the same extensions? The falsehood of 'My neighbour's three-year-old child is an adult' need not be construed, that is, as revelatory of a relationship between the *meanings* of 'three-year-old child' and 'adult'. It may just reveal that the extension of 'three-year-old child' and 'adult' exclude one another. To make any serious impression upon a Quinean who chooses to argue in this way, we need a clear criterion for distinguishing between empirical and conceptual revision. Appeals to linguistic intuition are useless unless intuition can somehow be got to yield such a criterion.

Dummett points out[14] that the sharp distinction, which Quine draws in 'Two Dogmas', between peripheral and non-peripheral statements in the 'net' of theoretically linked statements comprising 'total science', is inconsistent with Quine's claim that any statement is equally open to revision in the fact of recalcitrant experience. If the second claim is true, then it is open to us to prefer to maintain the truth values of peripheral sentences at the cost of theoretical revision in the interior of the net, in which case the interior must presumably be said to 'impinge upon experience' more directly than the periphery. But it is not at all clear at first sight that or how far the

① Q's claim is that they cannot be "empirically distinguished" (by behavioral criteria) from one another — and so rests upon a metaphysical prejudice

for the observable

periphery–interior distinction is essential to Quine's position. What is essential, I think, is the claim (1) that the statements of a theory 'face the bar of experience' collectively, and the correlative claims (2) that the adjustment of theories to take account of recalcitrant experience is a holistic process in which the truth values of individual statements can be bargained off against general considerations of the simplicity and coherence of the whole theory; and (3) that alternative total adjustments to recalcitrant experience are always possible: that the totality of a theory is always underdetermined by the observations which provide the evidence for the theory. All three claims do, it seems to me, clearly depend upon the Inextricability Thesis: the claim (4) that linguistic considerations and empirical considerations affecting the truth and falsity of statements cannot ultimately be distinguished from one another. But it is not obvious that they depend upon the maintenance of the periphery–interior distinction, and perhaps they do not.

false — the converse is supposed to be the case

4. Meaning and translation

In *Word and Object*, and in the essays in *Ontological Relativity*, Quine reformulates his position as a theory about translation.

Quine's concern is with *radical* translation – translation between languages of widely differing families – where the translator is not able to appeal to the web of loan words and common grammatical structures which aid us in translating between two closely related languages. The examination of the conditions for radical translation brings out the nature of the fundamental relationships between language and experience, just because the radical translator is not able to rely on any of the clues which are available to him when he is translating from one language into one with a common history and common assumptions.

In this situation, the radical translator has access to only one category of data. When changes occur in the environment, he can utter what he takes to be an appropriate comment on the situation and see whether a native speaker assents or dissents to his remark. Thus, if, when a rabbit runs by, the natives say 'Gavagai', the linguist makes a note of this and tries to discover whether his own tentative venture of 'Gavagai' in more or less similar situations will elicit assent or dissent. To know this he needs to know the native words for 'yes' and 'no'; but he can elicit these by echoing the native's own pronouncements, or by seeing which of two words tentatively identified as 'yes' and 'no' elicit the emotional response of a man absurdly contradicted.[15]

The total class of stimulations which prompt native speakers' assent to 'Gavagai', or some such one-word sentence, Quine calls the *affirmative stimulus meaning* of the sentence. The total class of stimulations which prompt dissent comprise *negative stimulus meaning*. The *stimulus meaning* of 'Gavagai' is the ordered pair of the two classes of stimulations.[16]

Quine is prepared to say that, in terms of the notion of stimulus meaning, we can define the *stimulus synonymy* of two expressions. This may seem to be a concession, a partial weakening of the scepticism of 'Two Dogmas'; but in fact it is not. 'Gavagai' looks, indeed, superficially like an observation sentence or a Carnapian *Protokolsatz*. Quine's account of stimulus meaning thus looks superficially like an attempt to define, in experiential terms, *the meaning of* the individual sentence 'Gavagai'. Thus, it is possible to misinterpret Quine's account of radical translation as embodying a retreat from language empiricism, or 'organic verificationism', as Dummett calls it, to some form of sentence empiricism. Quine rebuts this interpretation most clearly, to my mind, in the essay 'Epistemology Naturalised'.[17] 'Gavagai' would be an observation statement if the verdict as to its truth or falsity 'depended only upon the sensory stimulation present at the time'. But how could it depend only on that? It depends also upon all the sensory information which went into learning the language to which it belongs. But how can we distinguish between information that goes into learning a language and information that goes beyond learning a language? This is the problem of analyticity again. Perhaps we can say at least that knowing a certain piece of information cannot be essential to knowing a language if not all the speakers of the language assent to it. But all speakers of a language possess in common an enormous amount of general information about the world. This Quine calls *generally shared collateral information*. The problem of analyticity arises anew as the problem of distinguishing between information relevant to meaning and generally shared collateral information.

Seen from this point of view, it is evident that a native's assent to, or dissent from, some utterance of 'Gavagai' must depend not just upon sensory stimulation present at that moment, but upon the entire body of information which the native brings to the business of speaking his language and interpreting his experiences. And it is evident also, I think, that the technique of tabulating the stimulus conditions which prompt assent or dissent to an individual sentence offers us no means of isolating a specific body of empirical information correlated with that specific sentence as its *meaning*, or its *cognitive content*, because such a technique offers us no means of distinguishing between generally shared collateral information and semantically relevant information. All that the stimulus meaning of 'Gavagai' reveals, in effect, is how the entire language is related to experience through the medium of this particular sentence. 'In giving up hope of [reductionist] translation', says Quine,

the empiricist is conceding that the empirical meanings of typical statements about the external world are inaccessible and ineffable.

How is this inaccessibility to be explained? Simply on the ground that the experiential implications of a typical statement about bodies are too complex for finite axiomatisation, however lengthy? No; I have a different explanation. It is that the typical statement about bodies has no fund of experiental implications it can call its own.[18]

In *Word and Object* Quine makes what is essentially the same point more controversially, as a claim about the underdetermination of translation by stimulus meaning. Radical translation depends entirely upon the correlation of assents, dissents and stimulation to arrive at estimates of stimulus meaning for segments of the native language, the identity of which is not given beforehand (we cannot determine even what counts as a word in a native language without something in the way of a scheme of translation, however tentative and rudimentary) but arrived at as part of the process of establishing stimulus meanings. Stimulus meaning is thus the only empirical justification we can offer for any translation from the native language into English. How much will it justify?

The problem about collateral information may prompt us to answer, 'Hardly anything'. Quine suggests, however, that, if there is no such thing as a purely observational statement, even so some statements are more observational than others in the sense that speakers' assents and dissents to them are less subject to the interference of collateral information – or, at any rate, of such collateral information as is not generally shared. 'Red' is less subject to such interference than 'Rabbit', and far less so than 'Bachelor'.[19] The most 'observational' native utterances can be treated as observation statements; though I think it must be emphasised again that they are not observation sentences in the sense required by reductionism of the traditional empiricist kind. We can, then, translate observation sentences on the basis of stimulus meaning subject only to the usual uncertainties which affect any inductive, empirical inquiry. Apart from this, only truth functions can be directly translated. Stimulus analyticity, stimulus contradictoriness and stimulus synonymy can be recognised in the native language, but the sentences concerned cannot be translated.[20]

If he wants to get beyond these limits, the linguist has only one option. He must make a list of short, recurrent native utterances and begin tentatively and hypothetically matching these to English phrases in such a way as to preserve native stimulus analyticity and contradictoriness, native stimulus synonymy, truth-functional relationships and the status of native observational sentences. Quine calls these tentative matchings *analytical hypotheses.*

Analytical hypotheses, now, are underdetermined by stimulus meaning, and this creates a radical indeterminacy in the translation of all sentences except for the comparatively small class of highly observational ones. In the case of 'Gavagai', for example, we have the option of equating the native sentence with 'Rabbit'; 'Stage, or brief temporal segment, of a rabbit'; 'Undetached rabbit part'; 'Rabbit' taken as a mass term (such as 'water' or 'meat'); and no doubt other options besides.[21] Stimulus meaning in itself gives us no empirical warrant whatsoever for choosing between them.

But, if we grant this last point, then it seems to follow that the truth value of an individual statement in the native language can never be determined by reference to observation, except relative to a specific translation scheme which has the effect of assigning truth values to all the sentences of the native language. For the indeterminacy of radical translation opens the possibility that two different schemes of translation may equate one native sentence with two English sentences, one true, and the other false. It is not necessary, in order to envisage this possibility and see the indeterminacy, to suppose that the users of the two translation schemes know definitely which of the English sentences is true, as Quine has recently pointed out:

the point is that the two translations of a native theoretical sentence may have unknown truth-values, known only to be unlike. Two speakers can have had completely identical experiences, and can agree in withholding verdicts on both sentences, and can agree to the truth of the biconditional which connects one of these sentences with the other. It's as simple as that. [22]

It is important to see that the indeterminacy that Quine takes himself to be demonstrating is not just empirical indeterminacy, the sort of indeterminacy which prevents us from answering the question how many herrings are at this moment located on a line drawn between Beachy Head and Cap Gris Nez. It is not that we cannot find out what the English equivalent of a native sentence really is; rather it is that the question 'What is the *real* English equivalent of a native sentence?' is unanswerable in principle – has no sense – unless we specify that it is to be asked in connection with some total scheme of translation which matches up *all* the sentences of the native language with *all* the sentences of English.

It may seem tempting to object at this point that, if all the sentences produced by each translation scheme derive all their meaning from their collective relationship to the same array of stimulus meanings, then it is difficult to see what could lead us to regard the two sets of sentences as in any way different from one another – unless we drop Quine's fundamental principle that the meaning of a statement is to be understood in terms of the empirical conditions for assent or denial. But there is an obvious reply to this. The two translations have to be recognised as distinct precisely because it is not possible to translate from one to the other on a word-by-word basis.[23] Word-by-word translation, in other words, could not proceed *salva veritate*. It is this negative relationship, and only that, which enables us to speak of a difference in content between the two ways of rendering what the natives say and believe.

5. *Naturalism and relativism*

We are now in a position to consider some of the general philosophical consequences of Quine's holism. As he makes clear at the outset of his essay 'Ontological Relativism', originally given as a John Dewey lecture at Columbia University, Quine is fundamentally a philosophical naturalist.

Philosophically I am bound to Dewey by the naturalism that dominated his last three decades. With Dewey I hold that knowledge, mind, and meaning are part of the same world that they have to do with, and that they are to be studied in the same empirical spirit that animates natural science. There is no place for a prior philosophy.[24]

'Prior philosophy' concerns itself characteristically with meaning and with ontology: that is, with problems concerning the proper analysis of such terms as 'knowledge', 'causality', 'identity'; and with the question of what sorts of entity (sense data? physical objects? minds? persons?) ultimately exist.

The effect of Quine's holism is to make the answers to all such questions 'ineffable and inaccessible'. Moreover, the inaccessibility and ineffability is a matter of principle. Once more, it is not that we are for some reason unable to discover the answers to such questions, but that there *are* no answers to them. Questions of meaning are, as we have already seen, always relative to some total translation scheme. And it is evident that this relativity operates not only between languages but also within one and the same language. Suppose we take our entire language, with its grammatical and logical apparatus, the predicates of identity and difference, other logical connectives, and such terms as 'rabbit', 'rabbit part', 'rabbit stage', 'formula', 'sense datum' and 'physical object'. We now try permutating the denotations of our terms, replacing 'rabbit' with 'rabbit stage' in all its occurrences, and so on.

We begin to appreciate that a grand and ingenious permutation of these denotations, along with compensatory adjustments in the interpretations of the auxiliary particles, might still accommodate all existing speech dispositions [i.e. all dispositions to assent and dissent]. This [is] the inscrutability of reference, applied to ourselves; and it [makes] nonsense of reference.[25]

Consider now, some characteristic ontological claims: 'Only minds ultimately exist'; 'Only sense data really exist'; 'Particulars exist'; 'Universals exist'; and so on. On Quine's view, neither the assertion nor the denial of any such assertion makes sense, *except relative to some total interpretation of the terms and logical apparatus of a language*. All ontological questions are relative to the linguistic convenience of language-users. Or, to make the same point according to another formula of Quine's, 'it makes no sense to say what the objects of a theory are, beyond saying how to interpret or reinterpret that theory in another'.[26]

We are thus brought finally to the famous Quinean tag, 'To exist is to be a value of an individual variable.' One consequence of Quine's thesis to the effect that truth functions are translatable but terms (except highly observational terms) are not is that formal logic can be used to provide a 'canonical notation' for theory. The thesis of the indeterminacy of translation can, as we have seen, be taken as a thesis about the possibility of interpreting and reinterpreting the bare logical scaffolding of a theory. Quine's canonical notation gives us, we are to hope, the structure of that logical scaffolding. A variable a may occur in a theory thus logically regimented without purporting to name an object. What makes it clear that a variable is being used, within a theory, to name an object, is that the theory cannot be stated without appeal to an existentially quantified statement $(\exists x)\,(x = a)$. But, of course, to say $that$ is simply to say that a certain theory has, as Quine says, certain ontic commitments. And as we have seen, we can always reconstruct in such a way as to change its ontic commitments the total theory in terms of which we interpret the world.

We can see Quine's relativism, if we wish, as representing an extension of Russell's Theory of Descriptions to its logical conclusion. The Theory of Descriptions was an ontologically parsimonious theory, designed to show how reality can be described without appeal to such apparent entities as the Present King of France, and, in general, to all the entities which populate Meinong's theory of objects. But Russell still retained, in his early work, a commitment to certain classes of individual (sensory particulars, universals and relations) regarded as real, and as known to us by acquaintance, as distinct from by description.

Quine has, in effect, dispensed with these remaining objects by appeal to essentially Russellian procedures. We are left, on Quine's account, with a description of the world which proceeds quite adequately in terms of predicate constants linked by the ordinary logical machinery of quantificational cross-reference. Symbols for individuals appear only as individual variables carrying the cross-references needed for quantification. There is thus no need to postulate individuals as real entities at all. We are thus left with a theory which is nominalist in the sense that it refuses to grant a privileged ontological status to any *category* of particulars (it refuses, that is, to grant reality to physical objects, persons, species, substances, and so on: the list is endless), and so avoids all philosophical controversy about which categories deserve to be granted this status over others.

Meaning, as we have seen, is similarly relative, if Quine is correct, to the totality of native theory and empirical knowledge. Hence, there is no possibility of a philosophy of language, at least if we construe the philosophy of language as we have construed it so far in this book, as a study of the constitutive rules which determine meanings in a natural language. 'Meanings' are simply not isolable objects of study. Talk about meanings, if such talk means anything at all, is simply, as Russell argued in 'On Denoting', talk about sentences.

A further consequence of Quine's holism is the collapse of epistemology as traditionally conceived: that is, as the study of the conditions of justification of claims to know. For, if Quine is right, there is no sentence – or at best only a few relatively observational sentences – to which we can attach either a determinate meaning or a determinate set of empirical truth conditions. What is left to us at this point is the move, introduced into philosophy by David Hume, of transforming philosophy into psychology. Epistemology becomes 'a chapter of psychology'[27] which investigates, by the methods of empirical psychology, the processes by which human beings transform sensory input into structures of theory.

Quine's position thus achieves many of the traditional goals of empiricism. The Deweyan naturalism from which he begins has its roots in Locke: in Locke's respect for science and disrespect for metaphysical speculation, and in Locke's desire for a philosophy capable of directing men's minds towards the empirical study of the natural world.

The eighteenth-century empiricism founded upon Locke failed in this endeavour because it took ideas – the mental contents associated with individual words – as the units of empirical significance. The logical positivism of the Vienna Circle improved upon earlier forms of empiricism by taking statements as the units of empirical significance. We catalogued its failures in chapter 6, and Quine's own arguments add some new and formidable defects to the list. Quine's achievement is to have shown how much can be rescued and restored of the fundmental doctrines of empiricism by taking the unit of empirical significance to be language as a whole.

6. Some paradoxes of radical translation

The achievement, however, is not without its price. Quine's thesis of the indeterminacy of translation is as counterintuitive as his denial of a distinction between analyticity and coextensionality. This is scarcely surprising, since the two theses are closely connected. To say that two expressions can be compared only in respect of their stimulus meaning is to say that they can be compared only in respect of coextensionality: the stimulus meaning of a term *is* its extension construed in terms of assent- and dissent-prompting stimulations.

Thinking of coextensionality in terms of translation increases both the power and the counterintuitiveness of Quine's position. If Quine is right, it seems that we can never know whether two languages differ in their conceptual schemes, for in constructing translation schemes for alien languages I necessarily impose the conceptual scheme of my own language upon them.

> There is a notion that our provincial ways of positing objects and conceiving nature may be best appreciated for what they are by standing off and seeing them against a cosmopolitan background of alien cultures; but the notion comes to nothing, for there is no που στω.[28]

Further, Quine's position makes it very hard to give any satisfactory account of linguistic change. Intuitively we seem to be able to distinguish between changes in language – in the content and structure of the conceptual scheme in terms of which we interpret the world – and changes in knowledge. On Quine's view, no such distinction is ultimately tenable.

One consequence of this is that we have to treat conceptual change as being very much commoner than we ordinarily suppose. Another, more serious consequence, is that we are left without any possibility of giving an account of the mechanisms of conceptual change, as distinct from change in empirical belief.[29] Thirdly, and still more seriously, it gives rise to well known paradoxes concerning the commensurability of scientific theories. The proponents of two opposing theories presumably entertain different beliefs by virtue of holding those theories. But, if the meanings of the terms used in stating the theories in question cannot be specified without reference to the beliefs of proponents of the theories, we cannot, it seems, be sure even that the two theories are addressed to the same subject matter. Mary Hesse,[30] indeed, has suggested (1976, p. 197) a possible solution which would, if successful, be compatible with Quine's position. Her suggestion is that commensurability requires only that the majority of the descriptive predicates do in fact remain extensionally stable, and does not require that we know *a priori* which ones these are going to be. What assures commensurability, in other words, is the fact that language in general is, extensionally speaking, more stable than theory, so that the theoretically distinctive predicates of two opposing theories can be compared against the general background of language. But, of course, this still gives us no more than extensional comparability, and it cannot be denied that we take ourselves, intuitively speaking, to grasp the meanings of theoretical terms in some stronger sense than this.

And, finally, Quine's position seems to entail that we can make no sense at all of the idea that one speaker of a language attaches the same meaning, or sense, as another speaker to a particular expression of a language. The most we can say of two speakers is that, over the whole range of the language, their linguistic dispositions (that is, primarily, their dispositions to assent to or deny assertions) more or less coincide. But general coincidence of linguistic dispositions can give no empirical warrant for the assumption that the two speakers ascribe the same meanings to individual expressions.

Quine has here abandoned a central element in Frege's doctrine of sense. Frege held that, if a sentence does not have the same sense for two speakers, there can be no question of their engaging in a common inquiry into the truth or falsehood of the statement which it expresses, since manifestly it expresses a different statement for each speaker. There is, as is evident, a strong intuitive plausibility about this argument; and I think, in fact, that it can be made to yield at least the beginnings of a critique of Quine.

7. Stimulus meaning and observationality

There is a tension in Quine's thought about the foundations of language over which I have passed comparatively lightly in expounding Quine's views, since to do otherwise would have hindered the exposition. It concerns the notion of an observation sentence, and of observationality in general, and their relationship to the notion of stimulus meaning. On the one hand, Quine wishes to say that no statement possesses a determinate empirical significance in its own right: that language, and not the sentence, is the basic unit of meaning. On the other hand, it would hardly be possible for a linguist to penetrate an alien language at all – even to begin constructing a translation scheme, that is – unless there are some short native utterance types which correlate in a consistent way with fairly sharply defined recurrent patterns of stimulation.

In practice, then, as we have seen, Quine is forced to make a partial exception to the operation of indeterminacy of translation in the case of observation statements: 'The observation sentence, situated at the sensory periphery of the body scientific, is the minimal verifiable aggregate; it has an empirical content all its own and wears it on its sleeve.'[31]

As we have already shown, this admission is not *in itself* damaging to Quine's general position. It does not, for example, compel Quine to withdraw any part of his case against reductionism or the analytic–synthetic distinction, since the meanings of observation sentences are not supposed to attach to them analytically. Here as elsewhere, we have no insight into meaning, only an insight into coextensionality: the possibility of *generally shared* collateral information prevents, even in the case of observation sentences, a clear distinction between the empirical and the linguistic components of the truth conditions of a statement. Observation statements are simply those the behaviour of which with respect to native assent and dissent depends least on collateral information and most on present stimulation. Quine, in 'Epistemology Naturalized', offers the following succinct definition: 'an observation sentence is one that is not sensitive to differences in past experience within the speech community'.[32]

Observation sentences are those the meaning of which can be to all intents and purposes wholly grasped by 'pure ostension'. Quine gives the colour word 'sepia' as an example. 'Sepia' can 'certainly be learned by an ordinary process of conditioning, or induction'.[33] By contrast, the meaning of even a mildly 'theoretical' term such as 'rabbit' cannot be wholly grasped in this way.

> ... the big difference between 'rabbit' and 'sepia' is that whereas 'sepia' is a mass term like 'water', 'rabbit' is a term of divided reference. As such it cannot be mastered without mastering its principle of individuation: where one rabbit leaves off and another

begins. And this cannot be mastered by pure ostension, however persistent.[34]

Indeterminacy begins with 'rabbit' and with terms of divided reference generally.

> Such is the quandary over 'gavagai': where one gavagai leaves off and another begins. The only difference between rabbits, undetached rabbit parts, and rabbit stages is in their individuation. If you take the total scattered portion of the spatio-temporal world that is made up of rabbits, and that which is made up of undetached rabbit parts, and that which is made up of rabbit stages, you come up with the same scattered portion of the world each of the three times. The only difference is in how you slice it. And how to slice it is what ostension, or simple conditioning, however persistently repeated, cannot teach.[35]

At the same time, 'rabbit' largely meets Quine's 'social' criterion for observationality; that 'an occasion sentence may be said to be the more observational the more nearly its stimulus meanings for different speakers tend to coincide'.[36] As Quine says, 'If "Red" is somewhat less susceptible than "Rabbit", there are other sentences that are vastly more so.'[37] ('Bachelor', which 'draws mainly on stored information and none on the prompting stimulation except as needed for recognising the bachelor friend concerned'[38] is the example Quine gives.)

In short, what enables the linguist to get his translation manual off the ground is that for many short occasion sentences such as 'Rabbit!', or 'Red!' or 'Table!', stimulus meaning will vary comparatively little from speaker to speaker. In effect, in such cases, stimulus meaning can be treated, for all practical purposes of communication, as equivalent to 'meaning' in the ordinary sense.

I am very sceptical as to whether this account of translation-manual construction will wash. Stimulus meaning is supposed to give the linguist a firm footing for the construction of analytical hypotheses in the case of relatively observational occasion sentences, even though it fails to do so in the case of more 'theoretical' sentences. I do not find it at all obvious, however, that stimulus meaning affords the linguist a firm footing even in the case of observation sentences, if we define 'observation sentence' as Quine defines it.

Let us suppose for a start that the natives do assent to the one-word sentence 'Gavagai!' only when current stimulation includes a rabbit, and that they never dissent from it when current stimulation includes a rabbit. Even given this degree of consistency of response from speaker to speaker, the linguist still knows only how the natives respond to 'Gavagai!' in a limited range of situations. Some unforeseen variation of circumstances may reveal that 'Gavagai' has an *entirely* different meaning from 'Rabbit': that it is not even an animal name, but a word, connected with the religious vocabulary of the tribe, meaning 'sacred beast' – only rabbits and one other, extremely rare species being sacred in that way. Such a possibility, indeed, is implicit in what Quine has to say about generally shared collateral information. But, as long as such possibilities exist, the linguist cannot venture any translation of 'Gavagai' at all.

The reason why he cannot is that he does not know what 'Gavagai' contrasts with *in native usage*. He does not yet know what is implied by saying of something that it is *not gavagai*: whether, for example, what is implied is that it is some other kind of animal, animal part or animal stage; or that it is not sacred. He needs, in short, to know *what possibilities are left open* by the denial that something is *gavagai*.[39] Knowing the meaning of 'Red', for instance, involves *inter alia* knowing that, when a speaker denies that something is red, the possibilities his denial leaves open include the possibility that the thing is orange, or blue, or some other colour, and not the possibility that it is square or made in Taiwan. Similarly, fully to grasp the meaning of 'liquid', I must grasp that, when a speaker says that something is not a liquid, the possibilities left open are that it is a solid or a gas, not that it is a rabbit or a watch.

It seems clear, too, that, unless I know what possibilities the denial of an assertion 'leaves open' in this sense, I do not know how to go about ascertaining its truth; for I do not know what would or would not count as falsifying it, and hence I do not know what would or would not count as making it true. This is essentially Frege's point that a common understanding of sense is necessary to the common pursuit of truth.

It may be objected that the conditions of falsification of an observation statement are specified by the negative component of stimulus meaning. This is a serious mistake. The point I am making, in fact, is precisely that negative stimulus meaning does not provide an adequate functional analogue for negation in natural languages, although it can perhaps be taken as a functional analogue of negation in an extensional language. Negative stimulus meaning simply contributes one half of the specification of the extension of 'Gavagai' in terms of stimulation. It does not in any way determine the force of the assertion '*x* is not *gavagai*' – for example, whether it is to have the force of '. . . but some other kind of animal', or the force of '. . . but a common, non-sacred thing'.

If the linguist knew the force of '*x* is not *gavagai*', then he would know the principle of individuation for the term – where one *gavagai* leaves off and another begins. If such matters 'cannot be mastered by pure ostension, however persistent', then meaning, '*tout court*', cannot be mastered by pure ostension, however persistent. Quine has committed himself, in short, to a false partitioning of the content of the concept of meaning between the empirically determinate and the supposedly empirically indeterminate. If the considerations which Quine takes to be empirically indeterminate are not *on some level of linguistic description* (not necessarily any allowed for by Quine) empirically determinate, then the meaning of observation sentences is not empirically determinate either. And this, I think, confirms our suspicions of a tension in Quine's thought which centres upon the concept of observationality. Either the indeterminacy of radical translation is, after all, a philosophical chimaera, or else the indeterminacy does not stop short at the boundaries of the relatively observational.

8. Linguistic autonomy and the bilingual speaker

The force of these arguments can be seen more clearly if we connect them up with our discussion of linguistic autonomy in chapter 1. There we argue that it is a trivial condition of anyone's being said to understand a language that he should be able to predict the linguistic responses of other speakers even in unfamiliar circumstances. In the case of a term ϕ, he must be able to sort things into ϕs, non-ϕs, and dubious cases for the application of ϕ, even when the things concerned are not exactly similar to the things previously sorted into the three categories. A boy who continues to hesitate over the application of the French word *plume*, say, as his teacher holds up one diverse object after another, simply does not understand the meaning of *plume*.

If we define the capacities of a competent speaker in this way, then it is very hard to see how Quine's linguist could ever become a competent speaker of the native language. As long as the possibility remains open of generally shared collateral information exerting an influence over the native's assents and dissents, the linguist cannot be sure that the very next occasion on which a native, or he himself, uses the term *gavagai,* will not be the one which breaches the hitherto completely general applicability of the collateral information in question, and places an altogether different construction on the entire preceding pattern of native assents and dissents. The occasion may be one, for example, upon which the hitherto omnipresent rabbit fly (which is the real referent of the term *gavagai*) is absent, because the rabbit in question has accidently been sprayed with insecticide by the linguist. In such circumstances the linguist can never predict with certainty what the native speaker's next response will be.

It may be objected here that certainty about native speaker's responses is too strong a condition for understanding, since it is surely possible even for a native speaker of English to misapply a general name. Just as a duck, which can presumably normally recognise other ducks, can be led astray by a decoy duck, so an English-speaker who knows the meaning of 'duck' perfectly well will sometimes misapply it, to the same lifelike decoy, or to a goose seen in a failing light, or to a shadow on the water. But this objection misses the point. It confuses proneness to perceptual error with linguistic incompetence. Certainly a native speaker of English may be in doubt as to what, perceptually speaking, something *is*; but provided he is in a situation where such doubts can, for all practical purposes, be excluded he cannot, *qua* native speaker, be in doubt about what, linguistically speaking, the thing in question *ought to be called* (would be called by any other native speaker). For if he is in doubt we have no option but to say that, after all, he does not know English (or perhaps does not know some specialised dialect of English: is not a duck-hunting man, for example).[40]

It is this purely linguistic certainty which Quine's argument fails to account for. Quine's anthropologist remains with respect to the natives' linguistic performances in the same position as that occupied by the experienced but not infallible duck with respect to a world which contains not only other ducks but also cunningly contrived decoys. Just as the experienced duck makes his perceptual judgements on the basis of past experience, and sometimes errs, so the Quinean anthropologist makes his linguistic judgements, when it comes to actually using the native language, on the basis of past experience, and sometimes errs; and for that very reason can never attain to the status of a native, or competent, speaker, who never errs on *linguistic* questions, just because he *is* competent, and because linguistic error implies linguistic incompetence.

These considerations, finally, throw some doubt on Quine's treatment of bilingual competence. Here again, we are accustomed to make a distinction, which Quine's arguments erode, between the scholar who has an empirical knowledge of a language and the bilingual person who 'speaks it like a native'. A modern English-speaker can never become bilingual in Old English, for example, because our knowledge of Old English is based upon a finite body of texts. For that reason we cannot be sure, on many points, what the linguistic judgement of a native speaker of Old English would have been: our judgement, as modern English-speakers, is worthless unless bolstered by empirical evidence derived from some text. One who is bilingual, on the other hand, would not need to refer to textual evidence to tell us 'what any speaker of Old English [we can specify one of, say, AD 800, to allow for linguistic drift] would say'. He knows, *because* he is bilingual.

Quine is at times prepared to use the notion of bilingual capacity in a full-blooded way. Sometimes he talks as if the *real* native meaning of *gavagai* – not just the meaning ascribed to it by one or another translation manual – is accessible to the bilingual speaker or the child who has learned the language at his mother's knee. But, of course, in reality talk of 'real' meanings is foreign to the whole tendency of Quine's thought, and at other times he takes a far tougher and quite explicit stance.

> It makes no real difference that the linguist will turn bilingual and come to think as the natives do – whatever that means. For the arbitrariness of reading our objectifications into the heathen speech reflects not so much the inscrutability of the heathen mind, as that there is nothing to scrute.[41]

This is all very well if it is impossible to state any clear criterion for what counts as being bilingual. But the notion of linguistic autonomy gives us such a criterion, and it is one which, it appears, the Quinean linguist cannot meet.

9. *Pelicans and half-brothers*

All the same, Quine might seem to have, in the shape of the Inextricability Thesis, an unanswerable reply to these criticisms. If the empirical and the linguistic considerations bearing upon the truth of a statement cannot be disentangled from one another, how can our grasp of linguistic relationships – or of what we like to think of as linguistic relationships – be anything but an empirical grasp?

We need to see, I think, that the scope of the Inextricability Thesis is limited to some extent by the terms of Quine's arguments. What Quine is arguing is that linguistic and empirical considerations cannot be differentiated from one another by reference to the only available evidence we have for judgements about the truth and falsity of statements: that is, by reference to observed conditions for assent and dissent to sentences. It does not follow, however, that there are no phenomena by reference to which we may define linguistic relationships independently of all questions of the truth and falsity of statements. Quine himself mentions one such possibility. The example he chooses is that of 'certain islanders' who speak of pelicans as their half-brothers. In such a case there is an objective 'cultural difference' between the islanders and English-speakers which consists in the fact that 'the islanders have a short occasion-sentence that commands an islander's assent indiscriminately on presentation of any pelican or any half-brother, and presumably no comparably short one for the case of half-brothers exclusively, whereas English is oppositely endowed'.[42] This difference, Quine says, 'does objectively manifest itself in language without intervention of analytical hypotheses'.[43]

It is clear why this kind of difference manifests itself objectively. It does so because we are interested not in discovering English sentences the truth conditions of which correspond to those of native sentences, but in charting differences in the way in which the same empirically locatable subject matter (pelicans and half-brothers) is divided up between, on the one hand, English sentences, and, on the other hand, native sentences. We are looking at internal relationships within the native language and contrasting them with internal relationships within English. Admittedly, these relationships are established in the first place by reference to stimulus meaning. But to assert that such relationships exist does not involve asserting the existence of *meaning* relationships between English sentences and native sentences; and so the problem of shared collateral information does not arise; is not relevant to the determination of the differences in question.

I am inclined to think that a great many of the conceptual differences between languages which Quine affirms to be empirically indeterminate, and to form part of a hypothetical native semantic consciousness which is not so much inscrutable as just not there to be scrutinised, might prove to be empirically specifiable upon what we might call the pelicans-and-half-brothers level of linguistic description. If so, would that achievement constitute a refutation of Quine? In one sense it would, and in another it would not.

Quine's theory as it stands offers, as I have tried to show in the last two sections, an entirely inadequate account of what is learned in learning language. If what is learned is primarily stimulus meanings, then we have no way of explaining linguistic autonomy: the ability of other native speakers to predict each other's linguistic responses, even in circumstances when the psychological capacity to generalise responses over a range of broadly similar stimuli cannot possibly be held to account for community of linguistic response. In order for one speaker to predict what another speaker will call *gavagai*, for example, all the speakers must possess common criteria for determining what things are *gavagai*, what things are not *gavagai*, and what things are dubious cases for the application of *gavagai*. As we argued in chapter 4, such criteria cannot just take the form of a list of properties which things must have in order to be *gavagai*. Each speaker must also grasp the logical category of *gavagai*: whether, for example, it is supposed to be the name of a kind of stuff, or a colour name, or the name of a kind of animal – or animal part or animal stage. Certainly, then, since language is learnable, and Quinean linguists, however tentative and empirical their first encounters with a language, do, in the real world at least, enter in the end into the full capacities of native speakers, something or other must determine conceptual questions which Quine holds to be intrinsically indeterminate. The common pursuit of truth, as Frege saw, requires common access to sense. If so, then meaning, in some sense, does – must – attach to individual expressions; the Inextricability Thesis must, strictly speaking, be false; and the paradoxes we canvassed in section 6 of this chapter may prove to be avoidable. In particular, it may prove possible to specify the meanings of theoretical terms without reference to any assertion about the world made by the theories in question.

But, on the other hand, the Inextricability Thesis would remain

MB

entirely untouched by these achievements, if we take it as the thesis that the meaning of individual sentences is not fully determined by the empirical conditions of assent and dissent attaching to them. That seems undeniable. And, if that stands, then much of Quine's argument against older forms of empiricism, against many ways of conceiving the analytic–synthetic distinction, and against the possibility of philosophical ontology, stands with it. These parts of Quine's position to my mind resemble large parts of Hume's philosophy, in being so well constructed that they are very unlikely ever to fall to a direct assault. Indeed, the criticisms which I have been levelling against Quine in the last few pages are not intended as a direct assault upon the Quinean fortress; rather as an attempt to envelop and outflank it.

Finally, then, let us try to see briefly how we might extend the scope of Quine's pelican-and-half-brother example. Quine believes, for example, that colour names can be learned by ostensive definition. To see that this must be wrong, it is only necessary to reflect that the human eye can discriminate about 7 million distinct shades of colour, that these discriminable presentations form complex qualitative series which can be displayed as colour wheels, charts and solids of various kinds; and that a colour name in a natural language picks out not a single discriminable shade of colour, but a very large, and open-ended, sub-class of discriminable shades of colour, each member of which is qualitatively distinct from all the rest. The remarkable, and really puzzling, facts, as we saw in chapter 1, are that each speaker of a given language can extend the open-ended class of shades marked by a given colour name in a way which matches that in which other speakers of that language are independently prepared to extend it, and that the colour vocabularies of different languages divide up the total colour array differently (in other words, that the contents of the class of discriminable shades attaching to one and the same colour word cannot, as we argued in chapter 1, be wholly physiologically or neurologically determined).

The reader may grant that this is a puzzle, but feel at a loss to say what kind of theory of colour-naming could provide an answer to it. It is not too difficult to suggest at least the outlines of how such a theory might go, however. Wittgenstein asks, in his *Remarks on Colour*

How do I learn the use of the word 'yellowish'? Through language-games in which, for example, things are put in a certain order.

Thus I can learn, in agreement with other people, to recognise yellowish and still more yellowish red, green, brown and white.

In the course of this I learn to proceed independently just as I do in arithmetic.[44]

Wittgenstein's learner is learning how to apply various relational predicates: 'is a yellowish ϕ'; 'is more yellowish than ϕ', and so on. Let us suppose that at the same time he is learning, in the same way, other sets of predicates, 'is more greenish than ϕ', 'is more reddish than ϕ', and so on. The series of 'yellowish and still more yellowish' reds, that of 'yellowish and still more yellowish' greens, that of 'yellowish and still more yellowish' browns, and so on, will all converge, given the phenomenal character of the contents of the colour solid, upon the area of the colour solid occupied by yellows which are neither particularly reddish, greenish, brownish or whitish: in other words, by the 'pure' yellows. Similar considerations will give a meaning to the predicates 'is a pure red', 'is a pure green', and so on. The end result will be that, for the learner, the three-dimensional colour solid – the entire array of possible colours – comes to be divided up linguistically (that is, for purposes of linguistic reference) between two types of volume:

(1) volumes occupied by 'pure' shades of colour: 'pure' reds, 'pure' blues, and so on; and

(2) volumes occupied by 'intermediate' shades of colour: reddish blues, bluish reds, yellowish greens, and so on.

The total collection of volumes of both types exhausts the contents of the colour solid.

Once a speaker has learned this system for linguistically tabulating relative qualitative distance between shades of colour (for that is what it is), he can, of course, predict where, within the system, an unfamiliar shade of colour will be placed by any other speaker of the language – any other speaker, that is, who has mastered the same system of tabulation of qualitative distance. All he has to do, to make the prediction, is to compare and contrast the shade with other shades until he finds a place for it relative to other shades – perhaps in the pure yellows, for instance, perhaps in the reddish yellows, or elsewhere. Wherever he finds a place for the particular shade in question, the system of linguistic tabulation will yield a linguistic designation for it – 'yellow', or 'reddish yellow', for instance – and this designation will be necessarily the one given by any other competent speaker, except in volumes of the colour solid occupied by the most marginal shades for discriminations marked in a given language, where disagreement may arise between speakers over, for instance, whether something is a greenish blue or a bluish green.

Such a system of linguistic tabulation of relative qualitative distance may be expected to yield different results depending on the number of basic colour names a given language introduces, for the colour-naming system of any language must divide up the colour solid exhaustively, even if only with a few basic colour names. For this reason we cannot regard the colour-naming system as something 'natural', in the sense of pertaining to the physiology or neurology of colour perception. But, even if we disregard cross-cultural differences, the colour-naming system is manifestly not something 'natural' in this sense. It is a *linguistic* device, or construct. To learn it, the learner must learn certain procedures of 'putting things in a certain order', as Wittgenstein says. These procedures, and not the physiology or neurology of colour, are what give a sense to such relational predicates as 'is a yellowish ϕ', 'is yellower than ϕ', and so on; though no doubt the possibility of carrying out these procedures in a standard, uniform and reproducible way *is* dependent upon the facts of human neurophysiology.

If colour-naming is learned in this way, *what* is being learned is manifestly not the stimulus meaning, in Quine's sense, of sentences such as 'ϕ is red', 'ϕ is blue.'

In the process of learning to find our way about within the colour vocabulary of a new language, we may indeed, of course, find ourselves tabulating what appear to be positive and negative stimulus meanings: native judgements to the effect that while *this* is *vair*, *that* is not *vair*, and so on. We shall not, however, at least if we think of colour-naming in the way I have just indicated, be using these native assents and dissents to confirm or disconfirm analytical hypotheses. Most likely, in any case, there will be no precise equivalent for *vair* in the English colour vocabulary. We shall be using them to determine the system of contrasts which enables one native speaker to predict another native speaker's judgements in assimilating colour presentations to one or another colour name of the native language. In other words, we shall be detecting differences between English and Native which are discoverable in the same way and on the same level of linguistic description as the differences in Quine's pelicans-and-half-brothers example. In particular, the natives' negative judgements do not function as the negative components of specifications of extensions; we shall be using them to determine *what is to contrast with vair*: to determine what possibilities are left open by the judgement, '*x* is not *vair*.' The upshot of the whole procedure is that we can attach a clear empirical content to the statement that the natives have *different* colour concepts from English-speakers, and that they have *colour* concepts; for what makes *vair* and the other words in the native colour vocabulary colour words is that we can predict native speakers' uses of them by carrying out various sorting and contrasting procedures with respect to the visual qualities of coloured objects, and not otherwise.

In *Word and Object* (1960, p. 100), Quine gives the following account of how we might learn the use of the proper name 'Nile':

> Say we want to teach the name 'Nile'. The hard way would consist in protracted training similar to what went into 'mama' and 'water'. We might expose our pupil to bits and stretches of the Nile from Kenya to the sea, schooling him in the proper applications of the word and discouraging its abuse, until satisfied that he was prepared to apply the term throughout the intended portion of the world and not beyond.[45]

As in the case of colour words, I do not think that Quine here describes a possible way of learning the meaning of the name 'Nile'. A knowledge of the meaning of 'Nile' involves more than an ability to say 'Nile' at every point in space occupied by some part of the waters of the Nile and to refrain from saying it at every point in space not so occupied. To have grasped the meaning of 'Nile' is to know at least that 'Nile' is the name of a river. The concept of a river cannot be explained by pointing to 'bits and stretches of rivers': what has to be explained is not even that the bits and stretches must be spatially connected, but that the connection must be of a particular kind; that a long sinuous lake, or a low-lying valley which becomes filled with seawater at exceptional spring tides is not a river, for example. No doubt Quine's account gives a description of a training process from which a particular child or anthropologist might, by putting two and two together, arrive at a grasp of the meaning of 'Nile'; but *the meaning of* 'Nile' is surely not to be identified with the training process, but whatever it is that the learner *arrives at*: the two and two which he puts together.

What he arrives at must make the difference, whatever *that* is, between treating 'Nile' as a cry which one utters on coming to the margins of a particular body of water the limits of which one has established by beating its bounds, and treating 'Nile' as a name: the name of a river. It is not hard to see the kind of consideration that would make the difference. We need to know, for example, whether the native is prepared to apply 'Nile' to a little lake adjacent to the river, but cut off from it by a sandbank. He may be using 'Nile' as a name for all bodies of water within certain limits of proximity to one another, although perhaps two of these bodies belong to different river systems – in which case 'Nile' is not functioning for him as the name of a *river*. Such questions can be settled, in the same way as Quine's natives' linguistic dispositions towards pelicans and half-brothers can be; but, once settled, they also settle questions about the content and structure of the native's conceptual system.

Again, suppose we want to know whether the terms for animals in a native language are terms for animal species or terms for morphological types. Part of the answer will depend upon whether the native terms follow the limits of interbreeding populations, and this too is an empirically determinable question.

There is no point in multiplying examples further. They all point in the same direction: towards a 'use' theory of meaning like that characteristic of Wittgenstein's later theory of language. But it is by no means clear how Wittgenstein's later writings ought to be interpreted; and to begin to identify the points at which it bears critically upon the tradition of formal semantics to which Quine belongs we shall need to examine the relationship of Wittgenstein's thought to the common ancestor of both traditions: Gottlob Frege. That will be the task of chapters 13 and 14.

8

Truth and Interpretation

1. Meaning and T sentences

Quine's outlook is destructive of most earlier programmes for philosophical analysis. Russell, for example, at one time conceived of analysis as a process in which complex denoting expressions are replaced successively by definite descriptions, analysed according to the Theory of Descriptions, until the process terminates in sentences containing only logically proper names and truth-functional operators. Quine's holism, ontological relativism and scepticism about particulars makes nonsense of talk of logically proper names (experience, in the shape of stimulus meaning, does not suffice to determine reference to particulars and so cannot determine the reference of a logically proper name) and in thus destroying the goal of Russellian analysis makes it pointless. Similar arguments, as we have seen, defeat the programme of phenomenalist analysis characteristic of Vienna Circle positivism and Carnap's *Aufbau*. And Quine's strictures against quantifying into modal contexts raise reverse difficulties for any conception of analysis founded upon modal logic and the notion of a possible world.

At the same time, the general reasons for pursuing the study of meaning in natural languages by attempting to construct rigorously formalised models, as we stated them in chapter 6, section 7, remain untouched by Quine's arguments. What seems to be needed is a new general strategy, or rationale, for the application of formal semantics to problems of meaning in natural languages.

There are other difficulties, besides those raised by Quine, which have to be confronted in constructing a rationale for the formal analysis of natural languages. The aim of formal semantic analysis must be to explicate the concept of meaning in terms of the concept of truth; but the concept of truth is not an entirely well-defined one, to say the least. Strawson has argued[1] that we cannot hope to define truth except by bringing in the concept of belief, and with it the notion of the content of an assertion, in which case any definition of meaning in terms of truth would be circular. Moreover, an explanation of the concept of meaning runs the risk of circularity in quite another way. It may fail to break out of the circle of intentional concepts, by presupposing at some point in the analysis some intensional concept which raises the same problems as the concept of meaning itself. Such a problem obviously arises in the case of analyses of 'meaning' which appeal to the concept of a rule, if the rules in question have to be formulated in a language before they can be understood. And, finally, any account of the nature of meaning in natural languages must give some account of how a speaker of a language attaches a sense to a language which he has never encountered before: how new sentences can be built from the basic vocabulary of the language without the need for the truth conditions of each sentence constructed in this way to be explained afresh to each speaker who encounters it.

Donald Davidson has shown how we can avoid most of these problems and still, astonishingly, get a non-trivial interpretation of the concept of meaning in terms of the concept of truth, if we confine ourselves to explicating the meaning of a sentence in terms of that very same sentence. Such elucidations play a large part in Tarski's theory of truth (the so-called 'redundancy theory'). Davidson calls such sentences T sentences. They take the following form.

'It's raining' is true if and only if (iff) it's raining.

'There are a million stars out tonight' is true iff there are a million stars out tonight.

T sentences offer a way of dispensing with the concept of truth; by replacing each statement of the form 's is true' with a statement 'p', which is either identical to, or a translation of, s. The reason why explication of truth conditions in terms of T sentences is not a trivial procedure is that T sentences offer an alternative to talk about truth for certain logico-grammatical contexts only. T sentences are of no help if we want to state the truth conditions of, for example,

Every sentence Aristotle spoke was false.

What you said last Tuesday was true.[2]

For such sentences, the notion of a T sentence provides us with a goal of analysis, in terms of which we can say in a reasonably clear and precise way what it would be to understand the logical structure of them. We should understand their logical structure, and be in a position to state their truth conditions, if we were in a position to replace them with equivalent T sentences. We thus have a new way of conceiving of the methodology of a truth-theoretical inquiry into the bases of a competent speaker's grasp of sentence meaning. The aim of such a theory would be the discovery of a principled and systematic way of mapping the totality of sentences of a given language onto some set of T sentences. And, putting this another way, we could then take the totality of T sentences as fixing 'the extension, among the sentences of the language, of any predicate that plays the role of the words "is true"'[3] which is why Tarski's theory of truth, for all its apparent triviality, can be regarded, when taken together with the complementary Tarskian notion of satisfaction, as offering a non-trivial explication of the concept of truth.

Davidson, in fact, would not claim to be putting forward a theory about 'the nature of meaning', and would not in any case, if I read him correctly, consider such theories sufficiently precise or specific to be worth putting forward. He is proposing, rather, a certain view of what it is to state the truth conditions of a sentence. It is among the advantages of this view that it is 'translational' in nature, and that the process of translation which it proposes can proceed *within* one and the same language. A Tarskian theory of truth has ordinarily been conceived as specific to a given language (regarded as an object language to which the theory in question stands as a meta-language); as defining not the concept 'true', but a concept of truth, 'true in L', specific to a given object language. Davidson's concept of truth, defined extensionally in terms of the totality of T sentences, is language-relative in the same way.

The goal of pairing off sentences of a language with correlative T sentences in a principled, non-*ad hoc* way offers us, then, a criterion of success, or adequacy, for formal semantics conceived as a way of studying meaning in natural languages. And the criterion, as one would hope, is a highly restrictive one. As yet, as Davidson points out in his essay 'Semantics for Natural Languages' (in Davidson and

Harman, 1975, p. 23), there is no clearly understood way of achieving such a goal in the cases of 'modal sentences, sentences about proposi- tional attitudes, mass terms, adverbial modification, attributive ad- jectives, imperatives and interrogatives; and so on through a long list familiar, for the most part, to philosophers'.[4] If this can be read as a lexicon of failure on the part of formal semantics, it can also be read as a rebuttal of the notion that to state truth conditions in terms of T sentences would be a trivial exercise.

Difficult as it might be, indeed, to meet the demands of a theory in accord with Tarski's Convention T, success would carry with it certain distinct advantages. We should have a theory which would account for 'the meaning (or conditions of truth) of every sentence by analysing it as composed, in truth-relevant ways, of elements drawn from a finite stock'.[5] And we should also possess a method for deciding, of any given sentence, what its meaning is. A theory which satisfies these two conditions, says Davidson, shows 'that the lan- guage it describes is *learnable* and *scrutable*'.[6] Davidson is perhaps right about the second of these claims: the first, as we shall see, raises problems. Finally, and perhaps most importantly, we should have a theory in which these goals would be achieved without any appeal to unanalysed semantic notions, such as those of *meaning* or *denotation*. It is obvious how this would work for a theory based on Tarski's Convention T, if we regard the object language as contained in the meta-language. In a statement of the form, 's is true iff p', the sentence which replaces p is s itself: hence, understanding p requires no appeal to concepts which are not required in understanding s. Thus, in understanding p we shall only need to appeal to semantic concepts if such concepts occur in s. There are, as Davidson admits, difficulties about extending this feature of a Tarskian truth theory to natural languages; but at this point, so far as that goes, we are simply discussing conditions of theoretical adequacy for a semantic theory of natural language. We can require it as a condition of adequacy that any such theory have this property; and it seems clear that any theory which meets this condition will, as Davidson argues,[7] be superior to theories such as Montague's, and other systems of 'possible-world' semantics, which appeal an unanalysed concept of denotation. Ideally, then, we have a way of disposing of the more metaphysical philosophical problems about meaning by simply disposing of the' entities, 'meanings', over which such problems arise. We are left with problems, indeed, but they are problems of the sort which logical analysis can fruitfully tackle.

Matters are not, of course, quite as simple as that. The application of a Tarskian theory of truth to an actual natural language cannot be merely a matter of logical analysis. Indeed, it might be cited as one great merit of Davidson's work that he is keenly aware of the gulf between logic on the one hand and natural languages on the other. Davidson's view, however, is not at all that there is any essential difference of kind between formal and natural languages which might prevent the discussion of the latter in terms of the former.

It would be misleading . . . to conclude that there are two kinds of language, natural and artificial. The contrast is better drawn in terms of guiding interests. We can ask for a description of a natural language: the answer must be an empirical theory, open to test and subject to error, and doomed to be to some extent incomplete and schematic. Or we can ask about the formal properties of the structures we thus abstract. The difference is like that between applied and pure geometry.[8]

We need, therefore, to supplement the description of the formal properties of a theory of truth adequate to the study of a natural language with an account of how such a theory is to be put into empirical relationship with its object. Davidson's view is that this requirement can only be met by a theory of what he calls *radical interpretation*.

2. *Radical interpretation*

To interpret a sentence is according to Davidson to analyse it 'as composed, in truth-relevant ways, of elements drawn from a finite stock'. But how are we to begin imposing such an interpretation on the sentences of an unknown language? It makes little difference to this question whether the language is supposed to be a foreign one or our own. In the one case we can envisage ourselves in the situation of a Quinean anthropologist; in the other, in that of a prelinguistic child. In either case all we have to go on – the fundamental data for any interpretation – is the set of uninterpreted sentences of the language taken in conjunction with the circumstances in which they are uttered by competent speakers. 'Uninterpreted utterances', says Davidson (1974, p. 310), 'seem the appropriate evidential base for a theory of meaning.'[9]

If we can sustain a theory on that sort of evidence, then we have a theory of meaning which rests upon evidence which can be described without appeal to semantic notions. There is an initial difficulty which arises because of the existence of indexical expressions in English and other languages. But that is not a serious problem for Davidson's theory. If speakers can interpret sentences involving indexical expressions, such expressions in a given language must be governed by definite rules of use, and we can supplement the sentence description which replaces p in a T sentence with an account of these rules; so that we get, in effect, a T sentence 'relativised' to time, place and speaker: for example,

> 'Es regnet' is true in German when spoken by x at time t iff it is raining near x at t.

Much more serious problems arise over belief. Suppose a speaker, Kurt, utters the so far uninterpreted sentence 'Es regnet' when it is in fact raining near him. Does this piece of evidence justify our writing down the following T sentence (or some suitably relativised version of it)?

> 'Es regnet' is true iff it is raining.

Only if we can be sure not only that it is raining, but also that Kurt believes that it is raining. Moreover, this difficulty is quite general. The ascription of beliefs is indispensable to the interpretation of meaning. But, unfortunately, the assumption that utterances bear one or another interpretation is also indispensable to the ascription of beliefs. Belief and meaning, precisely as Strawson argues in 'Meaning and Truth' (in Strawson, 1971b), are locked into a hermetic circle.

The problem of constructing a viable theory of meaning now appears as the problem of breaking into this circle. In his papers 'Radical Interpretation' and 'Belief and the Basis of Meaning', Davidson considers the main philosophical 'theories of meaning' and rejects them all as inadequate to this task for reasons which are by now familiar to us. Causal theories, which attempt to give behaviourist analyses of the meanings of individual sentences, fail in this enterprise and in any case give no account of the interpretation of any. but the simplest sentences. Theories which take naming as the fundamental linguistic operation fail because no account of naming will work unless we give a prior account of the role of names in sentences. And theories of use or function, under which Davidson lumps (1974, p. 311) such diverse theorists as Mead, Dewey, Wittgenstein and Grice,[10] are rejected because they appeal to a knowledge of beliefs, intentions and purposes which cannot be assumed without assuming that we already possess an interpretation of the sentences of the language for which we wish to construct a theory of meaning.

Davidson's conclusion is that interpretation is necessarily *radical* interpretation, in the Quinean sense. We cannot assume either antecedent knowledge of speakers' beliefs upon which to base hypotheses about the interpretation of their utterances, or antecedently given interpretations of utterances upon which to base hypotheses about beliefs. The investigation of belief and intention must proceed hand in hand with the construction of truth-theoretic procedures of interpretation for the language. But, if this is so, what criterion can we have for success in this joint enterprise? Davidson's reply (1973a, p. 324) is that the only possible solution is that of 'holding belief constant as far as possible and solving for meaning'.[11] To do this we have to adopt, as a 'principle of charity', the assumption that the native speakers' beliefs are correct more often than not and that they speak the truth more often than not. We then assign truth interpretations to sentences in such a way as to maximise true belief and truth-telling by our standards. Such a methodology, Davidson argues, is not unduly trustful or incautious; in fact, the assumptions we make in adopting it are not even empirical assumptions.

> The methodological advice to interpret in a way that optimises agreement should not be conceived as resting on a charitable assumption about human intelligence that might turn out to be false. If we cannot find a way to interpret the utterances and behaviour of a creature as revealing a set of beliefs largely consistent and true by our own standards, we have no reason to count that creature as rational, as having beliefs, or as saying anything.[12]

The principle of optimising agreement in effect sets up connections between the truth conditions we assign to any given sentence, the assumptions we make about the beliefs of speakers who utter it in given circumstances, and the truth conditions we assign to other sentences. The assumptions we make about the truth-relevant internal structure of individual sentences obviously enter into the processes of radical interpretation, but only in a secondary and derivative way. The primary process of radical interpretation is that of distributing truth conditions to sentences in such a way as to maximise agreement and truth across the widest possible range of utterances and contexts of utterance. Radical interpretation is thus essentially *holistic* in nature. That is, the interpretative options between which we have to decide are primarily and fundamentally not options involving single sentences, but options involving the systematic and, as it were, simultaneous assignment of truth conditions to the widest possible array of utterances in context (sentences 'relativised' to time, place and speaker), under the general control of a Davidsonian principle of charity. In this process, as Davidson puts it in 'In Defense of Convention T', the internal structure of sentences is 'up for grabs'.[13]

> A workable theory must, of course, treat sentences as concatenations of expressions of less than sentential length, it must introduce semantical notions like satisfaction and reference, and it must appeal to an ontology of sequences and the objects ordered by the sequences. All this apparatus is properly viewed as theoretical construction, beyond the reach of direct verification. It has done its work provided only it entails testable results in the form of T sentences, and these make no mention of the machinery.[14]

Radical interpretation thus provides a new set of reasons for rejecting traditional ways of formulating the problem of meaning. Davidson, like Quine, holds, in effect, that the notion of the meaning of an individual sentence is no more than fundamental or philosophically interesting than that of the meaning of an individual word. In neither case is there any way of determining absolutely or independently what 'the meaning' of a particular expression is. All such judgements are relative to a more fundamental level of decisions, which match truth conditions not to sentences *per se*, but to sentences relativised to time, place and speaker, and do so holistically, across the widest possible range of utterances and contexts.

3. Critique of radical interpretation

The originality and elegance of Davidson's work are undeniable. He has given both an unexpected new interpretation and a new justification of the Fregian maxim that to know the meaning of a sentence is to know under what conditions one who utters it says something true. If Davidson is correct, Frege's maxim is the key to a wholesale replacement of the traditional problems about meaning by a new set of problems surrounding the construction of informative and empirically testable theories of truth, the point of the change being that the new problems will very likely turn out to be soluble piecemeal by known methods of logical analysis, without appeal to mysterious intensional entities or unanalysed semantic notions.

Nevertheless, doubts can reasonably be raised about the general strategy of Davidson's theory, with its curious yoking of a Tarskian theory of truth with Quinean scepticism about radical translation. But the doubts are difficult to drive home. Putnam,[15] for example, attacks Davidson for bypassing, rather than solving, the problem of intension. An agreement-preserving assignment of truth conditions might, for example, yield as a T sentence

'x is water' is true iff x is H_2O

which is extensionally correct, but not, intuitively speaking, intensionally correct. Putnam points out that Davidson's appeal to a theory of radical translation (or interpretation) is designed to remedy this, by making it unlikely that such a T sentence would appear in an interpretation of the language of, say, a prescientific community. But Putnam regards the attempt as a failure, because radical interpretation is unlikely to yield semantically informative T sentences in any case: we are most likely to end up with T sentences such as

'x is water' is true iff x is water.

We can see, I think, why this need not worry Davidson much. As he remarks somewhere, it is not individual T sentences which enlighten us about meaning, but the recursive processes which relate the whole web of sentences of the language to its T sentences. Davidson's holism, in short, like Quine's, offers a genuine refuge at least from the traditional problems about intension and extension, if we are prepared to accept its essential counter-intuitiveness.

Putnam is on firmer ground, it seems to me, when he observes that the method of radical interpretation, proceeding as it does from sentences to words, runs counter both to intuition and to the actual

practice of anthropologists, schoolboys and the decipherers of hiero-
glyphics or Linear B.

> It is noteworthy that the procedure that Quine and Davidson claim
> is the only *possible* one – going from whole sentences to individual
> words – is the *opposite* of the procedure upon which every success
> ever attained in the study of natural language has been based.[16]

I think this point can be developed further. When we start learning a
foreign language, for example, questions of truth seem to have a
minimal bearing upon the process. No doubt this is because I already
dispose of the resources of my native language, the truth conditions of
whose sentences I already know. I thus do not need to be told the
truth conditions of 'Jean et Marcel sont dans le jardin', if I know it
means 'Jean and Marcel are in the garden.' But the fact remains that
the giving of sentence-by-sentence statements of truth conditions of
this sort is quite unhelpful when it comes to grasping the syntactic and
semantic mechanisms of the language. I do not, in other words, start
with some set of putative T sentences such as

> 'Jean et Marcel sont dans le jardin' is true iff Jean and Marcel are in
> the garden

and go on from there to build up, by trial-and-error methods, an
empirically founded and approximate truth theory for French, proceeding on the assumption that most French speakers believe and
speak truth more often than falsehood, and treating French grammar
and the meanings of individual French words as 'up for grabs' or as
'theoretical constructions beyond the reach of direct verification'. It is
difficult to say what would become of me if I did. I should certainly
not stand much chance of learning French within a finite span of time.
   Actual language-learning starts, as Putnam rightly says, from the
meanings of individual words and the internal logico-grammatical
structure of sentences, and what I learn of such matters at the outset
of the course is not treated as a theoretical proposal open to an
indefinitely extended process of revision and reformulation in the
light of experience. There is, it is true, a period when my grasp of a
meaning or a construction may still be fluid and uncertain, and new
contexts of use, together with the explicit explanations of my teacher,
may change my appreciation of the force of those words. But it

changes it only in the course of hardening it. I arrive at a point at which I can be said to have 'grasped' the workings of the tense system or the meaning of the word *fond*. And the test of this is that after that point the more I learn of the language the more the correctness of my understanding is confirmed.

It might be argued that learning to interpret a language as close to English as French is not truly *radical* interpretation. But French is, after all, not all that similar to English, and I can see no grounds at all for claiming that there is some absolute change in quality between the differences which separate French from English and those which separate Kwakiutl or Cantonese from English.

In any case, there is, I think, a quite simple reason why, in language-learning, our first correct appreciations of the meanings of words or the force of grammatical constructions should stand, as it were, to eternity, as things absolutely fixed and final, rather than continue to be regarded as approximative theoretical constructions, subject to an indefinitely continued process of revision in the light of empirical data about the truth conditions of utterances. It is the reason which we have already raised in connection with Quine's account of radical translation. We, *as students of languages*, may if we choose rest content with an empirical and approximate grasp of the meanings of words or the force of grammatical constructions; and in some cases, where the languages concerned are very dead ones indeed, such as Ugaritic or Old English, we may have no choice but to do so. But we cannot, *as speakers of a language*, possess only an approximative, empirically corrigible grasp of its fundamental syntactic and semantic machinery, for if we did we should not really *know* the language in question; that is, we should not count as competent speakers of it. And therefore no theory which claims to represent what a competent native speaker knows in knowing his language, and which represents the fundamental semantic and syntactic knowledge of such a speaker as 'approximative' or 'theoretical' in Davidson's sense, can possibly be true. I shall now try to amplify this point a little further.

Let us return to Davidson's exemplary speaker Kurt and his utterance 'Es regnet'. I take it to be trivial that, unless we regard Kurt as speaking a language, there is no point in speculating about the truth conditions of his utterances. Without such an assumption, that is, we have no licence for regarding the sounds which he makes with his mouth as anything more than curiously patterned noise. This assumption, however, carries with it another: namely, that Manfred and Horst can independently read off from the utterance 'Es regnet' exactly the sense which Kurt in his turn would attribute to it if it were to be uttered by Manfred or Horst. The grounds for taking the second assumption to be implicit in the first are those discussed in chapter 1, sections 2 and 3. Only the sense which *any* competent speaker can read off from a written or spoken sign can be regarded as communicated by that sign or as part of the meaning of the sign. The ability to read off the same sense as any other speaker, which includes the ability to supply a statement, matching those independently supplied by other competent speakers, of the truth conditions of the assertion made by the utterance in the mouth of a given speaker, at a given time and place, is, indeed, a test of competence in the language. There are, of course, bound to be marginal cases where competent speakers fail this test: cases where minor differences of dialect obtrude, or where Kurt and his friends are using high-flown language which none of them properly understand. But these cases are marginal precisely because they contrast with the normal ability of competent speakers to predict each other's linguistic judgements with perfect accuracy over very large tracts of discourse, so we can disregard them for the purposes of the present argument. If they were more than marginal cases, natural languages would not exist.

Unless we can assume a shared competence, in this strong sense, on the part of the community of speakers we are investigating, radical interpretation cannot get started. Davidson's account of radical interpretation is, as we have seen, that we 'hold belief steady and solve for meaning', and the assumption of a methodological principle of charity about the distribution of true belief and truth-telling is supposed to be sufficient to 'hold belief steady'. But the notion of truth-telling is itself derivative from the notion of an utterance, since only an utterance in a language can convey an assertion, and only an assertion can be true or false. And the supposition that a sound or mark constitutes the vehicle of an utterance is dependent upon the assumption of an absolute, and not just an approximative, community of judgement about the meanings of individual words and the force of individual grammatical constructions. 'Solving for meaning', in other words, implies the assumption that there is a single, unique *solution* which, once discovered, will enable us to interpret speakers' utterances with the perfect, automatic accuracy of a native speaker, and in ways which fail to match other speakers' independent interpretations only in a few special cases involving, say, dialect or the assumption by a particular speaker of 'cultured' turns of phrase which he does not properly understand. Indeed, if there is not supposed to be a unique solution, in this strong sense, then what are we supposed to be 'solving for'? On the supposition that no single unique solution exists, we have to suppose that different native speakers cannot ever read off the sense of each others' utterances with complete certainty that what they are reading off is what any other competent speaker would read off. We might think of this situation as a sort of limiting case, in which worries about possible differences of dialect infect *every* act of verbal intercourse between one speaker and another. It is difficult to imagine such a situation, if we keep the assumption that the two speakers construct their utterances using materials drawn from the same fund of words. But, if we make the effort to imagine this improbable state of affairs, it seems clear that the situation we have imagined is equivalent to the situation in which the two speakers simply do not speak the same language. But, if the supposition that a community possesses a common language turns out in this way to have been made vacuous by the terms in which we have stated the methodology of radical interpretation, there can be no question of 'solving for meaning' with respect to that language.

This is perhaps a surprising conclusion, given that one of Davidson's main arguments in favour of a theory of truth as a means of understanding meaning in natural languages is that such theories enable us to understand the ability of native speakers to attach a sense to sentences which they have never encountered before.

The step which leads to this outcome is, of course, Davidson's decision to treat the relationship between the proposed truth theory and the corresponding natural language as analogous to the relationship between, say, a partly formalised physical theory and the evidence supporting it. What is fundamentally needed to explain the capacity of a native speaker to understand an unfamiliar sentence in the way that any other native speaker would understand it is, as Davidson rightly sees, common access by all speakers to recursive mechanisms of some kind. Once a speaker has a viable Davidsonian truth theory for his language, he has access, of course, to recursive principles of just the kind he needs. But to acquire such a theory he has to set about 'solving for meaning', keeping belief steady: to do that he must already have a conception of truth: for that, it seems, he has to have some grasp of the distinction between an utterance and a mere noise, and, as we argued in chapter 1, the notion of linguistic autonomy, of the sense of a sentence as something which can be 'read off' from the sentential sign in the same way by independent speakers, seems to be essential to that distinction. It is thus very difficult to see how the process of radical interpretation could get off the ground for a child learning his native language, and thus hard to see how Davidson can give any account of language-learning at all. Davidson's and Quine's reversal of the natural order of language-learning is thus perhaps, as Putnam suggests, symptomatic of a more profound inadequacy in both theories.

MB

The step from a Tarskian truth theory to a theory of radical translation is central to Davidson's position: it is what secures him from, for instance, Strawsonian objections concerning the relationship between truth and belief.

Davidson has, indeed, two arguments which seem to show that such a step is not only feasible but unavoidable. The first is the Quinean argument that the only data available to us – that is, the utterances of speakers taken together with their contexts of utterance – are insufficient to determine uniquely the meanings of individual words or the structure of individual sentences. This argument seems to me to involve an elementary mistake: the mistake of supposing that the 'power' of data to determine theories is a sort of property, or virtue, inherent in 'the data' themselves. So far as I can see, epistemological animism of this sort has nothing to be said for it whatsoever. Not only is the power of nature to determine our theories entirely relative to the power of the theories we address to her, but in addition our judgements about what constitute 'the data' in a given area of inquiry are necessarily also relative to what actual or possible theories we suppose to be relevant to that area of inquiry. It is certainly true that we cannot determine the meanings of individual words or the structure of individual sentences by appeal to the circumstances of utterance of whole sentences. But we do not determine such questions by appeal to data of that sort when learning a second language, and at present we lack even the beginnings of a theory about how such questions are determined for a child learning his native language, precisely because we lack a theory of meaning which would tell us, among other things, what sort of questions they are.

This argument of Davidson's, then, offers no obstacle at all to the possibility that a viable theory of meaning begins from individual words and the internal structure of sentences, rather than from the truth conditions of sentences taken as unstructured wholes.

Davidson's second argument is, I take it, that only an empirically testable theory of truth offers us the possibility of a non-circular theory of meaning which proceeds without appealing either to 'intensional entities' such as 'meanings' or 'objects of reference', or, in a more or less covert way, to the very intensional concepts which it is supposed to elucidate. This, too, seems to me to be a *non sequitur*. Davidson has indeed here identified a crucial criterion of adequacy for theories of meaning in natural languages. Davidson's theory would, if it worked, satisfy this criterion; and I think he is right when he argues that other formal semantic theories – for example, those based on the notion of a possible world – fail to satisfy them. But I see no reason why they should not equally well be satisfied by a theory of some radically different kind: for example, a theory of 'criteria', or 'use'.

Certainly, such theories have in the past often been formulated in a very loose way, without being addressed to any precisely formulated problem other than that of representing some feature of linguistic intuition. But there is a quite clear and precise problem to which such a theory might be addressed: namely, the problem of explaining the autonomy of language, as we have defined it in chapter 1. And, as I shall argue in chapters 13 and 14, this question is fundamental to a good deal of Wittgenstein's work, and is the key to understanding his application of the terms 'use' and 'criterion'.

① The distinction *can* be made, it is just characteristic of headaches that two headaches are never the same, or two spatio-temporally designated + distinct occurrences of head pain are not the same headache; even if similar.

9

Naming, Necessity and Natural Kinds

1. Realism and indexicality

Phenomenalism is, historically, the doctrine that we are acquainted in experience only with sensations, or sense data. The contrary doctrine that we are directly acquainted in experience with *particu-* physical objects which have their own existence independently of being perceived by us, and is known as realism or, to distinguish it from realism about universals, epistemological realism.

The contrast between phenomenalism and realism can be formulated in a more abstract way, according to which realism becomes the doctrine that we are directly acquainted in experience with *particulars*, or *individuals*. A particular is something to which it is possible to ascribe numerical identity. The distinction between 'the very same x as a' and 'a very similar x to a' can be drawn, common sense tells us, in the case of chairs, stones or ships; it cannot be drawn in the case of after-images, for example, or in general in the case of sensations or sense data. Phenomenalism now becomes the doctrine that the distinction between numerical identity and qualitative similarity cannot ultimately be drawn: to say that two sensations are *the same* can only mean that they are qualitatively similar; it cannot mean that they are numerically one and the same.

② False

This thought opens the way to a third, and still more abstract, way of formulating the contrast, according to which phenomenalism becomes the doctrine that reference to particulars is a derivative and secondary feature of language, and not an ultimate and primary feature; while realism becomes the converse doctrine, that reference to particulars is a primary and underivative feature of our conceptual scheme. On this level the dispute between phenomenalists and realists evolves into a dispute between those who believe that indexical expressions, of which the most obvious instances are proper names, can be analysed in non-indexical terms, and those who believe that they can not.

Seen from this point of view, phenomenalism is closely connected with nominalism. The nominalist, as we have seen, wishes to deny, *inter alia*, that *categories* of things, as well as the things that fall into them, are real. He wants to deny that the *substance* 'gold' is real, over and above this or that sample of gold, and that the *species* 'tiger' is real, over and above this or that particular tiger. To begin with, his intention may, as with Locke, be anti-phenomenalist. He wants to say that 'all things that exist are particulars', where by 'particulars' he means things to which it makes sense to ascribe numerical identity. But to grant that some terms name particulars in this sense is to grant that some terms correspond to a real 'essence' or principle of unity (whatever in nature gives us the criteria by appeal to which we detect the recurrence in our experience of a particular of the required sort) – in other words, to a universal which is not, as Locke would say 'the work of the mind'. Ultimately the drift of nominalism is, therefore, towards a theory, such as Quine's, which denies ontological status (other than a purely relative and conventionally assigned ontological status) to *all* classes of particulars. The nominalist thus ends by agreeing with the phenomenalist that reality is to be equated with the patterns of stimulation which affect our sense organs.

Jonathan Bennett succinctly expresses a nominalist point of view of this kind when he says that, since 'all our concepts are tools for the intellectual handling of our sensory intake, we cannot make sense of any statements about the world except ones admitting of a broadly phenomenalistic analysis'.[1]

2. Proper names and criteria of identity

The question of whether indexical expressions are indispensable to a natural language becomes, at the simplest level, the question of whether proper names have qualitative criteria of identity attached to them.

Mill, in the *System of Logic*, held that they do not: that a proper name such as 'John', although borne by many persons, 'is not conferred upon them to indicate any qualities, or anything which belongs to them in common; and cannot be said to be affirmed of them in any *sense* at all, consequently not in the same sense.'[2]

Russell's doctrine of logically proper names shows him to have been, at that stage of his intellectual development, in agreement with Mill at some fundamental level. Logically proper names are the only genuine proper names, according to Russell, just because their bearers cannot be identified by description but only by deixis in a context of direct acquaintance. They have, in other words, no qualitative criteria of identification attached to them.

Russell, like Frege, however, did not believe that Mill's account held true for ordinary proper names, such as 'Bismarck' or 'Manchester'. He held with Frege that ordinary proper names were, logically speaking, shorthand for descriptions such as 'The first German Chancellor' or 'The second largest city in Lancashire'. And a majority of logicians, subsequently, have continued to hold that ordinary proper names are disguised definite descriptions, while for the most part rejecting the purely Russellian doctrine of logically proper names.

There are, indeed, some very powerful reasons for taking the Russell–Frege line about ordinary proper names. Most such names, for most of their users, cannot easily, or even intelligibly, be defined by pointing at anything, as we observed in chapter 3. Then, again, problems arise over negative existential statements involving proper names, if we construe the names in question as pure denoting expressions. On such an interpretation, 'No such horse as Pegasus ever existed' becomes senseless if true, because in such a case there is nothing to be denoted by 'Pegasus', which in consequence becomes merely an empty noise (the requirement of a context of acquaintance for the use of Russellian logically proper names ensures that *they* never lack denotata).

Again, identity statements involving proper names, such as those involving definite descriptions, seem often to express contingent matters of fact. 'Hesperus is identical with Phosphorus', like the more familiar Fregian version about the Evening Star and the Morning Star, says more than just that a certain planetary body is identical with itself.

Admittedly, it may be difficult to fix on a precise description as intended by a given proper name. Russell held that the description may vary from user to user;[3] so that, for example, one user may attach to the name 'Lord Russell' the description 'The co-author, with Whitehead, of *Principia Mathematica*', while another may attach to it the description, 'The thin gentleman who buys his tobacco in my shop on Wednesdays.'

This thought, however, has not generally deflected philosophers from the conviction that some description or other must be necessarily connected with each proper name; it has merely made them think either that the description in question must in fact be a cluster of alternative descriptions; or else that there must be a rather complicated 'fundamental' description known to some privileged subset of users from which all the other descriptions known to the rather heterogeneous company of users of the proper name in question are derived by some process or processes of inference. The first of these options is defended by John Searle, for example, in a frequently quoted article (1958);[4] the second by Michael Dummett, in his book on Frege:

> It is not possible that none of those who use a name have any criterion for identifying the bearer of the name, that all of them use it with only a partial criterion in mind, but with the intention of referring to the commonly agreed referent: for there would, in such a case, be no commonly agreed referent. It is conceivable, for example, that a wide circle of people were in the habit of using the word 'Easthampton' as the name of a town in England, say with the vague impression that it was somewhere in the East Midlands. . . . But, if we suppose that there is no single person who knows, and no printed reference-book which supplies, any determinate way of identifying a town as being Easthampton, then the name has no referent and no definite sense.[5]

If we assume that the alternative descriptions of the 'cluster' theory are uniquely identifying descriptions, the two options are compatible; otherwise they are not.

3. Naming and necessity

It seems intuitively that it would have been possible to identify the bearer of a proper name even if events in the world had taken a different course. If Britain had never entered the Second World War, it would still have been possible to identify Churchill. If Moses had never ascended Mount Sinai to receive the tablets of the decalogue, never led Israel out of Egypt and so on, he would presumably still have been identifiable by reference to some or other of his properties, even in the guise of a highly placed Egyptian of Jewish descent. We can, as modal logicians say, identify Churchill or Moses 'across possible worlds'.

If the Frege–Russell account of proper names is right, and Mill's account wrong, then it is presumably the qualitative criteria of identity attaching to a proper name which enable us to identify its bearer across possible worlds.

But this yields a curious consequence. To say that a proposition remains true in all possible worlds is simply to say that it is necessarily true. If the properties which constitute the criterion of transworld identity for a proper name a are symbolised F, then the statement that if anything is F it must be a, and *vice versa*, or

$$(x)\left\{ Fx \equiv x = a \right\}$$

must be necessarily true. But then that has the consequence that anything which happens to have the property F in a given possible world *is* the individual a. And it certainly seems that there is a strong sense of identity in which something might possess F and yet not be identical with a. If we take it as a criterion of transworld identity for Moses that he led Israel out of Egypt, ascended Mount Sinai, and so on, then it certainly seems possible that, in another possible world, some other person, numerically distinct from Moses, though perhaps also called 'Moses', did all these things, while the *real* Moses – *our* Moses – stayed at home and did none of them.

4. Identity and rigid designation

Saul Kripke, in an influential article, states this problem in terms of what he calls *rigid designation*.[6] A rigid designator designates the same (numerically the same) object in all possible worlds. Non-rigid, or *accidental*, designators do not. The trouble is, now, that, whatever qualitative criterion of transworld identity we fix on for the bearer of a proper name, we seem to end up with an accidental and not a rigid designator.

Suppose, for example, we take it as part of a qualitative criterion of transworld identity for Nixon, a necessary if not a sufficient condition, at least, that he be a human being. It does seem empirically possible that the being we call Nixon may turn out not to be human. Similarly, if we make it the criterion that he be the man who won the 1968 election (and *that* looks uniquely identifying, and so a necessary *and* sufficient condition of something's being Nixon), it appears that Nixon the man might very easily *not* have won that election, though it is not the case that the man who actually won the election (Nixon) might not have been Nixon.

This is one of the problems which the 'cluster theory' is supposed to deal with, by making the necessary propositions required by a criterion of transworld identity disjunctive propositions. Searle offers this solution:

> Suppose we agree to drop 'Aristotle' and use, say, 'The Teacher of Alexander', then it is a necessary truth that the man referred to is Alexander's teacher – but it is a contingent fact that Aristotle ever went into pedagogy (though I am suggesting that it is a necessary fact that Aristotle has the logical sum, inclusive disjunction, of properties commonly attributed to him).[7]

But this will not do either. *All* the things commonly attributed to Aristotle are things he might not have done or suffered; which may not be true of him. But even to identify such counterfactual situations we have to think of them as situations in which *Aristotle* failed to do, or to undergo, certain things.

5. Necessary – contingent: a priori – a posteriori

All these problems can be rephrased as problems about necessity; about what propositions we are to take as necessarily true, and in what senses. The description 'The man who won the 1968 US Presidential election' identifies Nixon, at any rate in the actual world. It is therefore certainly necessarily true of the man who won the 1968 Presidential election that *that man* is Nixon. But it does not at all follow from this that Nixon *necessarily* won the 1968 Presidential election, and therefore it does not follow either that the description 'The man who won the 1968 US Presidential election' *necessarily* identifies Nixon (that is, identifies him in all possible worlds). Kripke argues, I think correctly, that this illicit transition is supported by a widespread tendency among philosophers to proceed as if the distinction between necessary and contingent truth, and the distinction between *a priori* and *a posteriori* knowledge were to all intents and purposes one and the same distinction, with the automatic consequence that all necessary truths are known *a priori* and all contingent truths known *a posteriori*, and *vice versa*. Kripke argues that the two distinctions are neither equivalent in sense nor extensionally equivalent. If we decide to call the man who won the 1968 election 'Nixon', then we know *a priori* that Nixon won the 1968 election. And it is tempting to conclude, on the assumption that only necessary truths can be known *a priori*, that therefore 'Nixon won the 1968 election' is necessarily true. But both the assumption and the conclusion to which it leads are false. 'Nixon won the 1968 election' is a contingent truth, from which it follows *a fortiori* that there are contingent truths which can be known *a priori*. And, similarly, there are necessary truths which can be known *a posteriori*. Nixon could not have been other than the man who won the 1968 election (for the man who won that election was, as it happens, the man we call Nixon); but the knowledge that Nixon won that election is (such are the defects of rational intuition) *a posteriori* knowledge. Similarly, if the length of a rod in Paris defines the metre as a unit of measurement, then it is a piece of *a priori* knowledge that that rod is one metre in length, although it is a contingent truth that it is a metre in length (i.e. is the length that it is), since it might have been a different length (an accident in its manufacture might have brought that about, for example). On the other hand, the proposition that a metre is a certain length, x (the length of that rod), *is* necessarily true, but can only be known *a posteriori*, since we must examine the rod in order to know the value of x.

Philosophical resistance to the idea of *a priori* contingencies is quite strong, and as a result the force of Kripke's main point is often obscured in discussion. But I am inclined to think that this objection is a red herring, as least as far as the adequacy of the Frege–Russell theory of proper names is concerned. Kripke's fundamental point is that, unless a description can be shown to attach necessarily to an individual, the phrase which expresses the description in question does not rigidly designate the individual in question. A description may uniquely identify a particular individual in one possible world, without necessarily identifying him in other possible worlds. And yet reference to individuals does cross the boundaries between possible worlds. We speak quite happily of what might have become of *Aristotle* if he had never studied philosophy – and so on; and, indeed, it is difficult to see how, if we could not refer 'rigidly' to individuals in this way, any talk of counterfactual possibilities could get off the ground.

At first sight this is such a baffling conclusion that we may feel tempted to try to resuscitate the Frege–Russell doctrine by appeal to belief. Aristotle may not be the man, in fact, who taught Alexander; and maybe Nixon did not *really* win the 1968 election (the Republican ballot-rigging machine perhaps got there ahead of the Democrats for just that once). But they are generally *believed* to have done those things (and others). So perhaps we can identify them for the purposes of reference across possible worlds by appeal to these generally held beliefs. And, indeed, it sounds reasonable to say, for example, 'The man whom most people believe to have been the teacher of Alexander in fact lived out his life as a happy Macedonian cowherd.' But if that is taken as a model for all singular reference it is simply circular.[8] For *to whom* is the status of Alexander's tutor being attributed? According to our new version of the Frege–Russell doctrine, to the person to whom most people attribute it. But this identifies nothing at all, unless it turns out that most people think that *Aristotle* (or Plato, or Anaximenes) was Alexander's tutor; and then we are back with proper names again.

We are left, it seems, with two conclusions: first, that proper names, since they rigidly designate individuals, are not analytically replaceable by descriptions; and, secondly, that we never dispose of a 'full' criterion for the application of a proper name (that is, a description which uniquely identifies across possible worlds) but dispose of only a 'partial' criterion: some description which is, or is believed to be, true of the individual in question, but which is never uniquely identifying across possible worlds, and often is not uniquely identifying even with respect to the actual world we live in.

> . . . most people, when they think of Cicero, just think of a famous Roman orator, without any pretension to think either that there was only one famous Roman orator or that one must know something else about Cicero to have a referent for the name.[9]

6. Baptism and criteria

How can this fairly extraordinary state of affairs be possible? Kripke's positive account of the use of proper names, which he himself feels to be inadequate, turns not unreasonably on the notion of a specific baptism at a particular point in time.

> Someone, let's say, a baby, is born; his parents call him by a certain name. They talk about him to their friends. Other people meet him. Through various sorts of talk the name is spread from link to link as if by a chain. A speaker who is on the far end of this chain, who has heard about, say Richard Feynman, in the market place or elsewhere, may be referring to Richard Feynman even though he can't remember from whom he first heard of Feynman or from whom he ever heard of Feynman. He knows that Feynman was a famous physicist. A certain passage of communication reaching ultimately to the man himself does reach the speaker. He is then referring to Feynman even though he can't identify him uniquely. . . . a chain of communication going back to Feynman himself has been established, by virtue of his membership in a community which passed the name on from link to link, not by a ceremony that he makes in private in his study: 'By "Feynman" I shall mean the man who did such and such and such and such.'[10]

All of this, although it does not help much with our present question, is undoubtedly quite true. And it makes proper names a further locus for the linking up of meanings to particular contexts of utterance; for the 'indexicality', in short, which has been an abiding source of difficulty and confusion for logicist and truth-conditional theories of meaning since Frege.

But, for all that, it will not do. It explains how proper names acquire currency, but it does not explain how proper names *are used*; how different speakers, lacking any uniquely identifying description, can use proper names in discourse with at any rate a practically sufficient certainty that different users of the same name are referring, when they use it, to one and the same individual. It is open to the most telling objection levelled by Michael Dummett in his discussion of Kripke, in the passage quoted at the end of section 2 of this chapter. As Dummett says, it seems at first sight just impossible that *everyone* who uses a name could be using it with only a partial criterion of identity in mind. At some point there must be somebody who has access to what Dummett calls a *determinate way of identifying* the bearer of the name.

I think, though, that there is a way round this objection of Dummett's. Any contingent property of an individual may serve as a perfectly satisfactory and determinate way of identifying that individual *in a particular context*. Thus, for example, 'The man who is wearing a white carnation and carrying a copy of the *Washington Post*' may, for practical purposes, serve perfectly effectively to discriminate Nixon from among a crowd of fellow passengers at Kennedy Airport on a particular day, though it would not identify him at any other time or place. Dummett's objection is, presumably, that not all the criteria which govern the actual application of a proper name can be as local and context-bound as this. But why not? The problem is, I suppose, to see what brings it about that the name 'Nixon', say, has the same meaning in the mouths of different users, picks out one and the same individual no matter who uses the name or on what occasion if the criteria which determine the actual application of the name differ not only from user to user but also from context of use to context of use. But, in fact, this burden need not be borne by the *criteria of application* of the name 'Nixon'. It can be – and, I think, is – borne jointly by (1) the continuity of reference, assertion and behaviour in actual situations of communication involving the name 'Nixon' and (2) certain considerations concerning the logic of proper names in general.

Let me explain what I mean by way of an example. I pick up Nixon, say, at Kennedy Airport by appeal to the criterion of the white carnation and the *Washington Post*. Nixon is travelling incognito and in disguise. As we are leaving the airport a man steps up and says, 'Sir, I believe I am addressing the President of the United States.' Nixon, dumbfounded, agrees that he is. 'I know you, Mr President', says the man, 'because I work in the White House, and the third button of your waistcoat has been loose for a week. I think you should tell your personal staff.' (Later the man hears from an independent source that heads have rolled.)

The day is not over for Nixon, however. Outside the airport he is accosted by his old nurse Anna-Luisa Mendoza, who has not seen him since August 1921, since when she has been in a remote mountain village in Mexico, cut off from television. She knew him by the strawberry mark under his ear, and in consequence is in an exalted state. In the absence of security men she cannot be restrained from telling him much about his childhood, some of which is confirmed by his blushes and his ineffectual attempts to quieten her, and some of which (like the discreditable affair of the teddy-bear with one ear) I know from independent evidence to be true, though Nixon has forgotten. And so on, and so on.

In short, where the identification of individuals is concerned, we

really are confined to criteria each of which, taken separately and on
its own, is no more than some trivial contingency. Such criteria never
are required, however, to stand separately and alone. The identifications we make with their help flow into a coherent fabric of expectations and satisfactions of expectations, fulfilled or unfulfilled beliefs,
behaviour and assertion. The coherence of this fabric then sustains, or
fails to sustain, the credentials of individual criteria of identity.
Failures in the coherence of that fabric are, indeed, the only sort of
grounds we have, or could have, for asserting the incorrect use of a
proper name. That Orsino's and Olivia's identifying descriptions of
'Sebastian' in fact identify Viola emerges in *Twelfth Night*, for example, because the Sea Captain's apparently sincere description of
Sebastian as the man who borrowed his purse cannot possibly be true
of Viola/'Sebastian'.

The relationship of mutual support which thus obtains between (1)
(partial) criteria of identity for individuals and (2) general considerations of the coherence of speech and action within communities of
speakers would not be possible if it were not taken for granted by each
speaker that a proper name picks out some numerically distinct
individual or other. The Sea Captain's test for whether Viola/'Sebastian' is Sebastian would not be crucial unless the Sea Captain took
'Sebastian' to designate a single individual, for it turns on the fact that
he cannot have lent his purse to more than one man.

The convention that a proper name names a single, numerically
distinct individual is a convention of *logic*, or *logical grammar*. As such,
it is part of the meaning that we attach to a word such as 'Sebastian' or
'Nixon', but a part which is quite separate and distinct from any
criterion of application – that is, from any perceptual criterion for
recognising the particular individual who bears the name – that we
may attach to a word of that sort. Once again, as in the case of our
discussion of general names in chapter 4, we have stumbled across the
distinction between something which, following Julius Kovesi,[11] we
may call the *formal element* of the meaning of a word – its logical, or
functional, category – and the perceptual criteria which govern its
application. This distinction between the formal and the perceptual
elements of meaning is often minimised or ignored by writers in the
analytic tradition, who tend to equate the meaning of a word with its
perceptual criteria of application; but I think that, nevertheless, it is a
distinction of quite fundamental importance.

For the moment it may perhaps help us to keep separate the

following quite distinct elements which work together as a single system to stabilise the reference of proper names from user to user and context to context, if we list them as follows:

(1) the logico-grammatical convention that each proper name designates a single, numerically distinct individual;
(2) the partial criteria of identity which individual users employ to single out the individual in question, and which may vary without limit from user to user and context to context; and
(3) the general considerations of coherence of discourse and action within a community which enable us as users to keep a constant running check on the accuracy of the identifications made with the aid of the criteria of identity mentioned in (2).

(1) and (3), working in concert, serve to keep the reference of a given proper name stable from user to user and context to context no matter how much arbitrary variation we introduce into (2). Holders of the Frege–Russell theory believe (in part, no doubt, because they fail to see that there is a distinction between the formal and the perceptual elements in naming) that the reference of a proper name can be stabilised only if the contents of (2) are stabilised: that is, if to each proper name there corresponds some uniquely identifying description or 'cluster' of descriptions. If this belief falls, then, so far as I can see, the last defence of the Frege–Russell thesis falls with it.

If this is correct, with what can we identify 'the meaning' of a proper name? Knowledge of meaning presumably includes only *linguistic* knowledge: that is, it excludes all knowledge which I possess independently of knowing a language. If I can recognise Nixon – by his face, a birthmark, the third button of his waistcoat, or whatever mark or sign serves me on a particular occasion – my ability to do so is clearly independent of my ability to speak English. The same goes for my ability to judge when people are talking coherently and making sense: it is not linguistic ability that enables me to say, for example, 'But, when you say you were lending your purse to Sebastian, *this* "Sebastian" was playing a lute to lovesick Duke Orsino', or other matter of the like sort, but the general ability to put two and two together. It looks, then, as if only (1) belongs to the meaning of a proper name; though to this we should add, I think, knowledge of the category of a proper name: it *is* a linguistic matter that 'Sebastian' may be a man's name, while 'Rover' can only be a dog's. But, if this is so, then Mill is vindicated. A proper name is indeed not affirmed of its bearers 'in any *sense* at all'; and we can continue to hold, as common sense would have prompted us to do in the first place, that proper names have reference but no sense.

If we wish to be awkward, however, we can put this another way by saying that any 'sense' we can attribute to proper names is a 'sense' which varies indefinitely from context of use to context of use. Putting it this way emphasises the 'indexicality' of proper names, and with it the inconvenience of the present view for any phenomenalist account of our conceptual scheme.

7. *Deixis and natural kinds*

The taint of indexicality has recently been further extended by Hilary Putnam to natural-kind names, by means of arguments not dissimilar to Kripke's, though independently conceived. 'Natural kinds', for Putnam, are 'classes of things we regard as of explanatory importance; classes whose normal distinguishing characteristics are held together or even explained by deep-lying mechanisms'. He gives 'gold', 'lemon', 'tiger' and 'acid' as examples.[12]

Putnam argues, as we argued in chapter 4 in connection with Locke's theory of meaning, that the meaning of a natural-kind name cannot be given by specifying a conjunction of properties. Natural kinds may have abnormal members. Moreover, all the exemplars we have so far seen of a given natural kind may be abnormal exemplars. There may, for example, be blue lemons; and it may even be the case that lemons are normally blue, but change colour as the result of peculiar conditions affecting their shipment to us. And the same Kripkean objections can be raised to any other putative defining characteristic of lemons. In short, 'There are no *analytic* truths of the form *every lemon has* [the property] *P*.'[13]

These arguments, redolent of Kripke (they were, in fact, developed independently of Kripke's work), are also redolent of Quine's attack on the concept of analyticity, but Putnam is not prepared to accept Quinean holism, for the reasons we discussed in chapter 9, section 6. One of the most fundamental presuppositions of modern philosophy, at least in the analytic tradition, is that the term 'meaning' has two senses: 'intension' and 'extension' – roughly, though by no means exactly, corresponding to Frege's terms 'sense' and 'reference'. And a great deal of ingenuity, as we have seen in the last five chapters, has gone into the enterprise of showing that everything which needs to be or can be said about meaning can be said in terms of the notion of extension alone.

Putnam's view is that this is a fundamental mistake, and that it leads directly to the absurdity of taking sentences and not words, or (to placate linguists, who believe that they have empirical grounds for regarding the concept of a word as entirely superstitious) some category of sub-sentential expression, as the fundamental bearers of meaning. He makes the shrewd point that 'extension' is not, except for philosophers of a certain school, one of the meanings of 'meaning' and that the notion of meaning is not in the least clarified by the introduction of the term 'intension'.

> The canonical explanation of the notions 'intension' and 'extension' is very much like 'in one sense "meaning" means *extension* and in the other sense "meaning" means *meaning*'. The fact is that while the notion of 'extension' is made quite precise, relative to the fundamental logical notion of *truth* . . . the notion of intension is made no more precise than the vague . . . notion 'concept'. It is as if someone explained the notion 'probability' by saying: 'in one sense "probability" means frequency, and in the other sense it means *propensity*'. 'Probability' *never* means 'frequency', and 'propensity' is at least as unclear as 'probability'.[14]

The development of any enlightening theory of intension requires, Putnam thinks, the displacement of the sentence from the centre of the philosophical stage and a return to the serious study of names as the fundamental bearers of meaning. He believes that the problem of how speakers attach a sense to an unfamiliar sentence is a relatively simple, though not unimportant, one, because he thinks, like Davidson and other formal semanticists, that its solution would be a by-product of a formal semantics for natural language. It is essentially the problem of how 'logical words . . . can be used to build up complex sentences' or of 'how the truth conditions of the complex sentences are related to the truth-conditions of the sentences from which they were derived'.[15]

The real problem for the theory of meaning, Putnam thinks, is a far older and nowadays rather stodgy-sounding one: how 'the meaning' of a word can be communicated by a short dictionary definition. How is it possible to go ahead and use a word perfectly sensibly and informatively in discourse on such a slender basis?

> The fact that one *can* acquire the use of an indefinite number of new words, and on the basis of simple 'statements of what they mean,' is an amazing fact: it is *the* fact, I repeat, on which semantic theory rests.[16]

This, of course, is simply another way of putting a double insight which is also Kripke's: first, that the reference of a term does not seem to be governed by any conjunction or disjunction of properties which analytically determine its meaning; and, secondly, that it could not be, because no criterion in the shape of a conjunction or disjunction of properties could possibly suffice to project the reference of the term *rigidly* across possible worlds.

Putnam is thus, in effect, engaged with the problem of the projection of meaning which we raised in chapter 6, section 3. He offers what I think is only a partial solution to it, but a genuine one as far as it goes, for the special case of natural-kind names. It is most easily explained in terms of an example of Putnam's which postulates two planets, *Earth* and *Twin Earth*. Earth and Twin Earth are very similar: so similar in fact that the inhabitants of both speak English. On each there is a substance which possesses all the properties of water so far as they can be detected by unaided human senses. This substance is called 'water' on Earth, and it is also called 'water' on Twin Earth. But the chemical formula of Earth water is H_2O, while that of Twin Earth water is quite different: call it XYZ.

When the first spaceship visits Twin Earth, its crew at first suppose that 'water' has the same meaning on both planets. But, once they discover the chemical formula of Twin Earth water, they revise this opinion, because 'water' on Twin Earth is the name for an entirely different substance. Let us now suppose that in 1750 neither planet possessed a developed science of chemistry. If $Oscar_1$ is a typical Earthian and $Oscar_2$ a typical Twin Earthian of that era, then every belief of $Oscar_1$ about water was shared by $Oscar_2$, and *vice versa*. So did 'water' then have the same meaning for $Oscar_1$ and for $Oscar_2$? No, because the term still picked out a different substance for $Oscar_1$ from the substance which it picked out for $Oscar_2$.

Meaning, in other words, is not in this case a function of belief, or of any psychological states of speakers. We have to explain the situation as follows. In defining a term such as 'water', we work initially from a *sample*. We say, holding up a glass of water, 'This liquid is called water.' This ostensive definition has a presupposition: namely, that the liquid in question stands in a certain specific relation of sameness (*sameness*$_L$) to all the other bodies of liquid which other English speakers call water. What actual properties define the relation *same*$_L$ can be determined only by the progress of chemical theory. If in the course of investigation it turns out that the constitution of some of the stuff called 'water' is radically different from the rest of the stuff called 'water', then the meaning of the term is tied down at that point solely by 'deixis'. We call water only the stuff which stands in the relation *same*$_L$ to *the stuff which most English speakers would indicate if asked to produce a sample of water*.

Putnam's theory is unique in that it combines (1) the notion of deixis, or ostension, with (2) a recognition that it is the actual structure of nature, as revealed by scientific investigation, which carries most of the weight of determining the extension of natural-kind names. What Putnam has done, in effect, is to produce not merely a new set of reasons for disputing Locke's claim that the meaning of a substance name is a *nominal essence* (a conjunction of properties which has, indeed, 'an union in nature', but a 'union' which in the end comes to no more than the regular *association* of those properties in our experience) but also a genuine alternative theory. Putnam's theory is closer to Leibniz's contention (*Nouveaux Essais*, III. xi. 25) that the meaning of a substance name is the internal constitution of the substance in question: the 'principle of activity' which explains the properties which it presents to experience.[17]

Putnam's theory has a number of other remarkably promising features. For a start, it manages entirely without appeal to the notion of analyticity. The relationship *sameness*$_L$ is never fully defined because its content depends upon the progress of scientific theory. What makes it serve to determine the extension of a term at any given point in time is simply the deictic indication of samples. What serves to fix the application of the term for speakers is indeed a small collection of perceptual properties, which Putnam calls a *stereotype*. But the contents of the stereotype corresponding to a natural-kind name do not constitute a set of necessary and sufficient conditions for the application of that name. In many cases, Putnam argues, the use of a natural-kind name is governed by what he calls a *linguistic division of labour*. Most speakers have only a stereotype to guide their application of the term *gold*. It refers to just a few obvious properties of 'gold' and it works – secures agreement in application of the term, that is – in most cases. The validity of the stereotype at any particular point in time is secured by the fact that there are experts on the assay of gold who have a very much more adequate and scientific grasp of the content of the relevant *sameness* relationship. But even their understanding of the content of that relationship may be found wanting as science progresses.

Putnam has thus abandoned the conventional conception of an intension, or a sense, as something like a description giving, analytically, necessary and sufficient conditions of application. But at the same time his abandonment of this traditional notion of sense does not lead him in the direction of treating the meanings of individual expressions as ineffable except in so far as determined by the outcome of a holistic process of assigning truth conditions to sentences. For Putnam the extension of 'gold' is determined, quite independently of any assignment of truth values to sentences in which 'gold' occurs, by certain acts of deixis and by the course of certain kinds of scientific inquiry.

At the same time, Putnam's theory is not verificationist in the classical sense. No determinate 'method of verification' is attached to the proposition '*x* is gold': what procedures confirm or infirm such a sentence will obviously depend upon the circumstances and the current state of scientific theory. For this reason, Putnam's theory explains precisely what nominalism and verificationism of all types, including Quine's, fail to explain: the problem of the projection of meaning; of how there can be common agreement between speakers on the meaning of a term in perceptual circumstances too new and unexpected to have been provided for by any previous teaching which the speakers can have received in the use of the word. Physical chemistry opens to the inhabitants of Earth and Twin Earth an altogether new set of perceptual properties of substances; but they do not in any way throw into doubt how the existing substance names employed by Earthians and Twin Earthians are to be employed in this new set of circumstances. What Putnam's account does, in effect, is to show us how our conception of *what it is to be an F* can change and develop without any fundamental change in the *meaning* of *F*; for 'water' for speakers of English on Earth or Twin Earth continues to mean *the stuff* which has turned out to be H_2O, or *the stuff* which has turned out to be XYZ, just as it did before these discoveries were made.

In one way, then, Putnam has not abandoned the concept of *sense* at all. As we saw earlier, one of the things which the term *Sinn* served to pick out for Frege was some set of considerations, possessed in common by all speakers, which serve to determine the reference of an expression. In this sense, 'water', 'gold' and other natural-kind names have a sense for Putnam. Their sense *is* the procedures of deictic identification of samples and the scientific investigation of those samples, which determine their meaning. Of course, *sense* construed in that way is something very much more like a *way of proceeding*, or a *language game*, than a description. Putnam, for this reason and for others which I shall explain later, is perhaps closer to Wittgenstein here than he thinks.

Finally, Putnam's theory is a realist one in several senses. First, it is a realist theory in the sense defined at the start of this chapter, in which realism is opposed to phenomenalism. A substance, or other natural kind, for Putnam, exists quite independently of any experiential grounds we may have for asserting its existence. Talk about substances, because of the irreducible element of deixis – reference to samples – which is required to get talk of substances off the ground, can never, in Putnam's view, be reduced to talk about the sensible properties of substances.

Secondly, it is a realist theory in the sense in which realism is opposed to nominalism, or to the nominalising tendency in philosophy which we have already encountered in discussing verificationism and the work of Quine. Putnam holds, that is, that the natural kind 'gold' exists in addition to, or over and above, particular samples of gold, or particular sets of stimuli which collectively constitute our acquaintance with such samples. In general, for Putnam, substances, species, persons and so on exist in addition to samples, individual animals or spatio-temporal slices of persons; and their existence is not just a matter of convenience. The combination of deixis and reference to an open-ended process of scientific investigation is what determines the reference of a substance word across possible worlds and both those referential mechanisms give *the substance* referred to by different groups of speakers at different times a reality which transcends anything which any particular group of speakers can say about it at any particular time.

Thirdly, the theory is realist in the sense in which Frege was a realist: that is to say, Putnam has found new reason for believing that the meaning of a sentence is defined not by reference to some set of procedures by which *we* determine its truth, but by reference to the conditions *which obtain in the world* in the event of its being true. What 'water' picks out as its extension, that is, is determined not by some antecedently (and conventionally) determined set of descriptive conditions, but by what turns out, in fact, to be water (or, to put it another way, by what the essence of water turns out to be by the light of the best science available) – which is another way of saying both why Putnam is not a verificationist, and why verificationism is not, as it has often seemed to be this century, the only tenable or possible theory of meaning.

8. Causality and description

Putnam connects his espousal of realism with the revival, by Kripke and himself, of a causal theory of reference. For example, the fact that 'Nixon' rigidly designates Nixon is explained for Kripke by the fact that the use of 'Nixon' by each speaker who refers to Nixon is causally connected, through a chain of speakers who have at various times used the name 'Nixon' in each other's hearing, to the original speaker who baptised, or 'dubbed', Nixon 'Richard Milhous Nixon'. Similarly Putnam suggests[18] that a dubbing theory, involving an historical chain of co-operating speakers between the present user and an original 'dubber', explains the reference of names of substances, species, theoretical entities such as electrons, and so on. What is 'realist' about such a theory is supposed, presumably, to be that it makes a connection between a referring expression and a real object, and that the connection runs *directly* from expression to object, without the mediation of any set of (supposedly) analytically specified sufficient and necessary conditions formulated in phenomenal terms.

I doubt, however, whether this kind of causal theory is any stronger than the more traditional kinds of causal theory which we discussed briefly in chapter 1. Nor do I think that such a theory offers a very sturdy prop to realism. Putnam's ideas do in fact give powerful support to realism, in all the senses of that term outlined above, but the support comes from elsewhere in his theory.

What is explained by the 'historical' connection between user and 'dubber' is simply the existence of a connection between *this* word and *this* man, substance, theoretical entity or whatever.

The existence of such a causal chain does not, however, at all explain how one speaker can predict another speaker's independent applications of the term in question. Just as indefinitely many chains of perceptual similarities can link one object to others of the most diverse kinds, so one and the same 'dubbing' can generate indefinitely many different causal 'chains' of acts of reference, depending upon what the speakers who form each 'chain' take the *intention* of the original act of dubbing to have been.

When I dub a man 'Nixon' or a glass with some liquid in it 'water', *what* am I dubbing: the man; or his status – as I might say of someone that he is not just Mr McKinnon but (the) *McKinnon*; or his condition – as when the village idiot is called by all and sundry 'loony'; or what? Is 'water' the name of a substance, or does it mean 'drink', or 'glassful', or 'potable', or 'fluid' (which is not a substance term), or what? May there not be a causal chain of reference acts stemming from the original dubbing of Nixon, in which the speakers involved in the chain take *what* was dubbed to have been a substance, so that such a speaker can reasonably respond to one who says 'I need Nixon urgently', by handing him a lock of the President's hair?

It is possible to derive a quite straightforward solution to these perplexities from Putnam's own discussion. This obvious answer is that the logical category of a term defined by a given act of dubbing depends upon what we *go on to do with* the term. If we proceed to investigate the liquid in the glass by tabulating those of its properties which are possessed alike by the whole liquid and by any fraction of its volume, pursuing the inquiry into *recherché* chemical investigations, and if we allow the application of the term 'water' to another sample of fluid only if it displays parity in all such properties, however *recherché*, with the fluid in the glass, then, evidently, we meant 'water' as a substance term.

If, however, we proceed by gingerly drinking some of the fluid and waiting for ill effects, only relaxing and saying with relief, 'Ah, yes, *water*' when none appear; and, if the same test moves speakers to say the same thing of other fluids of quite different chemical constitution, then clearly 'water', said of the fluid in the glass, means 'potable', or something of that sort.

The point is that the ostensive definition *in itself* does not suffice to fix a meaning. It fixes a meaning for a word *w* only when taken in conjunction with the form, or structure, of the investigation which links one sample ostensively labelled as *w* to other samples so labelled. We can, in short, reformulate our conclusion of chapter 3. Ostensive definition cannot give meaning to a name until we know what we are to do with the name: until we know, in the later Wittgenstein's terms, what language game the name is to be fitted into: for example, the game of investigating the properties of substances, or merely the game of checking whether ill effects attend the drinking of a fluid.

Putnam's and Kripke's arguments, in short, do not in the end weigh against the conclusion we reached in chapter 3, that there can be no naming without description.

Putnam and Kripke have certainly, I think, thrown considerable doubt upon the idea that the meaning of an expression is to be *equated* with a description, and it is natural, given their emphasis upon ostensive definition and 'causal' accounts of meaning, to suppose that their work therefore amounts to a refurbishing of the notion of a purely referential expression, the meaning of which is established solely by ostensive definition. This notion, I fear, will admit of no refurbishing, for the reasons we gave in Part I. It is possible for Putnam and Kripke to introduce an ostensive component into their theories only because, in the context of their theorising, the point of the ostension in question is made clear by the nature and structure of the investigation which extends the reference of the name in question to objects other than those included in the original dubbing or series of dubbings. However, Putnam's and Kripke's work does point forward to a fundamentally realist conception of the meaning of a term as neither an ostensively indicated 'object', or 'simple', nor a set of descriptive conditions of application, but as something like the relationship of the word to the pattern of investigative procedures which project its reference across possible worlds. And that conception, as I shall try to show later on, has much in common with Wittgenstein's notion of a language game.

III

Communication and
Intention

10

Speech Acts

1. Language and action

It is widely accepted that the most plausible – perhaps the only possible – alternative to a truth-conditional theory of meaning is a theory couched in terms of the beliefs and intentions of speakers and hearers in specific, concrete contexts of communication. I am not so sure about this. I think the options need to be, and can be, set up rather differently. The outlines of the revision I have in mind are perhaps already darkly visible, and will, I hope, become more sharply defined in the last three chapters.

All the same, it is not hard to see the force of the conventional estimate of the options at present facing the theory of meaning. A truth-conditional theory must treat a natural language, as far as possible, as a context-free calculus the expressions of which have meaning quite independently of the communicative purposes and intentions of speakers. Here, as frequently in philosophy, mathematics has been taken, more or less consciously, as providing a standard of clarity and rigour to which all discourse should approximate; or, rather, mathematical clarity and rigour have been taken as *unique paradigm cases* of rigour and clarity: philosophers, with the one exception of the later Wittgenstein, have seldom seriously or persistently entertained the possibility that there may exist rigour and clarity of quite other and different kinds, appropriate to one or another species of non-mathematical discourse.

But there seems something implausible about the idea that the gulf between the meanings of sentences and speakers' intentions in using sentences which appears to characterise mathematical discourse is, or could be, a general feature of all language. Strawson has argued[1] that on such a view there would be no *essential* connection between meaning and the use of language to communicate. It would simply be a curious contingent fact that the rules of language are 'public rules', accessible to all speakers in common.

Noam Chomsky has recently maintained exactly this (1976, p. 71): 'As for the fact that the rules of language are "public rules", this is, indeed, a contingent fact.'[2] Strawson's discussion does not, it seems to me, make it entirely clear why, intuition apart, such a supposition is absurd. But I think the discussion of linguistic autonomy in chapter 1 of the present book (a discussion which, for that matter, is partly rooted in Chomsky's own work) does. The capacity to predict other competent speakers' linguistic judgements is essential to the concept of a language. Without publicity, the responses of an isolated speaker would become simply a curious pattern of behavioural response, without linguistic significance.

This being so, the natural response to dissatisfaction to truth-theoretic accounts of meaning is simply to reject Fregian anti-psychologism, and in so doing to move to the opposite pole of the dichotomy of theoretical options which Frege's position defines. To put it more crudely, the natural response, for analytic philosophers who have thoroughly absorbed a Fregian outlook, and who find themselves persuaded that that outlook is mistaken, is to move to what Frege considered to be the opposite view to his own: that is, to the view that meaning can be understood only in terms of speakers' beliefs and intentions as these inform and direct acts of communication in specific contexts of social interaction involving discourse.

On such a view the theory of meaning must be construed as a part, or special case, of a more general theory of intentional action. John Searle has put the point particularly forcefully: 'a theory of language is part of a theory of action, simply because speaking is a rule-governed form of behaviour'.[3]

The assimilation of meaning – or, more generally, signification – to action is a leading *motif* of phenomenology, and it is not surprising that Searle's work has evoked a response from Paul Ricoeur[4] and other continental philosophers interested in hermeneutics. But the connection reveals a fundamental ambiguity in the position of those whom Strawson labels 'theorists of communication–intention'. Ricoeur takes Searle, and Austin, to be offering a contribution to a theory of the rules governing the interpretation of speech, or discourse

– as distinct from the rules governing the interpretation of the meanings, or senses, of sentence types (sentences taken independently of any context of utterance, that is). For Ricoeur, the central problem of hermeneutics arises precisely because the two modes of interpretation more or less coincide in the case of immediate, spoken discourse, but fall apart in the case of written text.[5] This problem can be formulated only in terms of the Saussurian distinction between a theory of *langue* (the timeless, virtual rules governing the syntax and semantics of sentence types) and a theory of *parole* (speech, discourse); and Ricoeur takes hermeneutics to be one sort of theory of *parole*, and the work of Searle and other 'theorists of communication–intention' to be a contribution to hermeneutics. Nor is Ricoeur alone in this. Strawson's defence of communication–intention theories also seems to identify them as theories of what Saussure would have called *parole*: 'We connect meaning with truth and truth, too simply, with sentences; and sentences belong to language. But, as theorists, we know nothing of human *language* unless we understand human *speech*.'[6]

This is doubtless true in some sense or other. But it is also true, indeed, a truism, that what *A* can *mean by* uttering *S* in a given context depends on what *S means*. If we allow *this* truism to weigh with us, it will seem unlikely that *intention in uttering* could prove a more fundamental or explanatory concept than *the meaning of a sentence*; or, what comes to the same thing, that *langue* could prove in the end to be explicable in terms of *parole*.

Searle is sensitive to this objection, and is careful to maintain that 'an adequate study of speech acts is a study of *langue*'.[7] But, as we shall see, the *langue–parole* distinction remains a weak point for any theory which assimilates the study of language to the study of intentional action.

Theories of this kind fall into two main classes. On the one hand there are those, such as Austin's and Searle's, which locate the distinguishing feature of language as a species of intentional action in the fact that it is *rule-governed*, and proceed to try to elucidate the rules in question.

On the other hand there are theories, such as those of H. P. Grice, Jonathan Bennett or David Lewis, which endeavour to avoid any reference to an unanalysed notion of *rule* at a fundamental level by analysing such notions as *rule* and *convention* in terms of speakers' and hearers' intentions and beliefs. We shall consider the two types of theory in that order.

2. Speech acts

The late Professor J. L. Austin, who first introduced talk of speech acts and performative utterances into philosophy in the course of his 1955 William James Lectures at Harvard,[8] did not, I think, at all intend what he said on these matters to be taken as a 'theory of meaning' in the sense in which we have been using that phrase in this book: that is, a theory of the constitutive mechanisms of a natural language. Nor, of course, was he simply drawing distinctions for the fun of it, as is also sometimes said: he *was* out after philosophical big game, but his main quarry was not ours. Austin's primary target was the verificationist presumption that the only meaningful sentences are those which express true or false statements, together with the supplementary error that if we are to regard a sentence as meaningful we must find some way of cramming it into the mould of 'descriptive' statement – for instance, by taking promises to be statements about an inner, mental state of commitment on the part of the promiser.[9] It seems to me that Austin was right to think that these are mistakes, and important ones, though they are not the only important errors for which verificationism has been responsible; but their rejection need not of itself lead to an adequate theory of meaning.

In the Harvard lectures Austin concentrates on a category of non-descriptive sentences which he labels variously 'performative sentences', 'performative utterances', or just 'performatives'. Performatives include such examples as 'I do [i.e. take this woman to be my lawful wedded wife]', 'I promise to be there at four', and 'I bet you sixpence it will rain tomorrow.' Such utterances do not describe or report anything; they cannot be true or false. Rather, uttering one of them constitutes *doing* something: taking a wife, making a promise, laying a bet. Although such utterances cannot be true or false, Austin says, they can be *infelicitous*. Infelicities, in Austin's account, take the form of *misfires* or *abuses*. For example, a marriage ceremony may misfire because of the existence of a previous unannulled marriage, or because the clergyman or the registrar is an impostor: the right words are said, but no marriage takes place. Or the conventions of speech-acting are abused: a promise is made in words, for example, but because the promise is made insincerely it is, though still a promise, hollow or worthless.

In the course of investigating performative verbs, Austin constructs a system of distinctions which have played a leading part in subsequent discussion. First, there is a tripartite distinction between *locutionary acts*, *illocutionary acts* and *perlocutionary acts*. A single utterance may constitute the performance of an act of each of these three kinds. A locutionary act is further analysed into the simultaneous performance of a *phonic act*, a *phatic act* and a *rhetic act*. All these six categories provide senses in which 'saying is doing'. A phonic act is the act of uttering certain noises: what is uttered is a *phone*. The distinction between a phatic and a rhetic act is, I think, somewhat less clear. What Austin actually says is that a *phatic act* is 'the act of uttering certain vocables or words, i.e. noises of certain types belonging to *and as* belonging to a certain vocabulary, in a certain construction, i.e. conforming to and as conforming to a certain grammar, with a certain intonation, etc.'[10] and that a *rhetic act* is 'the act of using that pheme [a *pheme* is the product of a phatic act] or its constituents with a certain more or less definite "sense" and a more or less definite "reference" (which together are equivalent to "meaning")'. The product of a rhetic act is a *rheme*.

This is, to put it mildly, extremely fuzzy. Passing over the large number of unexplained notions to which appeal is made, the inverted commas around crucial terms, and the indefiniteness imported by Austin's concluding 'etc.' into the definition of a phatic act, the most important obscurity concerns the question of whether *meaning* in some unitary sense enters at the level of the phatic or the rhetic act, or whether 'meaning' in different senses of the term is associated with each of two acts, and if so, in what senses? If, in a phatic act certain vocables (the hesitation between 'vocables', 'words' and 'noises *of certain types*' – emphasis added – does not help matters) are uttered *as belonging to*, or conforming to, a certain vocabulary and grammar, then presumably this means that they must be uttered with a certain meaning, for what does a *vocabulary* record, unless it is distinctions of meaning between words? Yet 'meaning' is then defined as the union of 'sense' and 'reference', and associated with the performance of a rhetic act. At times Austin seems to intend the phatic–rhetic distinction to correspond roughly to the distinction between what a *sentence type means* by virtue of the rules of the language, and what a *speaker means* (or affirms) by uttering a sentence token of that type in a certain context. 'He said "the cat is on the mat"', reports a phatic act, whereas 'He said that the cat is on the mat' reports a rhetic act.[11] But are we to take 'He said "the cat is on the mat"' as reporting *what sequence of noises he made* (in which case the sentence reports a phonic act), or are we to take it as reporting also *the meaning of the sentence type he uttered*, in which case meaning, in some unexplained sense, enters at the level of the phatic act, so that meaning cannot simply be identified with the combination of 'sense' and 'reference' with which words are used in a rhetic act? Perhaps reporting a phatic act is reporting merely that the sentence the phatic actor has uttered is grammatical? But grammatical sentences, as Chomsky has shown, can be senseless, and I am inclined to think that Austin would have wanted to say that 'He said "colourless green ideas sleep furiously"' reports a phonic, and not a phatic, act. Certainly Austin's inclusion of the proviso 'belonging to a certain vocabulary' in addition to 'conforming to a certain grammar' in his explanation of the term 'rhetic act' seems designed to exclude just such possibilities.

Part of the trouble is that Frege's terms *Sinn* and *Bedeutung*, at least in their conventional English dress of 'sense' and 'reference', can be applied equally well to the meanings of utterances or to their purport. We can say either, 'The sense of "The water is running under the door" is "l'eau coule sous la porte"', or, if John shouts, 'My God, the floor's all wet!', that the sense (or purport) of his remark is that water is running under the door. Similarly, we can say either, 'The term "water" refers to a type of liquid', or 'When I say, "Water is running under the door", I am referring (fool!) to that water there!'

Word or sentence *types*, in short, may have sense and reference in one pair of senses; speakers' utterances may have sense (i.e. purport) and reference in another pair of senses. Austin's example of a rhetic act is 'He said that the cat is on the mat'; but that, if it reports anything, reports the purport of a speaker's utterance (his *words* may have been 'You'll find Tibbles by the fire', 'That beast is on the mat again', 'When Mrs Calshott-Mortenhoe wakes up I won't answer for her aleurophobia, you know', or any of an indefinite number of other sentences). If sense and reference belong to vocables only in the context of a rhetic act, then, they have to do not with the meanings of sentence or word types, but with the purports of speakers' utterances. This (as well, incidentally, as being diametrically opposed to Frege's intentions in introducing the terms 'sense' and 'reference' in the first place) pre-empts the term 'meaning' in such a fashion as to leave us no way of talking about the meanings of sentence or word types: meaning in *that* sense is simply pushed to one side.

To be fair to Austin, we have the following indirect textual evidence that he took the rheme to be in some sense or other the bearer of meaning: 'The pheme is a unit of *language*: its typical fault is to be nonsense – meaningless. But the rheme is a unit of speech; its typical fault is to be vague or void or obscure, etc.'[12] But I do not find it easy to see how this can be squared with his remarks elsewhere on sense and reference as these concern the rhetic act.

Let us leave these questions hanging for a moment, and return to Austin's major distinction between locutionary, illocutionary and perlocutionary acts.

Austin takes the phonic act, the phatic act and the rhetic act to be three aspects of the locutionary act – the act of ' "saying something" in [the] full normal sense' (p. 94). When something is *said*, it may be *taken* as fulfilling one or another communicative function: as the answer to a sentence, as the expression of a promise, as a verdict or an expression of intention, for example. To take it in one of these ways is to take it as having a certain *illocutionary force*; to say something with a given illocutionary force is, *eo ipso*, to perform an illocutionary act. Such acts, like other sorts, have practical effects: advice is taken, the passing of sentences results in men being sent to prison, the uttering of the words of the marriage ceremony ties the knot of matrimony. In bringing about such consequences, the speaker who performs the illocutionary act, of advising or sentencing say, also and *eo ipso* performs a perlocutionary act; he convinces someone, or commits someone to gaol.

Austin's discussion now turns back on itself. The philosophical interest of performative verbs arose in the first place, we remember, because they seemed to offer a counter-instance to the verificationist claim that the only meaningful sentences are those which express true or false statements. Performatives, indeed, were supposed to be distinguished from descriptive statements by the fact that they could not be true or false, but could only be felicitous or infelicitous. But what are *stating* or *asserting* if not illocutionary acts, which also and *eo ipso* (quite a lot of the time anyway) count as performances of the perlocutionary act of instilling belief?

3. Speech acts and meaning

It is at this point, I think, that Austin's discussion of performatives has seemed to a number of philosophers to promise something more than a naturalistic examination of an interesting corner of the English language: to offer, in fact, the clue to a non-Fregian theory of meaning capable of doing justice to the communicative and intentional aspects of language. Perhaps the study of meaning ought simply to be regarded as coextensive with the study of illocutionary acting. An uncompromising expression of this view can be found early on in John Searle's book *Speech Acts*:

> a study of the meaning of sentences is not in principle distinct from a study of speech acts. Properly construed, they are the same study. Since every meaningful sentence in virtue of its meaning can be used to perform a particular speech act (or range of speech acts), and since every possible speech act can in principle be given an exact formulation in a sentence or sentences (assuming an appropriate context of utterance), the study of the meanings of sentences and the study of speech acts are not two independent studies, but one study from different points of view.[13]

On the face of it, the claim seems implausibly grandiose. If I state, for example, that Searle is a professor at Berkeley, the illocutionary act which I perform is, presumably, *stating*; it is not 'stating something about Searle', and certainly not 'stating that Searle is a professor at Berkeley', for these last two 'acts' precisely introduce the question of truth and falsity: criticism of them is not, that is, confined to their felicitousness or infelicitousness. Austin, for his part, is perfectly clear about the necessity to keep sentence meanings and speech acts apart in our minds if we are to regard stating as a speech act without falling into confusion.

> Once we realise that what we have to study is *not* the sentence but the issuing of an utterance in a speech situation, there can hardly be any longer a possibility of not seeing that stating is performing an act.[14]

But perhaps it could be argued on Searle's side that Austin himself produced some evidence which tends to blur the distinction between stating and other illocutionary acts (the distinction between *performatives* and *constatives*, in Austin's terminology). There is, as Austin says,[15] 'an obvious slide towards truth or falsity' in the case of such performatives as estimates, findings and pronouncements: though we may not speak of truth and falsehood in such cases, we do speak of correctness and incorrectness, for example.

No doubt, in any case, Searle's assimilation of the study of meaning to the study of illocutionary acts must be judged finally by its results, and not by these *prima facie* considerations. And perhaps, too, we are making a mistake in thinking of illocutionary force as something which stands outside the sentence or is added on to it, like the Fregian assertion sign. Searle wishes to carry the analysis of speech acts 'inside the proposition', by treating the utterance of even a simple declarative sentence as a complex of speech acts, the two most salient being the act of reference and the act of predication.

Searle's assimilation necessarily determines a certain methodology for the theory of meaning. If Searle is right, the study of meaning is primarily the study of what conditions are necessary and sufficient for a speech act 'to have been successfully and non-defectively performed in the utterance of a given sentence'. But a language, Searle wants to say, is a system of conventions: speech acting, unlike other forms of acting (knocking in a nail or lighting a pipe, perhaps) is 'a rule-governed form of behaviour'.[16] There is, for example, a *convention of promising* – Searle calls such conventions 'linguistic devices' – and it is the rules for operating this convention which ultimately determine when the utterance of a sentence does, and when it does not, constitute the making of a promise. The ultimate object of a Searlian theory of meaning is to elucidate these rules – the *constitutive* rules, as Searle would say – which define such linguistic devices as the institution of promising, using as data for this elucidation our intuitions, as native speakers, concerning the conditions of defectiveness or non-defectiveness of particular sorts of illocutionary act. 'The procedure which I shall follow', says Searle (ibid., p. 22), 'is to state a set of necessary and sufficient conditions for the performance of particular kinds of speech acts and then extract from those conditions sets of semantic rules for the use of the linguistic devices which mark the utterances as speech acts of those kinds.'

4. The anatomy of promising

It does not seem self-evident, however, either that it is feasible to state sets of sufficient and necessary conditions for the 'successful and non-defective' performance of speech acts, or that speech acting is, in some way which distinguishes it from other kinds of acting, 'rule-governed behaviour'. Both of these claims can be contested.

Searle's set of putative necessary and sufficient conditions for promising, for example, includes the following (I have in part paraphrased Searle's formulations for ease of exposition, I hope without serious distortion. I retain Searle's numbering.)

(3) A speaker, S, who makes a promise, says that he will perform some act A in the future.

(5) It is not obvious to both S and H [a hearer] that S will do A in the ordinary course of events.

(6) S intends to do A.

(7) S intends that the utterance of T [a sentence] will put him under an obligation to do A.

It is not difficult to show that none of the above conditions is a necessary condition of promising. What I promise need not, for example, be the future performance of some act. I may say to a sick child, in order to calm its fears and hasten its recovery, 'I *promise* that you will get better.' And perhaps the child trusts me and is reassured, but, if so, *what* he trusts in is not the future performance by me of any action but my adult knowledge of illness. And, if I am wrong, if I have promised lightly and ignorantly, just in order to be relieved of his complaints, and he gets worse, he can reproach me with 'But you *promised*', just as bitterly as if I had promised to perform some action.

Again, it may be obvious to my elderly mother and to myself that I shall take her to the hospital in the ordinary course of events tomorrow: who else would do it? I do it every week. But I say, 'I'll be back tomorrow – promise!' to cheer her up and confirm her feeling of security in my return. It is a light and scarcely necessary promise – but still a promise.

Finally, I need not utter the words 'I promise', nor have any intention of promising, nor of undertaking any obligation, for my words to have, as they say, *the force of a promise*. It depends entirely on the situation. A doctor attending a seriously ill patient says, 'I shall be passing this way again tomorrow.' He says the words abstractedly, because he is musing on the course of the next few days, but the sick man hears them and says, 'Oh, good, Doctor, I shall rely on that', and the doctor realises that he has inadvertently promised to call. He did not intend his words to be taken as a promise, but he sees that in that situation, given the patient's anxiety and his fear of death, those words could hardly be taken as anything *but* a promise to call. Or, more simply still, an auctioneer makes a mental note not to close the bidding too soon on a certain lot, although he is for other reasons in a hurry to finish the auction, which has otherwise come down to odds the ends. At the crucial moment his fluster betrays him and he slaps his desk out of habit, fractionally before a further bid is nodded. He curses his impetuosity: he had not intended to promise to sell a picture which just *may* be a Vermeer for £750; but that is what he has done (that is the effect – the illocutionary force – of his slapping the desk).

Searle's conditions for promising are supposed to be both necessary and sufficient. That is, they are supposed to exhaust the possible ways in which the act of promising can be *defective*. Searle says (ibid., p. 54) that his notion of defectiveness 'is closely related to Austin's notion of an infelicity', but he hardly discusses Austin's views on infelicity, and in particular he does not mention the Austinian distinction between *misfires* and *abuses*. This is important, I think, because misfires seem to be related to the meanings of illocutionary verbs, while abuses do not. It is part of the meaning of 'marriage' that marriage is a sacrament of the Church; that is why the marriage ceremony misfires if the marriage service is conducted by an impostor. On the other hand, Searle's conditions (6) and (7) appear to record abuses of the institution of promising rather than misfires of the act of promising. A promise which I do not intend to keep is not a *defective* promise (i.e. an attempt at promising which has somehow failed to come off; a saying of words which has somehow not resulted in the actual making of a promise): it is a false promise. Promises are, after all, contracts (a promise, to the extent that it is relied upon, binds both parties – remember that I insult you if I treat your promises as wind, and put myself in the wrong if they are not – and is thus to the advantage of the promiser as well as that of the person to whom he promises: that is why reproaches are in order if promises are not kept) and it is no part of the meaning of the term 'contract' that the parties to contracts should be honest men.

But, even if the distinction between misfires and abuses is kept straight, it is not obvious that the meaning of an illocutionary verb can be stated, even in part, by making a complete list of the sorts of misfire which can vitiate the act which the corresponding substantive names, and then representing the contraries of these as a set of sufficient conditions for the performance of that act. There seems no reason why knowing the meaning of 'promise' should enable us to foresee every possible way in which promising may misfire; nor does it seem reasonable to suppose that the meaning of 'promise' alters when a new ground of misfire is admitted. For example, promising may misfire because the promise is extracted in the course of a hoax; because it is founded upon a false presumption (I promise to speak to the chairman on your behalf, not realising that the department has adopted the principle of collective responsibility, abolishing the office of chairman); because it is made to someone who deliberately chooses not to rely upon it, or accept it as a promise; because it is made by somebody who is not entitled to make it; because it is a supererogatory promise to perform a feat of such difficulty that nobody would seriously hold a man to it; because the person to whom the promise was made turns out to be someone other than the person he and everyone else thought he was (the heir of Stair turns out to be a foundling and the son of a shepherd, so promises made to him as to the future master of Stair lapse retroactively); and for many, many other reasons, few of which seem to have all that much to do with the essential nature of promising. Nor need this surprise us very much. In promising I make myself *responsible* for the action or piece of information which the promise concerns, and the concept of responsibility is, as H. L. A. Hart argued long ago,[17] a *defeasible* concept: whether a man is responsible for his acts turns not on any positive criterion, but on whether or not any of the members of a list of *defeating pleas* can be successfully urged in his case against the normal presumption of responsibility. The list includes such things as insanity, minority or drunkenness, and it can be extended indefinitely, as the progress of case law and our knowledge of psychology, the effect of certain drugs, and so on, may happen to require. Promising works in a similar way. If a promise has been explicitly made, or may reasonably be held to have been made (as in the axe-borrowing case, for example), it stands, unless it can somehow be shown to have been defective; but the grounds of defect are not laid down in advance, and may multiply for the same sort of reasons which increase the number and variety of Hart's defeating pleas in court cases involving questions of responsibility. And, of course, matters are further complicated by the fact that reasoned disagreements may arise over whether certain circumstances cause a promise to misfire or not. Hobbes notoriously thought that a promise made under threat of death was still a promise, and, although most of us would disagree, perhaps, still most of us can see the force of his argument.

Philosophers who are very attached to the idea that meanings are given by sets of necessary and sufficient conditions may take these arguments as tending to show that the word 'promise' has no clear meaning at all, and thus they may be inclined to dismiss them as contributing merely to a nihilistic pessimism about the possibility of constructing any serious theory of meaning. But their tendency is in fact opposed to any such scepticism. What they show is that we can recognise a promise as having been made even where some or all of the common features of formal, ceremonious promising are missing – that, knowing the meaning of the term 'promise', we can project its reference to cover new and unforeseen kinds of promising – and that, similarly, we can recognise new sorts of ways in which promising can misfire. This argues not that the term 'promise' has no meaning, but that the rules which govern its application have the power to organise experience in ways which are beyond the power of a set of sufficient and necessary conditions.

Searle's account of the relationship of the rules governing speech-acting seems to me to come down to the following two propositions, which summarise, I hope not unfairly, a good deal of discussion in *Speech Acts*.

(1) The semantic rules which regulate the use of an illocutionary verb (for instance, 'to promise') are rules *for performing illocutionary acts* of the sort picked out by that verb.

(2) Such rules serve to *constitute* a mode of activity (promising, for example) in the way in which the rules of a game such as chess or football *constitute* the game. That is, just as the invention of the rules of chess brings into being the possibility of playing chess, so the invention of the rules for making promises brings into being the possibility of promising. The rules, therefore, express the very essence of what it is to promise, and so give us the *meaning* of 'promise'.

It is not at all clear, though, that illocutionary acts are rule-governed in the sense which Searle requires. Indeed, it is pretty clear that some of them, at least, are not. Searle's phrase 'rule-governed action' suggests *ritual*: the sense in which the actions of a priest saying Mass, or of Black Rod at the door of the House of Commons, are governed by rules. Strawson has observed[18] that some illocutionary acts are certainly not rule-governed in this sense. The idea that one must follow a special ritual in order to *entreat*, for example, is 'like supposing that there could be no love affairs which did not proceed on lines laid down in the *Roman de la Rose*'. But Strawson grants (ibid.) that

> the contention that illocutionary force is a matter of convention is easily seen to be true in a great number of cases . . . the fact that the word 'guilty' is pronounced by the foreman of the jury in court at the proper moment constitutes his utterance as the act of bringing in a verdict, and that this is so is certainly a matter of the conventional procedures of the law.[19]

This admission of Strawson's has, if one considers its implications, the curious property of demolishing Searle's entire position by partially granting one of its premises. For, granted that the rule of English court procedure which requires the verdict of the jury to be delivered by the foreman at a certain point in the trial constitutes (or in part constitutes) *the foreman's actual speech* as the delivery of a verdict, still that rule of procedure does not seem to be essential to, or constitutive of, *the concept of verdict-giving*. There are many ways other than those laid down by the traditions of the Common Law in which a verdict in a trial might be delivered, or for that matter arrived at, and many other sorts of authority can arrive at and deliver verdicts.

There are grounds here, in short, for suspecting that Searle's account of semantic rules as rules *constitutive of practices* may embody a radical confusion of two quite distinct questions.

(1) What considerations mark out particular utterances as having some specific illocutionary force?
(2) What enables one speaker of a language to apply a term such as 'promise' or 'verdict', independently of other speakers, in ways which match the linguistic judgements of other speakers, even in cases which do not exactly match the paradigm cases in which the use of the term was first learned?

The answer to (1) may on occasion be that some ritual has been observed, on other occasions not. But, even where the observance of some ritual *is* essential to the illocutionary status of an *utterance*, the ritual in question may not be at all constitutive of, or explanatory of, the corresponding illocutionary *concept*.

To drive this criticism home it would be necessary to supplement it with a positive answer to (2). I suspect that the beginning of wisdom so far as promising is concerned may be to see that 'promise' is not the name of a kind of action, or even of a *practice*, in the sense in which, say, urn-burial or crop-rotation are *practices*, but the name of a species of moral relationship between persons. To promise is to give a (formal or implicit) guarantee of the reliability of my words in order to bring it about that they are in fact relied upon. In promising there is thus always a notional, and very often an actual, exchange of advantages, and it is this which brings it about that reproach is in order equally if a promise is not kept or if it is kept but not relied upon by the party to whom it was made. Searle thinks that the fact that a promise creates an obligation requires no explanation, and he suggests that to ask such a question is like asking the question how scoring a touchdown can create six points (Searle, 1970, p. 35). Hence, one of his rules for promising (rule 5) simply states that the utterance of a promise counts as the undertaking of an obligation. Unless we take the concept of obligation as crystal-clear, this seems to me merely to shroud the whole topic of promising in obscurity. To understand promising just *is* to understand the source of the obligation which promising creates. Searle's promiser is like a man who says, 'You may reproach me if I step on the lines in the pavement.' We understand that *as a rule*, and we may even obey it, to humour him, but the *point* of reproaching him remains so far altogether obscure, and our hearts will scarcely be in the 'reproaches'.

This is a very rough account of promising, and would need to be refined a good deal before we could present it as an account of what a competent speaker knows in knowing the meaning of 'promise': it would need among other things to be set in the framework of a general theory of meaning. But even in its present rough state it seems to account for many of the features of promising which appear to provide counter-examples to Searle's treatment. It explains the existence of locations such as 'I promise you that it is so' (in effect, 'I give you a formal guarantee, as upon oath, that it is so'), which Searle has to explain away as 'emphatic assertions', so leaving it unclear why the formal words of a promise can function, without apparent homonymy, as a mere mark of emphasis, as well as obscuring the actual force of the English ('I promise you she is safe' does not at all come to the same thing as 'SHE IS SAFE', or 'God damn it, she is safe, I tell you').

Our account also explains how it is possible to promise inadvertently. On Searle's theory, promising involves the unilateral conferral by the promiser, upon the person to whom he promises, of a right of reproach which the latter can exercise in certain specified circumstances. On such an account promising must be an intentional act: rights cannot be conferred accidentally or by inadvertence. On our view, on the other hand, promising involves the acceptance by the promiser of certain goods in the shape of the reliance which others place upon his words. Even on occasions when these goods are not, as it were, goods I wish to purchase, I may find that I have taken delivery of them just the same, and so that I have to pay for them by an exercise of promise-keeping. Thus, the auctioneer has inadvertently taken delivery of the assurance that the bidder will not take his £750 to another auction, and the fact that the assurance is unwelcome, and secured only inadvertently, does not relieve him of the obligation to pay for it, by completing the sale at the agreed price.

Hence, also, a promise misfires unless it is accepted as such (unless reliance is placed upon it, that is); or if the person to whom it was made turns out not to be the person he was thought to be (*his* reliance upon the promise is of no value to the promiser).

5. *Reference and predication*

Searle's theory of reference, and his theory of predication, seem to me to suffer from defects which exactly parallel those of his theory of promising. They offer putative sets of sufficient and necessary conditions for referring and predicating, taken as acts, which are vulnerable to counter-example; and they offer no insight at all into the workings of the *concepts* of reference and predication.

Searle's account of reference, in fact, takes the concept of reference for granted, merely conceding (ibid., p. 72) that 'the notion of singular definite reference is a very unsatisfactory one, but one we can hardly do without' and explaining the notion, and some consequent ones, by appeal to example. Searle's discussion of the rules for referring lead him to the conclusion that reference is possible only if the speaker can, on demand, produce a uniquely identifying description of the entity referred to. We have already discussed this thesis, and no further discussion is required here.

Searle's account of predication is founded upon an interesting discussion of Frege and Strawson, which need not detain us here. In essence, Searle's general view is that predication is not in itself a speech act; the notion of predication is an abstraction formed by reflecting upon certain common features of many different kinds of illocutionary acts. Searle suggests that the sentences

(1) You are going to leave
(2) Leave!
(3) Will you leave?
(4) I suggest that you leave

can be represented by the following formal schema:

$$(5) \quad F \begin{pmatrix} R & P \\ \text{you} & \text{leave} \end{pmatrix},$$

where F marks the different illocutionary forces and R and P stand for a referring expression and a predicate expression respectively. So predicate expressions are neutral with respect to illocutionary force, but can occur only within the context of an illocutionary act.

Searle argues that there is no need to postulate universals or concepts as objects of reference for general names. General names have no reference. To understand the name of a universal it is necessary to understand the use of the corresponding general term, and to understand the use of 'red' or 'wise' is 'just to understand the use of the corresponding predicates' (pp. 119–20).

Everything turns, therefore, upon what it is to predicate something of something, and the root of the answer which Searle gives to this question is (p. 124) that 'To predicate an expression "P" of an object R is to raise the question of the truth of the predicate expression of the object referred to.'

The formula 'raises the question of' gives Searle a way of explaining how predication, which seems essentially connected with the concepts of truth and falsehood, can occur in, say, questions or commands, even though questions and commands cannot be true or false, and to that extent it is not trivial. But as an account of the nature of predication it does seem trivial. It in no way explains how predication is connected with the concepts of truth and falsehood, nor why predication is so connected while reference, or naming, for example, is not. The concept of predication, in short, is taken as much for granted, as an intuitively clear but unanalysed notion, as the concept of reference. Chomsky's recent remark to the effect that Searle's theory 'gives us no way to escape the orbit of conceptual space that includes such notions as "linguistic meaning"'[20] is thus, it seems to me, quite correct, despite Searle's various attempts at rebuttal.[21] For one thing, nothing in Searle's account explains what it is to know the meaning of a general name.

Searle's 'rules' for predicating are advanced tentatively, and perhaps should not be taken too seriously. But they include, as rule (5), 'X [the entity picked out by the referring expression to which the predicate attaches] is of a type or category such that it is logically possible for P to be true or false of X.'

What, now, does 'type or category' mean here? Is it a natural fact or a linguistic fact that objects of reference come in different 'types' or categories; and, if the latter, what are the linguistic mechanisms which bring it about? What kind of 'logic' governs the 'logical' (*sic*) possibility of attaching certain predicates to certain referring expressions? And what about the well known fact that metaphors cross such categorical boundaries, which makes it odd, to say the least, to talk about *logical* impossibility where questions of the intelligibility of predications are at stake? The intelligibility of a given predication is often relevant to context ('Friday is in the hut cooking dinner' makes sense in *Robinson Crusoe*). So whether it is 'logically possible for P to be true or false of X' apparently depends on context. That means that, unless it is open to each speaker to *decide* whether a given predication is intelligible in a given context, there must be some machinery of rules or conventions, shared by all speakers, which enables any speaker to *determine* (in a way which matches the independent determinations of other competent speakers) whether a given predication – which may be one he has never encountered before – is intelligible relative to a given context. The mechanisms which decide such questions must evidently be in some way essentially bound up with the nature of predication. I can see no very promising way in which they might be identified with Searlian rules: that is, with rules for the performance of illocutionary acts.

11

Meaning and Speakers' Meaning

1. Utterers' intentions

It is possible to hold that the concept of linguistic meaning is to be analysed in terms of communication and social interaction and yet to deny any *fundamental* role in the analysis to the concept of a *semantic rule*, or a rule of language. And it can seem a great relief, as it does also to Davidson, to be rid of the debased coinage which such phrases have often seemed over the past thirty years to have become.

The most currently celebrated theory of this sort is owing to H. P. Grice.[1] Grice begins by trying to find a ground of distinction between the meaning of 'meaning' in such contexts as 'Those spots mean measles', or 'The recent budget means that we shall have a hard year', and its 'non-natural' meaning – which Grice refers to as 'meaning$_{NN}$' – in such contexts as 'Those three rings on the bell (of the bus) mean that the bus is full', or 'That remark, "Smith couldn't get on without his trouble and strife", meant that Smith found his wife indispensable.'

Grice sees that 'means$_{NN}$' has, in fact, two senses, the first of which concerns, as he says 'particular occasions of use', while the second concerns the 'timeless meaning' of a sentence. The contrast between these two senses can be paradigmatically represented by the following schemata:

(a) U meant$_{NN}$ p by x at time T
(b) x means$_{NN}$ p

where U is an utterer, x is a sentence and p is a proposition. This leaves out of consideration statements of the form 'a means$_{NN}$ ϕ' which give the meaning of a single word: such statements give Grice peculiar difficulties,[2] but they are scarcely worth insisting upon here.

For reasons which I have been unable to find clearly or convincingly stated anywhere in the work of Grice, he thinks that (a) gives the more fundamental sense of 'means$_{NN}$'. That is, Grice thinks that the sense which 'means$_{NN}$' bears in contexts of type (b) is always ultimately to be explicated in terms of the sense it bears in type (a) contexts.

Many critics have found this move of Grice's perverse and arbitrary. The answer usually given by Griceans is Asquith's: 'Wait and see.' This is fair enough in one way: a programme of analysis is to be judged by its results. But more can be said about why one should want to make the attempt to produce an analysis of type (b) uses of 'means$_{NN}$' in terms of type (a) uses. Jonathan Bennett has recently given a very clear statement of the reason: it is that Grice's programme seems to offer the prospect of analysing the concept 'means$_{NN}$' without appeal to any semantic or linguistic notions whatsoever, provided we are prepared to accept quite a lot of quantifying over beliefs and intentions. The programme is yet another version of nominalism about meanings.

> H. P. Grice showed how to give a clear sense to 'By uttering x, U meant that P' without implying anything about any language – not that x meant that P in any language, or that U thought it did, or that U thought his hearers thought it did, or . . . etc. Grice's theory analyses the concept of meaning which is involved in language as distinct from the one involved in 'Those clouds mean rain' but the analysis itself presupposes nothing about language. . . .
>
> So now we can have a meaning-nominalist account of language, that is, one which treats as basic the individual instance of meaning, by one speaker at one time, and gives a derivative status to every kind of general statement about meanings – what the speaker usually means by x, what speakers generally mean by x, what x means in the language, and so on.[3]

Grice's final analysis of 'By uttering x, U meant$_{NN}$ P' goes like this. 'U means$_{NN}$ something by x' is roughly equivalent to 'For some audience, A, U intends (1) that his utterance of x should produce a particular response r in A; (2) that A should recognise that U intends (1); and (3) that A's response r should issue from A's recognition that U intends (1).' To ask *what* U means$_{NN}$ (that is, what corresponds to P on a particular occasion of utterance, or what the *context* of x is) is to ask, Grice says, for 'a specification of the intended effect'.[4] In the case of a statement, the effect intended may be that A should come to entertain a certain belief.

2. The standard counter-examples

Grice's analysis must run a very close second to certain forms of utilitarianism for the title of 'philosophical thesis most beset by counter-examples'. The counter-examples, although they attack different elements of Grice's thesis, all bear ultimately on the same question: has the concept of utterers' intentions any bearing at all on the meaning of 'means$_{NN}$' in contexts of type (b)?

There can be no doubt, I think, that Grice's analysis does give us some genuine insight into the nature of the distinction between the meaning of 'meaning' in 'Those clouds mean rain' and its meaning in 'Those cries (gestures, marks, words) are supposed to mean$_{NN}$ something.' Judging whether an utterance 'means$_{NN}$ something' in the latter sense often is, I think, in part a matter of judging whether the speaker has Gricean intentions *vis-à-vis* an audience.

The trouble is that there is another sense of 'means$_{NN}$' – the context (b) sense – in which the question of whether something means$_{NN}$ something seems entirely disconnected, or disconnectable, from all considerations concerning intentions, Gricean or otherwise. In that sense of means$_{NN}$, that is, the question of whether something means$_{NN}$ something can on the one hand be settled without appeal to Gricean intentions; while on the other hand no demonstration of the existence of Gricean intentions is sufficient to show that something means$_{NN}$ something.

Ziff,[5] for instance, invents an irritable academic, George, who is given a test to establish his sanity on being inducted into the army. On being asked how he would identify himself, George replies, 'Ugh ugh blugh blugh ugh blug blug.'

By this utterance George means to produce an effect in his audience: to wit, he intends to offend them; and he intends their offence to arise from their recognition that he intended to offend them. (The example can be tailored to cover various other provisos and caveats raised in Grice's discussions.) So George means$_{NN}$ something by his utterance in Grice's sense. But, of course, his utterance *means*, in itself, nothing.

Again, Searle[6] invents an American soldier captured by Italian troops who fondly imagines that he can give his captors the impression that he is a German by addressing them with the words 'Kennst du das land, wo die Zitronen blühen?' On Grice's analysis his words mean$_{NN}$, 'I am a German soldier', but, as we know, they really mean, 'Do you know the land where the lemon-trees bloom?'

Searle, to be sure, wishes not to overthrow Grice's analysis, but to take it over into a speech-act theory of meaning in a modified form. He takes Grice's notion of the 'effect' of an utterance upon an audience to involve a conflation of illocutionary with perlocutionary effects. Only illocutionary effects, Searle thinks, have to do with the linguistic meanings of utterances; linguistic intentions are therefore intentions to produce illocutionary effects. According to Searle's revised version of Grice's analysis, the effects of U's utterance on A must be produced through the mechanism of A's knowledge of the rules governing the use of the sentence type x which U utters.

This move of Searle's seems to me to throw away the advantages of a Gricean analysis of meaning while retaining its disadvantages. One leading advantage of Grice's theory, if it worked, would be that it would enable us to do without talk of meaning rules. One of its main disadvantages is that, like Searle's theory, it connects the concept of meaning *essentially* with the concept of 'intention to communicate', abandoning the Fregian principle that the meaning of an expression in a language must be independent of the psychological states of particular speakers.

Grice's thesis not only requires the concept of meaning to be essentially connected with that of communication intention; it also requires what Mill would have called a concomitant variation to obtain in general between P and r; between the response which U intends to elicit and what is meant by x. The counter-examples which we have examined so far work precisely because p and r can vary independently of one another. To use an example of N. L. Wilson's,

if I mean my guests to leave there are any number of different things I can say (and mean by what I say) in order to shoo them out. On the other hand, if I say, 'It's getting pretty late', meaning that it's getting pretty late, there might be any one of a number of different things I expect of my audience.[7]

But if p and r can fall apart in this way, Wilson argues, there is no reason why my intentions in uttering x should not be (1) to assert p, and (2) to avoid having an intention postulated by Grice in any of his published papers or any subsequent paper. Wilson's utterer, though fixed in his determination to affirm that snow is white, is otherwise virginal in his innocence of intentions towards his interlocutor (Grice).

> As a matter of fact I didn't even intend that you should alter your views. . . . You can only intend to produce an effect if you deem it possible to do so . . . and everybody knows it is not possible to persuade a philosopher to give up a cherished doctrine. . . . My only intention was to behave in a counter-exemplary manner.

The dilemma which all these arguments pose for Grice is this. A Gricean analysis of 'means$_{NN}$' achieves its aims of avoiding reference to rules of language, or to prior linguistic or semantic concepts, precisely by taking the individual utterance, by a particular speaker, as fundamental. Our ordinary use of 'meaning', on the other hand, involves an implicit appeal to *language*, conceived as something which determines meanings *in general*, independent of the intentions of particular speakers. Wilson, like Davidson, argues that attributions of meaning to sentences are always relative to a *corpus* of sentences: the meaning we give to a particular sentence is part of a general interpretation of the corpus designed to maximise truth among the sentences of the corpus according to a principle of charity. Ziff makes a similar point, though without basing it upon the idea of the maximisation of truth amongst the sentences of a corpus:

> Grice's analysis rings untrue. It was bound to; his alloy lacks the basic ingredient of meaning: a set of projective devices. The syntactic and semantic structure of any natural language is essentially recursive in character. What any given sentence means depends on what (various) other sentences in the language mean.[8]

On the other hand, the device of attacking Grice by finding counter-examples to his analysis has its limits. The counter-examples merely present Grice with the dilemma we have just outlined: they do not in themselves show that a Gricean approach cannot pass between its horns.

There is indeed, an obvious way in which a Gricean theory might do just that. It would do so if it could be shown that the general linguistic conventions which relate each sentence in a language to other sentences in that language are in some reasonably straightforward way outgrowths of, or developments of, essentially Gricean communicative relationships holding between particular speakers and hearers in specific situations of communication. Such a demonstration of the Gricean roots of linguistic convention would need, of course, in order to succeed, to go through without appeal to any unanalysed semantic or linguistic notion. But we have as yet found no conclusive reason which would exclude such a development of Grice's ideas. It is this option of theory which we must now consider.

3. Intention and convention

To begin with, the Gricean conditions do seem to describe the essential machinery of a mode of communication even if that mode of communication seems, *prima facie*, to be quite distinct from communication by means of language. Grice is talking – here I agree with N. L. Wilson – not about language but about *signalling*. If, from half-way up a cliff, I signal to you, by gesturing, that you are to stand back from the cliff-foot because of the danger of falling rocks, what makes my gesture a *signal*, and distinguishes it from the exactly similar gesture (the outflung arms flailing the air) which merely 'means' – 'natural' rather than 'non-natural' sense of 'means' – that I have lost my hold and am about to fall from the cliff, is, precisely, that I intend the gesture to have a certain effect upon you, and that I intend it to have that effect on you as a result of your recognition that I have that intention. When you ask yourself if in fact the gesture *is* to be regarded as a signal, or whether it is not just an involuntary movement made by a man in danger of losing his balance, what you are asking yourself is indeed whether or not I have the proper Gricean complex of intentions. And, similarly, deciding what the signal *means* is deciding what effect I must be intending it to have.

But, given that Gricean signalling is a quite commonplace and familiar mode of communication, why should it not become standardised? Why should not a gesture which was originally the impromptu invention of a Gricean utterer come to have a standard signification as part of a repertoire, or 'language' of signals? Once we have reached that point, the familiar gulf between meaning and intention revealed by the usual counter-examples to Grice's thesis opens up again. If a certain gesture is generally used to signal 'Stand back', then if I use it with the intention of signalling 'Start coming up the rope' my intention will fail in its effect: the rest of the party will be able to say 'That may have been what you intended, but it wasn't what your signal *meant*.' And, if I use an impromptu gesture to signal instead of the gesture which is provided by the repertoire for that purpose, my baffled fellow climbers will be able to say, 'But why didn't you use the proper signal? The gesture *you* made was *meaningless*.'

But now these possibilities do not seem any longer to count as counter-examples to Grice's thesis. *What* each signal signals is still a Gricean intention: it is just that the association between certain types of utterance and certain types of intended effect has become standardised by convention.

It may be thought that the introduction of the phrase 'by convention' conceals a covert and un-Gricean reliance upon the notion of a semantic rule. This is not necessarily so at all. As Jonathan Bennett[9] has recently argued, David Lewis'[10] theory of convention offers us, when coupled with Grice's theory, a way of understanding linguistic convention which is fully consistent with 'meaning nominalism'.

Lewis regards conventions as solutions to what he calls co-ordination problems. Co-ordination problems arise where two or more agents have interests which do not conflict, but which are such that, for each agent, the best way of pursuing them depends on what the other agents do. It is known to all the agents that on a previous occasion such a problem has been handled by adopting a certain procedure, *C*. Given that they all know this, and that each knows that all the others know it, any of them knows that he has a good chance of solving the co-ordination problem by initiating procedure *C*. When such behaviour becomes uniform and regular in the face of that sort of problem, the community has acquired a convention. A convention is thus more than a mere behavioural regularity, but it is nevertheless entirely explicable in terms of dispositions to behave in certain ways: no reference to 'agreements' or 'tacit agreements' or to 'rules' is needed.

Is there any insuperable barrier, now, to thinking of a natural language as a system of Lewisian conventions founded upon the Gricean signalling mechanism? The obvious objection is that the Gricean mechanism operates upon 'whole utterances'. It makes no allowance for the recursive interpretation of sentences in terms of their component expressions. Bennett sees this difficulty. He argues that, by combining Grice and Lewis,

> we reach the notion of the meaning that a certain expression – a certain product-kind – conventionally has; but the expression is still a whole utterance, something more like a sentence than like a word or phrase. The final big step is from that to
>
> (4) w means . . .
>
> where w is an utterance-part, and the completion is a word or phrase and not a 'that P' clause where 'P' stands for a sentence. . . . The term 'language', I believe, becomes fully appropriate at level (4) but not before.[11]

It seems to me, however, that there is a further, less obvious obstacle, which Bennett half sees, but passes over altogether too easily, and which is fatal to the programme of interpreting natural languages as conventionalised Gricean signal systems. The difficulty is quite distinct from that of passing from 'whole utterances' to structured ones: it already arises at the level of 'whole utterances', and it concerns Bennett's analogy between such utterances and sentences. The problem is to know what grounds we can possibly have for assigning to a signal – even a signal drawn from a conventionally accepted repertoire of signals – anything remotely analogous to the content, or force, or import, of a sentence? Certainly Bennett is quite correct to say that a signal does not function like a word, but that is, to say the least, an Irish reason for saying that it functions like a sentence.

At first sight, though, this may seem no problem. What can the import of my gesture from the cliff, say, be *but* 'Keep away!' or perhaps 'Look out for falling rocks!'? If it is intended to have an effect upon someone, it is intended to have a *meaning* – so much we have admitted – and *what* it means must surely be given by the content of the intention. We might say, perhaps, that the content of the gesture is the same as that of the sentence I should utter if I were close enough to the ground to be sure of being heard by you, and so did not have to rely on signalling.

But this last way of putting it gives the game away. If I have access to a language I have access to the concept *What U would say if he were to speak instead of signalling*. Bennett's admirable aim of giving an account of meaning which 'presupposes nothing about language' necessarily deprives him of access to such concepts. He therefore has to find some other set of grounds – and preferably behavioural ones – for ascribing sentential or propositional force to a non-linguistic utterance or piece of behaviour which expresses a Gricean intention.

Bennett encounters this problem obliquely, in the course of attempting to reformulate, in Gricean terms, the distinction between a statement and an injunction. According to Bennett, 'the essence of a statement is U's reliance on the Gricean mechanism to get A to believe something.'[12] Bennett's problem is now to find behavioural criteria for ascribing such intentions to people without appeal to linguistic considerations.

Bennett has two solutions to this problem. The first is that *iconicity* – the pictorial character of certain signals – offers us a direct insight into the nature of the belief which an utterer may intend to produce by his utterance. The second is that *regular association* may offer us a way of 'escaping from icons'. If we find that a certain gesture constantly correlates with certain environmental conditions, say the presence of a shoal of fish in the bay, or the onset of rain, and if the social circumstances in which it is produced are such that we can reasonably impute to the person who produces the signal a desire to produce in others beliefs about those conditions (people respond to the signal by getting out nets and joining the signaller in a fishing expedition, say), then we have grounds for treating the gesture as having a certain propositional content.

Let us begin with iconicity. Bennett says, apropos of a 'tribe of anthropoid mammals' invented for the purposes of his transcendental deduction of the concept of meaning,

> one day we observe a tribesman, U, stand in full view of another, A, and emit a snake-like hissing sound while also making with his hand a smooth undulating horizontal motion which resembles the movement of a snake. Why did he do this?[13]

Bennett argues that, given that U's performance 'naturally induces the thought of a snake', we can tentatively postulate that, 'if U is trying to make A believe something, it is something about a snake' and that U's further behaviour, combined with what we know about the context (that U has not just been bitten by a snake, that there has been no recent tribal snake encounter, and so on) can give us good grounds for concluding that U intends A to believe on this occasion that there is a snake nearby.

We can accept all of this, I think, for the sake of argument, and subject to the essential unreality of all such armchair anthropology, as a plausible enough description of a case in which we might have non-linguistic behavioural grounds for asserting the existence of a Gricean intention on the part of one creature to produce a state of belief about some specific matter of fact in another. What I question is the transition from asserting the existence of such an intention to the claim that the signals or gestures which manifest this intention constitute the making of a statement, and are thus, in that sense, equivalent to the utterance of a sentence in a natural language. I question, in short, Bennett's claim that 'the essence of a statement is U's reliance on the Gricean mechanism to get A to believe something'. I think, on the contrary, that it is possible to make a statement only by uttering some appropriate sentence in some natural language.

To begin with, Bennett radically misconstrues the role of what he calls 'iconicity' in his example. Why should the tribesman's performance 'naturally' induce the thought of a snake? Why should it not represent the motion of the waves and the hiss of the surf; or the wing movements of a wild goose landing and the goose's hiss; or the movement of a field of corn in a great wind, with the wind's sighing; or the quaking of the mudpools in a volcanic crater, with the escape of volcanic gases through fissures; or the escape of air from the tyres of a car, together with its lurching forward motion as the tyres deflate? The reason, of course, is that the context, including what we know or guess of the tribesman's beliefs and intentions, and including the tribesman's further behaviour, will not support these equally 'iconic' interpretations. But that shows that what we fix upon as the 'iconic' significance of non-linguistic signals depends entirely upon what assessment we make of the signaller's beliefs and intentions in a given context. 'Iconicity' does not offer us a *separate* route by which we may arrive at the intended 'reference' or 'propositional content' of a non-linguistic signal. The idea that 'iconicity' and the assessment of belief and intention do offer separate sorts of grounds for ascribing significance to non-linguistic signs is a very ancient mistake in philosophy (it gives rise, for instance, to the persistent attempt to account for thought in terms of mental imagery)[14] and it gives

Bennett's argument certainly a part of its plausibility. Once we get it out of the way, Bennett is left with the claim that the investigation of intention and belief can provide sufficient grounds for ascribing propositional content to a non-linguistic signal. This is highly implausible, for the following reason.

If another speaker of English says to me 'Look out, there's a snake next to you', I precisely do *not* need to undertake any investigation into his beliefs, or his intentions in producing this string of noises, in order to know what he has said. I simply read off the meaning of the sentence he has uttered from the spoken words themselves. I may indeed presume that his intention in uttering them was to warn me, and discover later that he merely meant to give me a fright, but such presumptions and discoveries about utterers' intentions are quite irrelevant, *prima facie*, to the question of what his words meant: I know that simply because I know English. Of course, given our special vantage point as speakers of a language, we can *describe* Bennett's tribesman's behaviour in propositional terms: we can say, 'Poor fellow, he is trying to say, "Look out, there is a snake!"' But this is really no more than a kind of pathetic fallacy; and what makes it so is that Bennett's tribesman's gestures are no more *intrinsically* correlated to that particular English sentence than to a host of others: for example, 'How I love the sea', or 'Isn't it fun when the tyres of a motor car all go down at once.' The tribesman's behaviour, that is, is not translatable in the way that, say, 'Faites attention! Voilà un serpent!' is. And, what is more, it does not need to be. The device of interpreting people's noises and gestures in terms of their probable beliefs, intentions and the general context is, within certain narrow limits, a perfectly satisfactory technique of communication in its own right. Only it is not language.

The same arguments apply against Bennett's second sort of behavioural ground for the ascription of propositional content to non-linguistic signals: regular and repeated association. Here it is even more evident that the ascription of significance depends purely upon the assessment of belief and intention.

Thus, the whole weight of Bennett's theory of language comes to rest upon the question of what account he can give of sentence structure. If the conception of language as a set of Lewisian conventions founded upon the Gricean mechanism were to yield a very informative and explanatory account of sentence structure, Bennett might then be able to argue that the *prima facie* disparity between the kind of interpretation we apply to signals and the kind we apply to sentences is an illusion – the interpretation of sentences being, perhaps, a process which operates through Lewis-type conventions which at bottom, if not in surface appearance, are founded wholly upon the Gricean mechanism.

But, so far as I can see, Bennett's theory yields no account of sentence structure at all. Bennett has two general theories of sentence structure. The first is that we assign 'meanings to *types* of utterance-part on the basis of what they contribute is the meanings of *types* of whole utterance containing them' (p. 272). But he also suggests (in section 80) that syntactic function can be ascribed even to parts of 'iconic' gestures which never recur, and so cannot be regarded as *types* of utterance. If I leave garbage and Smith's wallet on the floor, intending to make you angry with Smith, the garbage-leaving corre-lates directly with the angry-making, and the wallet-depositing with the Smith-involving parts of my total intention. So, if a native, in a moment of gestural inspiration, sketches a fish in the air, jumps and bites, his behaviour has not only the sense, but also the structure of, the English sentence 'The fish are biting', or at least a structure which is closely analogous, and analogous in a philosophically illuminating way.

Let us examine the first of these proposals. Suppose we do find that the tribesmen's gestures fall into recurrent types of gesture, and that each gesture type can be correlated, in all its recurrences, with a specific Gricean intention. We still do not have what is uniquely characteristic of sentence structure: namely, signs which have radi-cally different syntactic functions, and functions, moreover, which can be grasped only by grasping the relation in which signs expressive of one syntactic function stand *in sentential contexts* to signs expressive of other syntactic functions. We have no behavioural evidence, in other words, for postulating anything like the subject–predicate relation-ship, for example, or the relationship between verb and adverb. All the gestures are signs of the same type – that is to say, signals – and the evidence we have for assigning a meaning to each signal bears on each signal separately, without reference to any other signal. So the relationship in which each signal stands to the others in a sequence of signals is that of simple juxtaposition, thus:

$$S_1 + S_2 + S_3 + S_4$$

It is not difficult to think of examples of such signal sequences. In rock-climbing the leader on the face may give a sequence of two short followed by three long whistles, meaning 'test the rope' (two short whistles) and 'start climbing' (three long whistles). But there is nothing which resembles sentence structure here, nor, so far as I can see, any analogy with the way in which someone who knows the grammar and the vocabulary of a language can 'read off' the meaning of a sentence he has never encountered before. The important thing to notice is that the elements of the signal sequence signify *in exactly the same sense* in which the signal sequence taken as a whole signifies. Each subordinate signal evokes a specific response from a hearer who has been trained to respond to the signal type in question, and the composite signal evokes a response which is a simple additive sum of the responses evoked by the subordinate signals. In the case of a sentence, the component signs possess meaning in a quite different sense from that in which the sentential sign possesses meaning; and the meaning of the sentential sign is not merely the additive sum of the meanings of the subordinate signs which enter into the sentence, but also a meaning of a type which comes into being only at the level of the sentence, and exists at no deeper level of analysis.

My point here is essentially Frege's: 'For not all the parts of a thought can be complete; at least one must be "unsaturated" or predicative; *otherwise they would not hold together*' [author's italics].[15]

So far as I can see, Bennett's theory of sentence structure simply fails to take account of this fundamental Fregian insight. The source of this failure is, I think, Bennett's willingness to treat as unproblematic the ascription of propositional content to a non-linguistic utterance expressive of a Gricean intention. If we can assume such utterances to have the status of propositions, we can assume that they have the internal structure of propositions, and the problem confronting Bennett becomes simply that of finding behavioural criteria for linking one or another element of such an utterance with one or another element of propositional (sentential) structure. There is no reason, now, why we should not be able to find behavioural criteria which decide between one or another syntactic or semantic structuring of the tribesmen's utterances (the fact that it is possible to construct grammars for languages, such as North American Indian ones, very different in structure from Indo-European languages, demonstrates, indeed, that such criteria can be found). But in order to embark on the search we have to assume that the tribesmen are speaking a *language* (i.e. that we have an intuitive grasp of the notion of a language) and that is the one assumption which Bennett's methodology forbids him to make, since it trivialises his entire analysis. We have thus uncovered a circularity in Bennett's argument. The possibility of ascribing sentence structure to Bennett's tribesmen's gestural 'utterances' depends upon the possibility of ascribing to them the status of propositions, and the ascription of propositional status depends upon the possibility of ascribing sentence structure to them. Perhaps a Gricean analysis might be extended in some way which would avoid this and any related circularity, but I am unable to see how.

IV

Language and the World

12

Interlude: Stalemate and Revision

1. Strawson's 'Homeric struggle'

We have now toured the camps of both armies locked in Strawson's 'Homeric struggle' between truth theorists of meaning and communication-intention theorists. The issue between them does not seem an easily decidable one. Their conflict, in fact, like many another bitterly fought battle in philosophy, has all the distinguishing marks of a Kantian antinomy. Each side disposes of arguments which are, to say the least, very damaging to the other side. Neither side possesses the means of conclusively establishing, once and for all, the correctness of its own position. Worse still, each side displays internal conflicts – between Grice and Searle, for example, or between Montague's possible-world semantics for natural languages and a Quinean semantics which excludes quantification into modal contexts – which exhibit the same disquieting characteristic of intractable and irresoluble mutual opposition as the larger debate.

In summary, the terms of the stalemate go something like this. Truth theorists accept Frege's anti-psychologism. They accept, that is, (1) that meanings cannot be mental entities of any kind, and (2) that the sentences of a language have meaning independently of the identity or intentions of the speakers who utter them, and independently of the particular contexts in which they may be uttered. Truth theories are essentially founded upon recursive mechanisms. This appears to give them a *prima facie* advantage as theories of meaning in natural languages, since, as the work of Chomsky and other transformational–generational grammarians has made clear, natural languages must be supposed to contain very complex recursive mechanisms in order to account for syntactic relationships. Moreover, the recursive mechanisms of a theory of truth seem naturally fitted to address the problem of how a competent speaker attaches a sense to an unfamiliar sentence. Truth theories are precisely concerned with the logical mechanisms which derive the truth conditions of complex sentences from the truth conditions of simple sentences.

However, this promising parallel is perhaps less promising than it looks at first sight. If Quine's and Davidson's arguments hold, there can be no question of a unique match between a natural language and a formal theory of truth. The only way of matching a truth theory to the empirical facts of language use is through a process of radical interpretation which leaves meaning and grammatico-logical structure as matters to be (loosely) determined in the wake of a holistic process of matching truth values and the logical interrelationships of sentences to stimulus conditions for assent and dissent across the whole body of the language, considered as a collection of sentences.

We are thus left with a theory which throws very little light on the question of how language-learning is possible, on the distinction between conceptual change and language change (it is quite unclear, if Quine and Davidson are right, why we should ever have supposed it possible to draw such a distinction in the first place) and, in general, on the question of how languages are able to function as systems of communication.

Communication is, of course, the *forte* of communication-intention theories. They take their theoretical stand upon the specific, concrete context of communication, and upon the intensional states – the 'propositional attitudes', as Quine would say – of speakers and hearers in situations of communication: their beliefs, intentions, presumptions, and so on.

In making this radical shift of theoretical focus, however, communication-intention theorists lose sight of Frege's fundamental insight – the basis of his anti-psychologism – that the meaning of a sign is something which it possesses only in virtue of its place in a *system* of signs. Frege saw that if we possess a well constructed symbolic language, or conceptual notation, the meaning of a sequence of signs in that notation must be capable of being read off from the signs themselves. For, if it were dependent upon the *ad hoc* intentions of particular speakers in particular contexts, or upon the identity, beliefs, or circumstances of the speaker, the meaning of the same sentence would be subject to indefinite variation from context of use to context of use, which comes to much the same thing as saying that it would have no *meaning* at all, but would simply be a noise which different speakers use for different purposes, as one person may express anger and another incredulity by the same inflected grunt.

This conviction of Frege's that meaning is something objective and public, which inheres in the signs of a language, and not in the uses made of them by particular speakers on particular occasions, is one which carries conviction both intuitively and theoretically, as is evident both from the general tendency of the objections faced by Grice or Searle, for example, and the difficulties they encounter in meeting these objections. It would not be misleading to say that the entire effort of communication-intention theorists in constructing their theories is to reconstruct, upon the slender basis of the particular communicative situation, the Fregian concept of meaning as public, independent of intensional states, and inherent in the signs themselves. But neither Searle's rules for speech-acting, nor Gricean intentions, nor Lewisian conventions, seem quite powerful enough to carry a communication-intention theory from its anti-Fregian beginnings to its Fregian goal.

Truth theorists labour under an exactly opposite disproportion of starting point to destination. Intensions and intensional states constitute a stumbling block for the truth-theoretic analysis of natural language. At the same time it is very hard to see how we could begin to translate a wholly unknown language, if translation is to begin from the tentative assignment of truth values to sentences or putative sentences of the language, without making some assumptions about the beliefs, intentions, presuppositions and so on, of the speakers of the language. In that sense reference to the intensional states of speakers seems to be inescapable, at least if we are concerned with the *empirical* investigation of meaning in natural languages. But if we are forced in this way to admit reference to intensional states into the argument, we must (so truth theorists are forced by the nature of their enterprise to say) prevent them at all costs from infecting the extensional clarity of the truth-theoretic constructions in terms of which meaning in the language is ultimately analysed. The most effective *cordon sanitaire* against intensionality discovered to date is the semantic holism of Quine and Davidson.

And so the argument comes full circle. An adequate theory of meaning, it seems, would do justice both to Frege's insights concerning the objectivity and autonomy of meaning, and to the apparent indispensability, in the description of natural languages, of a whole family of intensional concepts of which the most salient and the most intractable member is, of course, 'meaning' itself. Truth theorists begin from Frege and run aground on the rocks of intensionality. Communication-intention theorists begin by taking intensionality for granted and run aground on the objectivity and publicity of meaning.

2. Names and sentences

Both truth theorists and communication-intention theorists start from the sentence as the fundamental unit of meaning. Sentences, as the vehicles of propositions, convey what can be true or false; prompt assent and dissent; are also the vehicles of speech acts and the focus of Gricean intentions.

Putnam has recently questioned this primacy (see above, chapter 10), and has argued for a revival of interest in naming as the most fundamental, and fundamentally philosophically puzzling, function of a natural language. In chapter 1, in discussing what we there called the autonomy of language, we formulated a problem about naming which is somewhat different from Putnam's, but which nevertheless, I think, is closely connected with it.

The problem is, in essence, that 'autonomy' or 'creativity' in language is a feature of name-using as well as sentence-using. A competent speaker can extend the series of objects – of whatever ontological category – which fall into the extension of a given general name N, in a way which matches the extensions of the series made by other, independent speakers. On the comparatively rare occasions on which a speaker is dubious about whether or not a given object belongs to the extension of N, other speakers will be independently dubious. The capacity of independent speakers to match performances in this way is essential to the concept of understanding a language. A speaker who cannot with certainty and consistency pick out objects which fall into the extension of a general name does not understand that name. Wittgenstein's dictum that to understand is to be able, independently of one's teachers, to *continue a series* as they continue it, has, it seems, a very general application to language. Understanding a general name is a matter of being able to *continue the series* of assignments of objects to the extension of the name.

To see this, however, is to bring about a very fundamental shift in the way in which we conceive the problem of meaning. The problem of meaning has very often, and indeed classically, been conceived as the problem of specifying the relationship which obtains between a meaningful sign and 'the world' or 'reality'. The presumption has been, in other words, that the meaningfulness of the sign arises from – consists in – its standing in a relationship of some sort to the world, and the task of the theory of meaning has been supposed to be the elucidation of that relationship. To conceive of understanding a general name as the ability to continue a series, however, is to see the problem of meaning not – or not primarily – as that of explicating the relationship between language and the world, but as that of explicating the relationship between one speaker and other speaker, in virtue of which the match between one independently generated series of applications of a name and another such series is achieved and sustained.

It is tempting to suppose that there is a psychological answer to this question; or in other words that the problem can be shifted wholesale from the province of philosophy, or general linguistics, in Saussure's sense, to the province of empirical psychology. But such a shift would solve nothing. It is absurd to suppose that the extension of a general name could be taught by expressly affixing the name to each object falling into the extension of the name. Once learned, the application of the name must, by the agency of some mechanism or other, generalise to new instances which are not exactly like the instances by reference to which the meaning of the name was originally learned. The question is merely whether we regard such mechanisms as psychological or linguistic mechanisms; and the former choice will be helpful only if there are psychological mechanisms, already well understood, to which the problem can be straightforwardly assimilated. The only immediately obvious mechanism is the generalisation of responses along natural dimensions of similarity in the perceptual space of an organism. Speakers, in other words, possess a fundamental ability to recognise one red, or one chair as 'naturally similar' to other reds and other chairs. Without such an ability, it is said, language could not exist: it is enough, however, to postulate such an ability to explain how independent speakers come to use general names within roughly the same limits of application, and the further investigation of the ability is a matter for psychology. General linguistics and philosophy end here.

I have already explained why this will not do, but it will do no harm to rehearse the argument briefly once more. Generalisation of response to perceptual similarities can in any case provide a *prima facie* explanation only for a comparatively restricted group of general names: colour words, names of animals or kinds of material object, for example. But even in these cases the explanation offered turns out to be vacuous, and to offer no explanation at all. Perceptual similarity is too ubiquitous and weak a relationship to connect independent speakers' applications of general names into series as rigidly defined as the observable facts of naming require.

Many chairs, for example, are quite similar to one another, perceptually speaking; others, such as the 'bean bags' sold in the more *chic* furniture shops are radically unlike 'conventional' chairs, but the difference creates no obstacle whatsoever for the application of the term 'chair'. Conversely, language dissevers things which are, perceptually speaking, very similar to one another: cups and chalices, fonts and bird-baths, dolphins and fish. Consensus between independent speakers does not follow the limits of perceptual similarity, and so cannot be reduced to consensus in the location of perceptual analogies.

Once the spurious 'solutions' offered by the postulation of unanalysed 'recognitional capacities' or 'natural similarities' are set aside, the problem of naming emerges as the problem of how independent speakers manage to preserve conformity of usage in contexts which *are not, in any simple or obvious way, mere repetitions of the contexts in which the meaning of the name in question was originally learned.* The contemporary logical vocabulary of 'possible worlds' thus has an immediate application to the problem. What competent speakers can do is to maintain conformity in the application of names *across possible worlds*. It is thus both natural and up to a point enlightening to speak, as Montague does for example, of the intension of a basic predicate as a function connecting the predicate to a range of extensions across possible worlds. But, of course, Montague's formula fails us because it says in itself nothing substantial about such functions. We need an explanation of how the intension corresponding to a basic predicate picks out extensions across possible worlds.

This is, essentially, the problem which Putnam raises in connection with natural-kind names. Rigidity of designation implies that the reference of a name such as 'chair' or 'water' to the kind *chair*, or to the kind *water*, remains stable even though the criteria by appeal to which we recognise chairs or water as belonging to those kinds may change.

We may begin by recognising water by its gross physical characteristics and end by recognising it by its molecular formula. Or we may begin by recognising a chair by its resemblance to 'standard' chairs, and end by seeing the same functional relationships manifested in the very unstandard appearance of a bean-bag chair. But in either case the reference of 'water' and 'chair' to a single coherent *kind* remains unchanged. Now, it seems to me that what we mean by the coherence of a *kind* in these cases is – to return to Wittgenstein's remark about understanding – precisely the coherence of a *series*. We can think of the applications of a given kind of name by independent competent speakers as a series, extending through time, of assimilations of objects of an appropriate ontological status to the extension of the name in question. Suppose the name is 'chair'. Then, at a certain point, the series comes to include bean-bag chairs, and the perceptual criteria by which we recognise such objects become, *a fortiori*, criteria of recognition for chairs. The kind 'chair', however, is not to be identified with any set of perceptual criteria for recognising chairs. The meaning of the kind name 'chair' – and this is why kind names are *rigid designators* in Kripke's and Putnam's vocabulary – is, rather, something like the *principle of continuity* of the series: the criteria, whatever they are, which enable independent speakers to maintain agreement in their extension of the series to new objects. The problem is to say, explicitly and clearly, what these criteria are and how they function.

It seems clear in retrospect that what is wrong with verificationism – and wrong with it even in Quinean dress – is that it absolutely fails to address this problem. No phenomenalist theory could possibly address the problem, since even to state it is to draw the distinction between thinking and perceiving, concept and percept, which Frege wished to sharpen, and which the empiricist tradition, from which all phenomenalist theories of meaning ultimately spring, has always endeavoured to blur over. Nominalist, or nominalising, theories are also ruled out in advance as possible solutions; for the nominalising impulse is precisely the impulse to deny that *kinds* have any reality over and above the perceptual criteria for assigning objects to their extensions. To suggest, as Dummett has recently done, that the best prospects for the philosophy of language lie in a revival of verificationism is therefore, I think, to espouse a forlorn hope.

Thus far I have argued in favour of Putnam's demand for a transfer of philosophical attention from the sentence to the name. But there is one potent reason why the demand should be resisted, at least in the form in which Putnam makes it.

To grasp the principle of continuity which governs, for independent speakers, the extension of the series of applications of a kind name, must be, in part, to grasp the logical category of that name. To see how the extension of 'water' must be extended, and limited, in the peculiar circumstances of the two planets Earth and Twin Earth in Putnam's example is in part to see that 'water' is a name for a *substance*, or a *kind of stuff*. The introduction of bean-bags into the extension of 'chair', again, surely has something to do with the fact that 'chair' is an artifact term, and so ultimately defined, somehow or other, in terms of function. In short, the real outcome of Putnam's argument is essentially the same as the outcome of our discussion of Locke in chapters 3 and 4: that the meaning of a term cannot be explained purely in terms of simpler and more concrete concepts – concepts with a richer empirical or perceptual content, that is – but requires reference to more general sortal categories (*substance*, *artifact*, *colour*, for example). It is difficult to see how we could come to grasp the complex interrelationships between the elements of our conceptual scheme at this level, except by studying the behaviour of terms in sentential contexts. Someone who asked, for example, 'What is the molecular formula of acid?' would show by that that he had misunderstood the logical grammar of the term 'acid'. Something similar would be true of someone who asked 'Where does "wood" appear on the Periodic Table of Elements?' An adequate theory of meaning should explain the nature of the misunderstanding in each case as a by-product of explaining the criteria which determine the extensions of substance terms across possible worlds.

3. Revising the options

Reconstructing the philosophy of language around the problem which we have just outlined may offer the best chance, it seems to me, of transcending the opposition between truth-theoretic theories of meaning and communication-intention theories. The criteria which enable competent speakers to match each other's linguistic performances must, by that very fact, be public and objective ones. Their operation cannot, by their very nature, be dependent upon variations in context or the identity of speakers. Nor, for the same reason, can their operation be responsive to the wishes or intentions of individual speakers. They must, in Saussure's sense, belong to *langue*, and not to *parole*.

But, at the same time, the existence of such criteria must, as we saw in chapter 1, be fundamental to the possibility of communication by means of language. What can be said to be *communicated* by means of language is precisely what can be read off from sequences of linguistic signs by any competent speaker; interpretations by one speaker which are not confirmed by other, independent speakers are not read off from, but read into, the signs. A theory of criteria would thus be both an *objective* theory of meaning, in the Fregian sense, and a theory of communication.

Such a theory may also go some way towards explaining what *intentions* or *senses* are. At present, as we have seen, the notion of sense enters philosophy either as a stumbling block for truth theories, or as an unanalysed assumption – under the guise of intensional verbs, attitudes, and so on – for communication-intention theories. Frege, who invented the modern notion of *sense*, defines it only in the most sketchy and metaphorical way. The sense of an expression, according to one Fregian formula, is any part of its meaning which affects the truth value of sentences in which it occurs: elements of meaning which do not affect truth belong to the *tone* (*Beleuchtung*) of the expression. According to another formula, the sense of a sentence is the way in which its reference is presented: we 'pass from a sense to a reference'.

This last formula, however, connects up the concept of sense with the problem which we outlined in the previous section. To extend the series of applications of a kind name across possible worlds is precisely to pick out the reference of the name – the extension of the kind. The criteria which enable competent speakers to match each other's independent extensions of the series thus have an excellent title to be regarded as constituting the *sense* of the name. They are, after all, what locates its reference for each competent speaker.

4. Frege and Wittgenstein

Are there any extant theories of criteria, in the sense we have outlined? I think the answer is yes. The work of Wittgenstein can be regarded as a sustained discussion of the problem which we have spent most of this book uncovering. Wittgenstein's work plays curiously little part in contemporary discussions of the philosophy of language, although one writer or another will occasionally think it worthwhile to claim Wittgenstein's authority for some favourite doctrine. Strawson, in describing the 'Homeric struggle', locates Frege and the Wittgenstein of the *Tractatus Logico-Philosophicus* as theorists of truth, and the post-1930 Wittgenstein of the *Philosophical Investigations* as a theorist of communication intention, committed to the proposition that 'the meaning of an expression is its use'.

I have already suggested that this siting of Frege is not an entirely happy one if we take into account Frege's doctrine of the objectivity of sense. Frege was not uninterested in language as a system of communication. He believed that sense must be objective, because he thought that otherwise there could be no communication and no common pursuit of truth.

I think that Strawson's classification of Wittgenstein as a communication-intention theorist is equally unhappy. The other writers whom Strawson classes under this heading are, as we have seen, united in nothing but opposition to Frege. Wittgenstein, on the other hand, remained an admirer of Frege to the end of his days, and claimed in conversation that Frege's ideas were a crucial influence, not only on the *Tractatus*, but on his later philosophy as well.

Michael Dummett, in a recent article (1976), does not see the transition from the *Tractatus* to the *Investigations* as a rejection of Frege, but as a development of certain Fregian themes. Moreover, he regards Frege as the direct ancestor of Wittgenstein's later doctrine of 'use': 'Frege's thesis that sense is objective is ... implicitly an anticipation ... of Wittgenstein's doctrine that meaning is use.'[1] I think this insight of Dummett's is substantially correct, and of the greatest importance. But it clearly needs documenting in detail. This task I shall try to perform in the next two chapters.

The interpretation I shall present shows, if it is correct, that Wittgenstein was never at any stage in his career a verificationist. This is in accord with Wittgenstein's own account of his intellectual development.[2] P. M. S. Hacker,[3] in his book *Insight and Illusion* claims that certain passages in the *Philosophical Remarks* and in Moore's lecture notes of the period 1929–32 show that Wittgenstein's memory of this period was inaccurate. The exegetical question is a complex one. I wish to claim here only that an interpretation can be given of Wittgenstein's discussion in the *Philosophical Remarks* as bridging the gap between the *Tractatus* and the *Investigations*, which removes the need to postulate either sharp discontinuity in his thought or a positivist interlude.

13

Objects and the
Determinateness of Sense

'The requirement that simple signs be possible is the requirement that sense be determinate.'[1]

1. Metaphysics and meaning

Wittgenstein begins the *Tractatus* with an extraordinarily bald and summary exposition of a metaphysical account of the world. The world is 'all that is the case' (1).* It is 'the totality of facts, not of things' (1.1). 'What is the case – a fact – is the existence of states of affairs' (2). States of affairs are combinations of 'objects', or 'things' (2.01). Objects, the nature of which constitutes one of the chief exegetical puzzles posed by the *Tractatus*, possess internal and external properties (2.01231). The internal properties of objects concern their possibilities of combination with one another in states of affairs. Wittgenstein makes it clear that the essence of an object is given by its possibilities of co-occurrence with other objects in states of affairs. 'If a thing *can* occur in a state of affairs, the possibility of the state of affairs must be written into the thing itself' (2.012). It would be 'a sort of accident, if it turned out that a situation would fit a thing that could already exist entirely on its own' (2.0121). This, of course, gives some preliminary sense, at any rate, to the claim that the world. is 'the

---

*The numbers in brackets refer to the paragraph number of the *Tractatus*.

totality of facts not of things': it follows from the claim that things, whatever they may be, can be specified only in terms of their possibilities of combination in states of affairs. If there were any other mode of specifiying objects, it would open the possibility that we might first identify an object independently of reference to any state of affairs, and then discover 'as a sort of accident' that it would fit into some states of affairs and not into others.

The nature of the external properties of objects is less clear from Wittgenstein's text. But we know that there is a difference between 'What is the case – a fact [*Tatsache*]' (2) and a mere state of affairs (*Sachverhalt*). And we know that what the difference consists in is that, whereas a state of affairs is 'a combination of objects' (2.01), a fact is 'the existence of [a] state of affairs' (2). A state of affairs, then, is what would, if it existed, or were actualised, be a fact; a fact is an actualised or existing state of affairs. And, since the essential properties of objects (those which are *internal* to them in the sense of determining their nature) concern their *possibilities* of combination in states of affairs, we may conjecture that their external properties concern the relationships to one another in which things *happen* to stand at any given moment in facts. For 'states of affairs are independent of one another' (2.061). Whether a given state of affairs exists or not has no implications for the existence or non-existence of any other state of affairs. The world as 'the totality of existing states of affairs' is thus an array of extensionally, or externally, related facts.

Against this bald and enigmatic metaphysic, Wittgenstein appears to set an equally baldly and dogmatically presented theory of propositions and names. A proposition is 'a picture of reality . . . a model of reality as we imagine it' (4.01). A proposition is a string of names; but over and above that, it is the way in which the names are articulated. 'One name stands for one thing, another for another thing, and they are combined with one another. In this way the whole group – like a *tableau vivant* – presents a state of affairs [*Sachverhalt*]' (4.0311). A proposition, in short, is not merely a string of names set one after another. 'It is only in so far as a proposition is logically articulated that it is a picture of a situation' (4.032). However, the possibility of the picturing relationship between propositions and state of affairs depends upon the relationship between objects and names, or 'simple signs'. 'The simple signs employed in propositions are called names' (3.202). 'A name means an object. The object is its meaning' (3.203). 'In a proposition a name is the representative of an object' (3.22). But, once we have attached the names in a proposition to objects in a suitable way, the logical 'articulation' or 'logical form' of the proposition mirrors the mode of configuration of the objects in the corresponding state of affairs. 'The configuration of objects in a situation corresponds to the configuration of simple signs in the propositional sign' (3.21). It is this isomorphism between the configuration of objects in the state of affairs and that of names in the propositional sign that enables us to use the sign either to affirm or to deny the existence of the state of affairs in question. 'A proposition can be true or false only in virtue of being a picture of reality' (4.06). For, 'A proposition communicates a situation to us, and so it must be *essentially* connected with the situation. And the connection is precisely that it is its logical picture' (4.03). Its status as a 'logical picture' is, indeed, what gives a proposition a sense, in Fregian terms. For 'What a picture represents is its sense' (2.221).

Cp
Black

2. *Determinateness of sense*

So viewed, as they inevitably are viewed by a reader who approaches the book for the first time, given Wittgenstein's uncompromising bareness of presentation, both the theory of objects, states of affairs and facts and, immediately following it in the book, the theory of propositions as pictures seem enigmatic, arbitrary and theoretically gratuitous. Why conceive of the world and of propositions in this way at all? What are the constraints bearing upon these theoretical constructions? What problems are they supposed to solve?

The order of paragraphs in the *Tractatus* is pretty clearly, I think, an order of exposition and not of justification. But if we are prepared to start in the middle, we can get the beginnings of an answer to these questions from propositions 4.026–4.03.

4.026   The meanings of simple signs (words) must be explained to us if we are to understand them.

With propositions, however, we make ourselves understood.

4.027   It belongs to the essence of a proposition that it should be able to communicate a *new* sense to us.

4.03   A proposition must use old expressions to communicate a new sense.

In these paragraphs Wittgenstein has seen, *inter alia*, that the exercise of linguistic judgement is creative, and, so seeing, has anticipated the most profound and seminal of Noam Chomsky's insights by almost half a century.

Chomsky's theorising about linguistic creativity is, however, conducted almost wholly in terms of syntax: in terms, that is, of the ability of a competent or native speaker to attach one or more phrase-structural descriptions (parsings) to a sentence he has never before encountered. For this reason, I think, philosophers have been slow to see the relevance of Chomsky's discussion of linguistic creativity to traditional philosophical problems about meaning; and as a result philosophical discussion of Chomsky has tended to confine itself to fishing in the – to my mind far less profitable – waters of the so-called Innateness Hypothesis.

Wittgenstein, however, poses the problem of creativity directly in terms of sense. To see the full force of the problem we must look at it from the point of view of the Fregian doctrine that to understand a proposition is to know its truth conditions. Wittgenstein accepts this doctrine and states it as follows:

> 4.024   To understand a proposition means to know what is the case if it is true.
>
> (One can understand it, therefore, without knowing whether it is true.)
>
> It is understood by anyone who understands its constituents.

The problem is, now, that we can understand, and hence know the truth conditions of, propositions which are new to us (which 'communicate a *new* sense', a new set of truth conditions), provided that they are constructed out of sub-propositional elements already known to us ('old expressions'). To use an example of Moritz Schlick's,[2] if we understand (can assign truth conditions to) the sentence

(a)   The ring is on the book

we can without further ado assign truth conditions to the sentence produced by rearranging the words of (a) to give

(b)   The book is on the ring

We do not, obviously, simply *invent* the truth conditions of (b) at the moment when we first encounter this hitherto unfamiliar sentence. Such a supposition is self-defeating, as we saw in chapter 1. A string of signs to which I can attach *any* sense and *any* truth conditions I choose is, by that very fact, not a proposition at all, but a mere sequence of marks or noises.

Something must therefore *determine* the sense, and hence the truth conditions, of (b); or to put it another way, must map the sense of (a) on to the sense of (b) in a definite and non-*ad hoc* way. Sense must, in short, as Wittgenstein says, 'be determinate'.

The doctrine of 'determinateness' of sense in the *Tractatus* is sometimes supposed to be simply the doctrine that a well formed proposition always, no matter what the circumstances of its use, possesses a definite truth value, either 'true' or 'false'. It is said that Wittgenstein abandoned this doctrine with the *Tractatus*, and that in abandoning it he abandoned the Tractarian doctrine of determinateness of sense *tout court*.

This is a very muddled view, both of the *Tractatus* and of Wittgenstein's later development, it seems to me. Wittgenstein, at the time of the *Tractatus*, certainly thought, I think, that the possibility of assigning a definite truth value to every proposition was entailed by determinateness of sense and *vice versa*. And the first doctrine is one that he certainly does drop in his later work. But the two doctrines are evidently distinct, and do not stand in the relationship of mutual entailment in which Wittgenstein perhaps thought they stood at the time of the *Tractatus*. As we shall see, Wittgenstein retained the doctrine of the determinateness of sense, as I have just characterised it, throughout his later work, although he finds new, and very un-Tractarian, ways of articulating it.

3. *The autonomy of the sentential sign*

But how can 'determinateness of sense' be guaranteed; and by what can it be guaranteed? Wittgenstein's answer to this question proceeds upon an icily austere level of generality and abstraction, and it is this, I think, which both defeats any attempt to give an experiential interpretation to the 'objects' of the *Tractatus* (to interpret them, for example, as sense data, sensory particulars, sounds, patches of colour, or whatnot) and contains the seeds of the difficulties which led to Wittgenstein's later dissatisfaction with, and repudiation of, the *Tractatus*.

The answer, I think, goes something like this. To begin with, grasping the considerations, whatever they may be, which guarantee the determinateness of sense of propositional signs, cannot possibly require assent to the truth of *further propositions*. For those propositions also must be understood if we are to know their truth conditions, let alone their truth or falsity, and hence, unless we are to appeal again to yet a third set of postulated propositions, their sense must be evident *simply from the identity of their elements and their mode of composition*. But, if we must, to avoid a vicious regress, assume that the sense of some propositions can be grasped in this way, then the sense of any can. This argument is clearly implicit in the following triad of propositions, taken together with 4.026–4.03 and 4.024:

2.021   Objects make up the substance of the world. That is why they cannot be composite.

2.0211   If the world had no substance, then whether a proposition had sense would depend on whether another proposition was true.

2.0212   In that case we could not sketch any picture of the world (true or false).

We must thus – so Wittgenstein's argument runs – confront the problem of guaranteeing determinateness of sense directly, as one which must be solved, not by appeal from one proposition to another, but by appeal to considerations inherent in the constitution of the propositional sign. We construct propositions which 'express a new sense' by, in effect, rearranging the parts of 'old' propositions (4.03). Now, clearly, the same cannot be true of the parts or elements of propositional signs, or, rather, cannot be true of them beyond a certain level in the analysis of propositions. The regress which we enter, if we try to suppose that it can be, is again a vicious one.

In short, at some level in the analysis of propositions we must come to what Wittgenstein calls 'simple signs', which are, precisely, signs the sense of which cannot be read off from the identity and mode of concatenation of still simpler signs which compose them. As Wittgenstein says (3.23), 'The requirement that simple signs be possible is the requirement that sense be determinate.'

But now, the requirement that 'simple signs be possible', taken together with the doctrine of the impossibility of any *propositional* explication of the meanings of simple signs, commits Wittgenstein to the entire Tractarian metaphysic of objects and states of affairs. What knowing the sense of a propositional sign does is to identify a state of affairs. The state of affairs is located by the propositional sign – the written or spoken sentence.

It must be possible to locate a possible state of affairs immediately on acquaintance with the propositional sign even when the sentence in question is an entirely new one. But the only possible way of connecting a fully analysed propositional sign with reality – with 'the world' – is by correlating the simple signs which occur in it with the members of some category of real 'objects'. The only sense we can attach to the concept 'knowledge of the meaning of a simple sign' is, therefore, 'knowledge of the identity of the object which it denotes'. But, now, if the question of what state of affairs a proposition picks out is decided by 'the meaning of' the simple signs which make up the proposition, it follows that it must be decided simply by the identity of the objects which the simple signs in question designate. Just from the knowledge of which objects the simple signs in a proposition designate, in other words, I must be able to read off the conclusion that p is the only proposition capable of being expressed by that particular string of simple signs. But in that case the 'objects' in question must be such as to determine 'in advance' (that is, before we actually set about *using* language to make any true, or false, assertions about the world) all possible states of affairs and, correlatively and in consequence, all the possibilities of sense, or 'propositional form'.

Wittgenstein summarises this part of his position in the following passage, which we have already quoted in part.

3.202   The simple signs employed in propositions are called names.

3.203   A name means an object. The object is its meaning. ('*A*' is the same sign as '*A*'.)

3.21   The configuration of objects in a situation corresponds to the configuration of simple signs in the propositional sign.

3.22   In a proposition a name is the representative of an object.

3.221   Objects can only be *named*. Signs are their representatives. I can only speak *about* them: I cannot *put them into words*. Propositions can only say *how* things are, not *what* they are.

3.23   The requirement that simple signs be possible is the requirement that sense be determinate.

The referents of 'simple signs' (objects), in other words, actually *enter into* states of affairs. Moreover, their nature, or essence, is determined solely by their possibilities of combination with one another in states of affairs. The nature of objects thus determines what states of affairs are possible. Objects, by their nature, determine a 'logical space'.

2.013   Each thing [object] is, as it were, in a space of possible states of affairs [*Sachverhalten*]. This space I can imagine empty, but I cannot imagine the thing without the space.

The existence of logical space, by determining what states of affairs are possible, determines what propositions are possible – that is, make sense. In short, we can attach a determinate sense to a proposition, because knowing the reference of the names which it contains, and knowing the possibilities of combination in states of affairs which identify the objects which they name, we know automatically what state of affairs the proposition 'pictures', or expresses.

4. Negation, sense and the picture theory

The conception of a proposition as a picture is essential to the theory of meaning in the *Tractatus*; and yet it is difficult to see precisely why the metaphor exercises such a powerful hold upon Wittgenstein's mind at this stage of his development. To see why it is such a crucial element in Wittgenstein's early thought we must look at the requirement of determinateness of sense from a new direction.

Determinateness of sense requires that, in grasping what a proposition asserts, we also automatically grasp what would be asserted by its denial. Wittgenstein was not original in making this connection. Frege, in his paper 'Negation',[3] sketched a closely related link between the concept of negation and the objectivity of sense. Frege held that a thought – what is asserted or denied – cannot be the same thing as a truth. It cannot, that is, be necessary to grasping the sense of an interrogative sentence that we know whether the answer is affirmative or negative. 'It must be already possible to grasp the sense of an interrogative sentence before answering the question; for otherwise no answer would be possible at all.'[4]

Moreover, if a thought were the same thing as a truth, objectivity of sense and the common pursuit of truth would be impossible, for a false thought would be a non-existent thought:

> The being of a thought may also be taken to lie in the possibility of different thinkers' grasping the thought as one and the same thought. In that case the fact that a thought had no being would consist in several thinkers' each associating with the sentence a sense of his own; this sense would in that case be a content of his particular consciousness, so that there would be no *common* sense that could be grasped by several people. Now is a false thought a thought that in this sense has no being? In that case investigators who had discussed among themselves whether bovine tuberculosis is communicable to men, and had finally agreed that such communicability did not exist, would be in the same position as people who had used in conversation the expression 'this rainbow', and now come to see that they had not been designating anything by these words, since what each of them had had was a phenomenon of which he himself was the owner ... they would not have been giving the question that they discussed a sense common to all of them.[5]

Wittgenstein makes precisely the same point in the *Tractatus*:

> 4.064 Every proposition must *already* have a sense: it cannot be given a sense by affirmation. Indeed its sense is just what is affirmed. And the same applies to negation, etc.

If sense is prior to affirmation and denial, then in knowing what it means to assert Fx we must automatically know what it means to assert $\sim Fx$. This is intuitively correct. If someone says to me, 'x is not red' I know automatically what possibilities in the world are compatible with the truth of this assertion. I know, that is, that x must be *some other colour*, blue, or pink, or brown and so on. Knowing that is essential to knowing the truth conditions of 'x is not red': knowing what the words mean involves knowing, *inter alia*, that it would

218   THE PHILOSOPHY OF LANGUAGE

establish the truth of the assertion that x is not red if x turned out to be blue, or orange, or green, and so on. But, suppose I were seriously troubled in my mind about whether the discovery that x was a dog, or a gas-stove, or schizophrenic, or reviewed badly in the latest issue of *Byzantine Studies*, and so on, might not establish the truth of 'x is not red', and suppose I could set no limit to this list of possibilities: that would mean that I was in doubt about the sense of 'x is not red', and thus about the sense of 'x is red' as well, or, to put it bluntly, that the expression 'x is red' had no determinate sense for me.

At *Tractatus* 4.463, Wittgenstein, in language only a little more oracular than my flat academic paraphrase, inserts precisely this move into the argument.

> 4.463 The truth conditions of a proposition determine the range that it leaves open to the facts.
>
> (A proposition, a picture, or a model is, in the negative sense, like a solid body that restricts the freedom of movement of others, and, in the positive sense, like a space bounded by solid substance in which there is room for a body.)

The totality of possible propositions, in other words, define each other's truth conditions by making it clear in advance of any affirmation or denial of a proposition what possibilities for the state of the world are closed (by assertion) or left open (by denial). That is the force of saying that there is such a thing as logical space, and that, 'The proposition determines a place in logical space' (3.4).

If we think in this way about determinacy of sense, we must take seriously Frege's dictum that a proposition (a thought, in Frege's terms) cannot be identified with a truth or an assertion: that propositions are prior to assertion, denial, and the assignment of truth values to assertions and denials. And so we need a way of graphically articulating the concept of a proposition that Frege's dictum seems to require. This is precisely the role played in Wittgenstein's thought by the metaphor of propositions as pictures. The proposition, conceived as a picture, simply *presents* a possible state of affairs. In itself it neither affirms nor denies anything, though we can make use of it to affirm or deny what it pictures, as a man might hold up a picture of a rainstorm and say, gesturing out of doors, '*This* is how things are', or '*This* is not how things are.'

If I am right, the theory of meaning in the *Tractatus* can be thought of as an attempt to state, in a very abstract way, the conditions which must be met if sense is to be determinate. The conditions include at least the following ones, connected in the ways I have suggested.

(1) Language must contain simple signs.
(2) There must be a 'logical space' determined by internal relationships between the referents of simple signs.
(3) Propositions must be conceivable as pictures.
(4) It must be the case that, in grasping what a proposition asserts, we also automatically grasp what is asserted by its denial.

Wittgenstein's rejection of the *Tractatus* certainly involved the rejection of (1)–(3). But it did not, I think, involve the rejection of (4). It is indeed, as we shall see, a process of reflection on the implications of (4) which leads him to develop his later account of meaning as 'use'.

5. *Frege and the* Tractatus

So far we have traced the general metaphysics of the *Tractatus*, the picture theory of meaning and the account Wittgenstein gives of determinateness of sense directly to Fregian sources, in Frege's doctrine of objectivity of sense and the account he gives of thoughts and their relationship to affirmation and denial. There is much else of Fregian provenance in the *Tractatus*. Wittgenstein accepts, for example, Frege's doctrine that to understand a proposition is to know what is the case if it is true, and continues to accept it, as we shall see, in his later work. He takes for granted, too, Frege's claim that names have reference only by virtue of their role in propositions. 'Only propositions have sense [*Sinn*]; only in the nexus of a proposition does a name have meaning [*Bedeutung*]' (3.3).

The distinction here between *Sinn* and *Bedeutung* is Frege's: these are the terms normally translated as 'sense' and 'reference'. The second half of 3.3 echoes the second of the 'fundamental principles' which Frege proclaims at the outset of the *Foundations of Arithmetic* (see above, chapter 5, section 2): 'Never to ask the reference [*Bedeutung*] of a word in isolation, but only to ask it in the context of a proposition.' But the first half makes it clear that Wittgenstein, unlike Frege, wants to claim that sense attaches only to propositions: names have reference, but no sense.

It may help us to see why if we recapitulate, briefly, the argument which we developed in sections 1 and 2.

Probably mistaken; Objectivity does not entail definiteness.

Unfamiliar sentences can 'communicate a new sense'. To that extent, therefore, sense is 'determinate': something which can be 'read off' from the sentential, or propositional, sign by any competent speaker. Something must, therefore, enable a speaker to 'read off' the sense of a new and unfamiliar propositional sign, constructed out of 'old' elements. Something must guarantee definiteness of sense.

What could make this possible? There seem to be only the following two possible answers:

(1) Basic signs are first given a meaning by referring them in some way to reality. Secondly, and independently of the meanings assigned to basic signs, a set of stipulative 'projection rules', or rules of logical syntax, determine in some systematic way how the meanings of new sentences are to be derived from the meanings of the basic signs which occur in them.

(2) The way in which basic signs are related to reality automatically determines their possibilities of combination in sentences, and the senses to be read off from well constructed sentential signs.

The first of these answers, I take it, is the one given by many philosophers who would give the label 'formal semantics' to the philosophical enterprise on which they are engaged. The second is the one Wittgenstein opts for in the *Tractatus*. I think that Wittgenstein was right: that only an answer which has the overall form of (2) can provide a satisfactory solution to the problem of how it is possible for a speaker of a language to construct and to understand new sentences. But the fact that Wittgenstein chose this answer at the time of the *Tractatus* means that that work belongs, in one fundamental respect at least, as little in the tradition of formal semantics as his later work belongs in the more recent tradition of communication-intention theories of meaning.

The theory of objects in the *Tractatus* is, I have argued, an attempt to give the most abstract and general account possible of what the world must be like if answer (2) is correct. As such it amounts simply to the claim that the world just *is* an array of facts the structure of which mirrors the structure of propositions, that these facts are combinations of objects characterisable only in terms of their possibilities of combination in states of affairs, and that such objects are the referents of the most basic names.

It is essential to this theory that the objects which names stand for should by their very nature determine the limits of possible states of affairs. This they can do only if they actually *enter into* states of affairs, and if it is not just *accidental*, but rather intrinsic to their very nature, what states of affairs they can and cannot enter into. It is important to see, I think, that the 'objects' of the *Tractatus* are theoretical entities, postulated simply in order to meet the series of theoretical requirements, originating in the problem of explaining 'determinateness of sense' within the framework of a referential theory of meaning, which we have just outlined. Seeing this we can see why it must be impossible, on Wittgenstein's account, to identify an object independently of the states of affairs which it enters, or, rather, can enter, into. If objects could be identified independently of states of affairs (if, contrary to the second sentence of the *Tractatus*, the world were the totality of things, not of facts) their relationship to one another in states of affairs would be external, or accidental, not internal and intrinsic to their nature. And thus knowledge of them would not automatically determine the limits of the array of possible states of affairs, nor, correlatively, those of the array of possible propositional senses.

To specify the reference (*Bedeutung*) of a name, we must, on Wittgenstein's account, locate the object (*Ding*) with which the name is correlated. We have seen why the nature of the grounds for postulating *Dinge* rules out the possibility that they could be identified independently of the states of affairs in which they stand conjoined. But that in turn means that the identification of states of affairs by means of propositions must be prior to the identification of the referents (*Bedeutungen*) of names, and hence that the reference of a name can be identified only relative to the role of the name in sentences. So names cannot have sense, since, if they did, the sense of a name would determine its reference. The reference of a name would thus be capable of being determined independently of the behaviour of the name in sentential contexts, and the possibility of accounting for determinateness of sense by the only means which appeared feasible to Wittgenstein at this stage of his intellectual development would simply collapse.

Wittgenstein has thus brought about a radical revision of Frege's doctrine of sense and reference. He has done it by combining two Fregian doctrines and developing each of them to a logical conclusion more radical than any envisaged by Frege. The first is the doctrine that the reference of names can be determined only in sentential contexts. The second is the doctrine of the objectivity of sense. What Wittgenstein has done is to make the conditions of the objectivity of sense a good deal clearer and more precise. The fact remains, however, that it is Frege's doctrine of the objectivity of sense which appears in the *Tractatus* as the concept of the determinateness of sense.

Wittgenstein's revision of Frege's account of sense and reference has certain immediate advantages. It makes it unnecessary to maintain the difficult distinction between concept and object, 'saturated' and 'unsaturated' expressions, at least on any fundamental ontological level. The structure of a proposition is conceived simply as a 'logical form' which mirrors the logical form of some possible fact. Objects are not ontologically categorised and their relationship to one another is spoken of merely as concatenation: 'In the state of affairs objects fit into one another like the links of a chain' (2.03).

Wittgenstein's theory of meaning preserves another Fregian doctrine, however: namely, the doctrine that meaning cannot be determined by appeal to empirical judgements and generalisations. For Frege it is not a sufficient answer to the question 'What is the meaning of "number"?' to present examples of numbers, or to gesture to such empirical facts of language use as that everyone 'knows what numbers are'. The only thing that will satisfy the demand for an explanation of the concept of numbers, for Frege, is the construction of a notation the symbolic manipulations of which are explicitly and rigorously defined in such a way as to make it clear that, and why, every well constructed proposition in that notation will have a determinate truth value. Frege would not, for this reason, I think, have accepted the Quinean appeal to empirical observations of stimulus meaning as capable of determining the sense and reference of expressions in a language.

Wittgenstein's attachment to this doctrine of Frege's stems directly from his conviction (itself, as I have suggested, an outgrowth of Frege's doctrine of the objectivity of sense) that at some level it must be possible to read off the sense of a proposition directly from the sentential sign. Clearly, when we do this, our judgement that the sign bears a certain sense cannot be an empirical one, for otherwise it would always be possible that the discovery of the *truth* of some *further* statement about experience would alter our opinion about what *this* sentence *says*; and for that matter, of course, about whether it says anything at all. But then, 'whether a proposition had sense would depend on whether another proposition was true' (2.0211).

This conviction of the necessity of a rigid link between sentential sign and propositions is evident in the treatment which Wittgenstein accords in the *Tractatus* to Russell's Theory of Types. The idea of a Theory of Types is that one specifies the possibilities of sentential co-occurrence of expressions in one language (the 'object language') by means of sentences in another language (the 'meta-language'), the point of the operation being to avoid various paradoxes of self-reference in formal languages.

Wittgenstein's objection is laconic in the extreme: 'It can be seen that Russell must be wrong, because he had to mention the meaning of signs when establishing the rules for them' (3.31). But the point of it should by now be obvious. Semantic ascents from one language to another, of the sort envisaged by the Theory of Types, merely launch us upon an indefinite regress of meta-languages. Sense must be read off either directly from the sentential sign or not at all.

A language, for Wittgenstein as for Frege, then, is a hermetically self-enclosed system, in the sense that all questions of the sense of propositions must be settled *from within*. That means that there must be a rigid division between the considerations which give meaning to propositions, and the empirical matters of fact which propositions state. The line between the linguistic and the empirical cannot be blurred as Quine, for example, wishes to blur it.

6. Saying and showing

This claim that simple signs lack sense has, of course, consequences of a highly paradoxical kind. The first concerns Wittgenstein's puzzling doctrine of 'elucidations' at *Tractatus* 3.263: 'The meanings [*Bedeutungen*] of primitive signs can be explained by elucidations. Elucidations are propositions that contain the primitive signs. So they can only be understood if the meanings of the signs are already known.'

Like the critique of ostensive definition in the *Investigations*, this passage seems to make it impossible that anyone could learn a language. Before we can know the meanings of names we must be able to understand sentences in which they occur; but before we can understand any sentences we must know the meanings (*Bedeutungen*) of the names which occur in them.

The paradox goes deeper than this, however. According to Wittgenstein, the considerations which assure the determinateness of sense have to do with the internal relations of objects. Is it possible to say anything about these relationships? Clearly not. If we could say anything about such matters, the sentences in which we said it would have to possess a determinate sense. And determinacy of sense for those sentences would have to be assured by some further set of considerations, and so on. The conclusion is obvious. If it is possible to read off the meaning of an unfamiliar sentence directly from the sentential sign, the considerations which make that possible must at the most basic level be ineffable. They cannot be stated, they merely *show themselves* mutely in the structure of propositions: in the logical grammar of our language, 'Whereof one cannot speak, thereof one must be silent.'

This has the immediate consequence that the *Tractatus* itself, since its subject matter is the relationship between language and the world, is itself nonsense. 'My propositions serve as elucidations in the following way: anyone who understands me eventually recognises them as nonsensical, when he has used them – as steps – to climb up beyond them' (6.54).

Finally, Wittgenstein is committed to a realism about objects of reference which is considerably more radical than Frege's. For Frege, as we saw in chapter 5, numbers are neither imaginary objects nor 'real' in the sense that chairs and tables are real. Numbers are in one sense mental constructions, but, nevertheless, questions about number are factual questions, and the facts in question are facts about the world and not facts about human psychology. Frege's theory of number allows us to see how such entities as numbers can come to be objects of reference for us.

Wittgenstein's 'objects', on the other hand, cannot have their ontological status explained in this way, since nothing can be said about them or about their relationships to one another. Reference to them simply has to be accepted as ultimate in our conceptual scheme. They are the fundamental reals, and they are real in the most absolute and Platonic sense.

7. *The breakdown of the* Tractatus

The later Wittgenstein rejected the *Tractatus*, though it is no longer clear, as was once generally supposed, that he rejected it root and branch. A good many of its features survive, in a more or less transmuted form, in the later work. We must now examine the reasons for the breakdown of the *Tractatus*, and the transformation of certain of its elements in Wittgenstein's later writings.

For Wittgenstein the break seems to have come[6] over an apparently trivial problem: that of explaining how one statement about colour for example '*x* is blue', can be the logical contrary of another, for example '*x* is red'. If the theory of meaning in the *Tractatus* is to work at all, it must be possible to maintain a distinction between simple (atomic) and compound propositions. Atomic propositions have their senses determined by the nature and mode of combination of the objects to which the names which compose them refer. But what about logically compound propositions, such as 'not *p*' ('it is not the case that *p*'), 'either *p* or *q*', 'All Fs are Gs', and so on? Such expressions, as we have seen, cannot count as *propositions* in the same sense as atomic propositions. There cannot, that is, be *facts* corresponding to them: if there could, any fact would have clustering about it, as it were, an infinity of other 'facts' generated by the infinite possibilities of trivial logical reformulation of the proposition expressing it, each quite distinct from the original fact. Wittgenstein's theory of truth functions and of formal operations, directed at solving this problem, need not concern us. We need consider only one consequence of the problem: namely, that no two atomic propositions can possibly be logically contrary to one another (4.211). If two propositions are contraries, if the truth of each entails the falsity of the other, this must mean that the two propositions are not atomic propositions.

The trouble, now, is that the propositions '*x* is blue' and '*x* is red' do seem to be atomic propositions if any are, do seem to be distinct propositions, and do seem to be contraries. In the *Tractatus* Wittgenstein chose the option of treating them as non-atomic propositions.

> 6.3751   ... (It is clear that the logical product of two elementary propositions can neither be a tautology nor a contradiction. The statement that a point in the visual field has two different colours at the same time is a contradiction.)

But in the lecture 'On Logical Form' (1929), he abandons this option. There he sees the problem as going beyond colour. Many concepts besides colour concepts involve the notion of *degree of a property*. And all such concepts yield contrary pairs of propositions, which, short of some radical programme of reductive analysis, must be treated as atomic propositions. Wittgenstein made various attempts to reformulate the *Tractatus*, but soon desisted. The problems posed by colour concepts and the like are indeed intractable. They show that, whatever the relationship between language and the world, it is more complex than can be grasped in terms of the Tractarian model.

14

Meaning and Use

1. The problem of colour

It is true, though not very enlightening, to say that the later Wittgenstein held that we should seek for the meaning of a word not by looking for some *object* corresponding to it, but by examining its *use* in discourse. That may appear to associate Wittgenstein with Strawson's 'theorists of communication intention', but the assimilation is a deeply misleading one, for two reasons: first, because it suggests that Wittgenstein was proposing an *analysis* of the concept of meaning in terms of some concept of 'use', analogous to Grice's proposed analysis of the concept of meaning in terms of the concept of intention, or Searle's in terms of the concept of a speech act; and, secondly, because it suggests that Wittgenstein's relationship to Frege in his later work was, like Grice's or Searle's, one of root-and-branch rejection.

Since the publication of *Philosophical Remarks*[1] the posthumously published book which Wittgenstein wrote between his return to Cambridge in early 1929 and the late spring of 1930, it is, I believe, possible to see how the set of later doctrines generally subsumed under the slogan 'Meaning is use' developed out of Wittgenstein's realisation that the existence of pairs of contradictory propositions which cannot be treated truth-functionally constitutes a fundamental and devastating objection to his entire position in the *Tractatus*.

In section VIII of the *Philosophical Remarks* he returns to the problem of colour predicates. The heart of the problem is this. In logic contradiction, tautology and various forms of logical construction of which conjunction and disjunction are the simplest are treated as truth-functional relationships between propositions. A contradiction, for example, is the conjunction of a proposition and its negation: p & $\sim p$. The essence of contradiction is that there is no way of assigning a truth value to p which can result in the assignment of any value but 'false' to the conjunction. It follows that, if a pair of contradictory propositions do not appear to exhibit the form p & $\sim p$, the propositions in question are simply not fully analysed: further analysis will reveal that the conjunction of the propositions in question is truth-functionally equivalent to some longer conjunction, one of the conjuncts of which is the negation of another. The same goes for contrariety and other truth-functional relationships.

That, however, as we saw at the end of chapter 13, does not seem to be true of the conjunction 'f is red and f is green'. If $f(r)$ and $f(g)$ contradict one another, it is because r and g completely occupy the f and cannot both be in it. But that doesn't show itself in our signs (*Philosophical Remarks*, 78).

Similarly, the fact that 'the colours have an elementary affinity with one another . . . makes it look as if a construction might be possible within the elementary proposition' (76).

> A mixed colour, or better, a colour intermediate between blue and red is such in virtue of an internal relation to the structures of blue and red. But this internal relation is *elementary*. That is, it doesn't consist in the proposition 'a is blue-red' representing a logical product of 'a is blue' and 'a is red'. . . .   (80)

The sentence, 'But that doesn't show itself in our signs' (78) strikes at the heart of Wittgenstein's predicament. Frege's work began in the effort to make mathematical reasoning completely explicit and perspicuous. As we have seen, it is an essential methodological assumption of this enterprise that statements asserting logical truths should be sharply contrasted with statements recording features of reality. Logic must belong not to reality but to the way in which we order the manipulation of signs in a calculus. The same assumption is essential to the *Tractatus*. If sense is to be determinate, then, in order to know the sense of a proposition, it cannot be necessary to know the truth of any further proposition, necessary or contingent: the sense must be determined by the signs themselves, once we have made some arbitrary set of provisions determining the use of each sign. This is the force of Wittgenstein's motto 'Logic must take care of itself.' The notebooks of 1914–16[2] begin with this remark, characterised a little way down the page as 'an extremely profound and important insight'. A page later, discussing the question of whether the subject–predicate form 'exists' ('Russell would say: "Yes! that's self-evident". *Well!*'), Wittgenstein says 'If the existence of the subject–predicate *sentence* does not show everything needful, then it could surely only be shown by the existence of some particular fact of that form. And acquaintance with such a fact cannot be essential for logic.[3]

Now, one might think that the effect of Wittgenstein's discovery of contrary pairs of elementary propositions *must* be to demolish this Fregian and Tractarian thesis of an absolute separation between questions of logic and questions about what exists or what is the case in reality, or in 'the world'. And, certainly, if we are to see the transition from the *Tractatus* to the *Investigations* as consisting in a reaction against a 'Fregian' truth-theoretic account of meaning in favour of an account in terms of communication intention, one would expect such a reaction to begin at this point if anywhere.

But Wittgenstein's argument in the *Philosophical Remarks* does not take this direction. Far from breaking with the Fregian separation of questions about logic and questions about reality, he reaffirms it. He is not prepared, for example, to grant that the statement that $f(r)$ and $f(g)$ contradict each other could be a statement about experience, or about the world.

> Immediate experience cannot contain any contradiction. If it is beyond all speaking and contradicting, then the demand for an explanation cannot arise either: the feeling that there must be an explanation of what is happening, since otherwise something would be amiss.   (74)

The problem which is raised by the relationship between 'f is red' and 'f is green', in other words, is not a problem about *coloured surfaces*, considered as objects of inspection. As objects of inspection we can inspect them: they are what they appear on inspection, no more and no less; and so long as we are content to *say* nothing about them, but just look, there is nothing *logically* problematic about them, and certainly nothing contradictory.

The problem is, rather, about *our propositions*: about what we can and cannot say in a particular language. What 'demands explanation', what 'gives us the feeling that there must be an explanation . . . since otherwise something would be amiss', is the relationship between two *propositions*, 'f is red' and 'f is green'. And what creates the feeling, and the demand for explanation, Wittgenstein argues, is the mistaken assumption that propositions can be used and understood as *separate entities*, in isolation from one another.

Fully analysed propositions in the *Tractatus* do function as significant units in isolation from one another. They are logically discrete, in the sense that the truth or falsity of one such proposition implies nothing about the truth or falsity of any other. If '*f* is red' and '*f* is green' were logically discrete in this sense, Wittgenstein argues, 'that would imply that I can write down two particular propositions, but not their logical product' (79).

The absurdity of this conclusion is evident enough. If each of the two propositions is, in itself, perfectly well formed and intelligible, why on earth should it not be possible to write down the logical product of the two? The only possible answer is that, contrary to appearances, intelligibility and well-formedness cannot be ascribed to single propositions taken in isolation, are not properties which belong to them in their own right, as it were, without reference to the ways in which they are related to other propositions. The ultimate units of meaning are not single propositions but systems of propositions.

2. Negation and possibility

This idea, that it is in the system of propositions and not in the single proposition that the foundations of language are to be found, makes a fundamental difference to Wittgenstein's treatment of truth and meaning in the *Philosophical Remarks*. Wittgenstein still cleaves, first of all, to Frege's equation of knowledge of meaning with knowledge of truth conditions. 'To understand the sense of a proposition means to know how the issue of its truth or falsity is to be decided' (43).

Secondly, Wittgenstein retains the idea that to understand the sense and hence the truth conditions of a proposition is to know automatically what is asserted by (the truth conditions of) its denial.

'I haven't got stomach-ache' may be compared to the proposition 'These apples cost nothing'. The point is that they don't cost any money, not that they don't cost any snow or any trouble. The zero point is the zero point of *one* scale. And since I can't be giving any point on the yardstick without being given the yardstick, I can't be given its zero point either.   (82)

Because, if I know the sense of an assertion, say 'x is red', I know what would establish the truth of 'x is not red' (x's being blue or green, for example) and what would not (x's being old or a horse, for example); I can give a negative description of something by saying what it is not. But, 'I don't describe a state of affairs by mentioning something that has nothing to do with it and stating that it has nothing to do with it. That wouldn't be a negative description' (82).

For negative descriptions to be possible, and distinct from the mere assertion of irrelevancies, each proposition has to determine one point in a space of alternative possibilities. Something like the Tractarian idea of 'logical space' must therefore survive the *Tractatus*.

> You can only search in a *space*. For only in space do you stand in relation to where you are not.

> To understand the sense of a proposition means to know how the issue of its truth or falsity is to be decided.

> The essence of what we call the will is immediately connected with the continuity of the given.

> You must find the way from where you are to where the issue is decided.

> You cannot search wrongly; you *cannot* look for a visual impression with your sense of touch.   (43)

Suppose, for example (Wittgenstein discusses this kind of supposition elsewhere), that it was a rational response to the question 'Is that red?' to investigate the thing in question by means of touch. If such an investigation were a rational response to the question, what response would *not* be rational? But if *any* response is rational, what determinate sense – what *sense*, that is – can we suppose the question to have? On the supposition of the rational possibility of such a response, the supposition that language exists at all is exhausted of content. The remark about the will, which may seem to sit rather oddly in the above sequence of propositions, is, I believe, strictly connected with this thought. To will is to project a new possibility upon the world; to envisage a way in which *things might be*, as opposed to *the way things are*. I can do this only if the way things are somehow intrinsically maps out in advance the basic possibilities of change: without such a preliminary mapping of possibilities I cannot say that such and such a change is possible, which means that I cannot say that it is not *im*possible. In such a case there would be no difference between willing that that door be painted red, for instance, and willing that hope be painted red. The first willing would be as idle as the second 'willing', in the sense that we should have as little idea of how it is possible to set about realising it. Propositional thought, Wittgenstein says, can be seen from this point of view as showing an essential feature of willing. To entertain a new proposition is to entertain a new picture of how things might be in the world. And, if we do not know whether, or how, what we envisage is possible (if our case is like the case of the man who says, for instance, 'Perhaps E-flat played on a clarinet might be red'), then *a fortiori* we do not know 'how the issue of its truth or falsity is to be decided', and what we say has no sense.

3. Propositions and yardsticks

'Logical space' in the *Tractatus* is defined in terms of the internal relationships of the objects which compose states of affairs (*Sachverhalten*), each of which corresponds to a single proposition. In the *Philosophical Remarks* it is conceived in terms of the relationship of systems of propositions to the ordinary material of sensory experience.

In the *Tractatus* Wittgenstein had written,

> 2.1512   It [i.e. a proposition conceived as a kind of picture] is laid against reality like a measure.

> 2.15121   Only the end-points of the graduating lines actually *touch* the object that is to be measured.

The names in a fully analysed proposition, that is, designate ('touch') the objects in a state of affairs, and the logical form of the proposition (the graduating marks of the ruler) mirrors the logical form of the state of affairs. Now, in the *Philosophical Remarks*, it is the system of propositions which is compared to a ruler, or yardstick.

> ... propositions turn out to be even more like yardsticks than I previously believed. – The fact that *one* measurement is right automatically excludes all others. I say automatically: just as all

the graduation marks are on *one* rod, the propositions correspond-ing to the graduation marks similarly belong together, and we can't measure with one of them without simultaneously measuring with all the others. – It isn't a proposition which I put against reality as a yardstick, it's a *system* of propositions.   (82)

The propositions '*x* is red', '*x* is blue', '*x* is green', and so on, do not correspond to independent states of affairs: they are intrinsically connected to one another as possible alternatives. This makes it possible for me to know quite definitely what possibilities would establish the truth of '*x* is not red', and so, equally, to know the truth conditions of '*x* is red'.

Syntax prohibits a construction such as '*A* is green and *A* is red' (one's first feeling is that it's almost as if this proposition had been done an injustice; as though it had been cheated of its rights as a proposition), but for '*A* is green', the proposition '*A* is red' is not, so to speak, another proposition – and that strictly is what the syntax fixes – but another form of the same proposition.

In this way syntax draws together the propositions that make *one* determination.   (86)

4. The transition to 'use'

What, in the new theory of the *Philosophical Remarks*, constitute 'logical space' and assure the determinateness of sense are the intrinsic oppositions between different propositions within the same system of propositions, taken together with the natural features of experience which make it possible for us to set up such systems of propositions. Frege's conception of the objectivity of sense, and of the essential connection between meaning and truth, still dominates Wittgenstein's thought. 'We could say: a proposition is that to which the truth functions may be applied. – The truth functions are essential to *language*.'   (85)

Along with these Tractarian elements, Wittgenstein's new position also retains the distinction between saying and showing, although in an altered form. The nature of the relationship between the proposi-tions which form a system of propositions – a 'yardstick' in the new sense – and the elements of experience with which the propositional 'graduation marks' of the system are correlated, clearly cannot be stated by any further propositions. To say, for example, that '*a* is blue-red' is not the logical product of '*a* is blue' and '*a* is red', or that '*a* is red' and '*a* is blue' yield no logical product, is precisely to say that at this point we have reached rock-bottom in the explication of meaning. All we can do, if we want to meet the demands of someone who *still* wants to know why such things are true is, as it were, to gesture dumbly towards the phenomenal nature of colour. If he can see colours, and if he grasps that 'red' and 'blue' are colour names, he will understand why '*a* is red' and '*a* is blue' yield no logical product: otherwise not. But how do we know when someone grasps that 'red' and 'blue' are colour names? How, in general, do we know that other speakers have grasped the relationship between systems of propositions and the aspects of reality which sustain and are mediated by such linguistic constructions? The only guarantee there could possibly be that others understand words as I understand them, Wittgenstein argues, is agreement in *use*: in what another speaker does with words in specific contexts of discourse.

> It cannot be proved that it is nonsense to say of a colour that it is a semitone higher than another. I can only say 'If anyone uses words with the meanings that I do, then he can connect no sense with this combination. If it makes sense to him, he must understand something different by these words from what I do.'   (4)

'In a certain sense the use of language is something that cannot be taught.' 'You cannot use language to get outside language.' These remarks can be seen as dying echoes of the *Tractatus*. The second recalls Wittgenstein's puzzling account of 'elucidations'; the first the related argument that understanding the sense of a propositional sign cannot require assent to any further propositions, with its consequence that there is a fundamental distinction to be drawn between what can be said and what can only 'show itself' in our use of language.

But they can with equal justice be seen as foreshadowing the *Philosophical Investigations*. The first becomes the doctrine that, at the most fundamental level, agreement about meaning is agreement about *what to do* in certain circumstances. Suppose, says Wittgenstein, at *Investigations*, I. 86, there were different ways of reading a table; on one occasion, perhaps, like this:

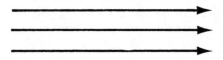

on another occasion, perhaps like this:

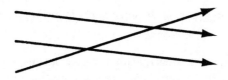

Such schemata, says Wittgenstein, are supplied with tables as rules for their use. But, now, 'Can we not now imagine further rules to explain *this* one? And, on the other hand, was that first table incomplete without the schema of arrows? And are other tables incomplete without their schemata?' In short, 'explanations must end somewhere'. And they cannot 'end in propositions'. Frege, as we have seen, took the primary and fundamental case of the understanding of meaning to be the case in which a speaker understands the meaning of a sentence: grasps a proposition, or a 'thought'. Wittgenstein, at the time of the *Tractatus*, accepted this view, but saw grave difficulties in it which were not apparent to Frege. The metaphysic of objects in the *Tractatus* was, as we have seen, introduced precisely to explain how it is possible for a speaker to read off a propositional content – a thought, in Frege's terminology – from a string of single signs, provided only that he knows the denotata of the simple signs in question.

Many philosophers in the analytic tradition have accepted Frege's position on this point, and, having accepted also Frege's general claim that to know the meaning of a proposition is to know its truth conditions, have concluded that knowing the meaning of a proposition is knowing *under* what conditions it is true; or, to put it another way, knowing, in fully and precisely observable conditions, *that* it is true. Quine's linguist, for example, although he must make do with a behaviourally defined notion of native assent and dissent in lieu of the concepts of truth and falsity, is essentially in this position with respect to the native language. He understands a native sentence (can attach a stimulus meaning to it) when he knows that, in certain conditions, it commands assent, while in others it commands dissent.

Wittgenstein's thought, after 1930, is in fundamental opposition to the idea that the understanding of meaning in natural languages can rest ultimately upon the knowledge that certain propositions *are* (say, in certain conditions of stimulation) *true*. The alternative view which he is putting forward is that the meaning of a proposition rests ultimately upon the use we make of it – what we *go on to do* with it; and that its truth conditions are determined by its 'use' in this sense. This, it seems to me, is part of the force of the following passage from *On Certainty*:

> Giving grounds, however, justifying the evidence, comes to an end; – but the end is not certain propositions' striking us immediately as true, i.e. it is not a kind of *seeing* on our part; it is our *acting*, which lies at the bottom of the language-game.[4]

This, then, is the way in which the idea that 'the meaning of an expression is its use' enters Wittgenstein's thought. It should now be clear why it is a mistake to regard Wittgenstein as the author of a theory to the effect that the concept of meaning can be analysed in terms of some concept of 'use'. He is not saying, like Searle, that the meaning of an expression is a set of sufficient and necessary conditions for using it correctly. Nor is he saying, like Grice, that assertions about the meanings of utterances can be replaced by assertions about the intentions of utterers. He is not trying to define the concept of meaning at all: rather, he is explaining it by saying something about the location and nature of the point at which explanations of meaning necessarily terminate.

5. Language games and 'the continuity of the given'

At the same time, Wittgenstein does seem, in the *Philosophical Investigations*, to be putting forward a theory of *some* sort about the workings of language. The central concept of this theory, if theory it is, is that of a *language game*. And Wittgenstein certainly does often speak as though the concept of 'use', and thus presumably that of meaning, is to be explicated in terms of the concept of a language game.

The concept of a language game remains, however, extremely

obscure. Strawson, in his review of the *Philosophical Investigations*,[5] raises the crucial question. At I.23 Wittgenstein speaks of the multifariousness of different *uses* of sentences, and gives a list which includes reading from a story, play-acting and translating from one language to another. Strawson observes that the sentence 'It was raining' may occur in the course of any of these activities, and points out that it would be absurd to speak of different *sentences* in such a case: the *meaning* of the sentence here seems precisely to be something distinct from the *linguistic activity* in which, at one or another time, it may occur. And what are the limits of a *use* of language, or of a *language game*? Does sending an old man to sleep by reading to him from a translation of a play count as a language game?

I think it may be possible to arrive at an understanding of the concept by reconstructing the transition in Wittgenstein's thought from the discussion of the colour problem in the *Philosophical Remarks* to the fully fledged notion of a language game in the *Philosophical Investigations*. What I am about to offer *is* a reconstruction, however. It can be tied down fairly firmly to Wittgenstein's text in a number of places, and I think that it throws a generalised light on a great deal that Wittgenstein says in the *Investigations*. But I cannot claim that the argument which I am about to offer can be found explicitly and sequentially stated in Wittgenstein's writings. Having entered these caveats, I think the transition may go something like this.

Wittgenstein at the time of the *Tractatus*, as we have seen, argued with Frege that to know the sense of a proposition is to know not only what is the case in the world if it is true, but also what possibilities in the world are left open by its denial. This principle also dominates the discussion of colour in the *Philosophical Remarks*. Negative descriptions are possible, and 'I don't describe a state of affairs by mentioning something that has nothing to do with it and stating that it has nothing to do with it' (82).

How can language meet the condition that a speaker who uses proposition *Fx* must know not only what is the case in the world if it is true, but also what possibilities are left open by its denial? What linguistic mechanism could account for such a capacity in a competent speaker?

One obvious possibility would be simply to decree – to establish a convention to the effect – that certain specific propositions, and those propositions only, may be true of a thing if *Fx* is false of that thing. Thus, we might stipulate that, if '*x* is red' is false, one or other of '*x* is green', 'x is blue', and so on, including 'x is colourless', must be true of x.

But this would be idle. Remember that unless we know what possibilities the denial of Fx leaves open we do not know the *sense* of Fx. Remember, too, that for Wittgenstein, as for Frege, 'to understand the sense of a proposition means to know how the issue of its truth or falsity is to be decided' (*Philosophical Remarks* 43); that a proposition has sense only if 'all the conditions necessary for comparing [it] . . . with reality' are satisfied. ('What belongs to grammar are all the conditions (the method) necessary for comparing the proposition with reality . . . all the conditions necessary for the understanding of the sense.') – *Philosophical Grammar* [*Philosophische Grammatik*], IV.45; (English trans. 1974).

The conventional stipulation we canvassed a paragraph ago would have to function, then, as an essential part of the conventions determining the *sense* of Fx. What we are saying, in effect, is, 'A speaker cannot know how to compare the proposition Fx with reality – how to decide its truth or falsehood – until he knows what possibilities its denial leaves open. So why don't we just tell him that the possibilities its denial leaves open are that Gx is true or that Hx is true, or that Ix is true . . . and so on.'

This move, clearly, will only work if the speaker in question already knows how Gx, Hx, Ix, and the rest are to be 'compared with reality'. He must thus presumably know what possibilities in reality the denial of each of *them* leaves open. If we now suppose that *this* is determined conventionally by stipulating that the denial of Gx leaves open the possibilities Fx, Hx, Ix, and so on, the circularity of the whole proceeding will, I think, be manifest. We are simply shuffling verbal counters. We are not making the slightest real progress towards specifying how any of these propositions are to be 'compared with reality'.

Putting this another way, if we *could* give sense to a proposition Fx by specifying that its denial left open the possibilities Gx, Hx, Ix, we could construct any picture of the world we liked. We could stipulate, for example, that '$\sim x$ is a noise' left open the possibility 'x is a colour'. But, as Wittgenstein says, 'Can anyone believe it makes sense to say "That's not a noise, it's a colour"?' (*Philosophical Remarks*, 8). What is at stake, here, of course, is not just the psychological possibility of believing or not believing such a thing. What is at stake, as we saw in the section 3 of this chapter, is the possibility of language as an instrument of communication. I cannot investigate whether or not something is a noise by investigating whether or not it is a colour. I do not know what the 'it' in question could conceivably be in such a case. No sense is given to the proposition 'x is a noise' by the 'explanation' that if x is a colour it is not a noise, but we can in part explain the meaning of 'harpsichord', for example, by explaining that a harpsichord is not really a small piano.

The sense of a proposition must in some way, therefore, be connected with the way things actually are, or can be, in the world. But at the same time I cannot explain the sense of a single proposition just by pointing to 'how things are in the world'.

> If I explain the meaning of a word 'A' to someone by pointing to something and saying 'This is A', then this expression may be meant in two different ways. Either it is itself a proposition already, in which case it can only be understood once the meaning of 'A' is known, i.e., I must now leave it to chance whether he takes it as I meant it or not. Or the sentence is a definition. Suppose I have said to someone 'A is ill', but he doesn't know who I mean by 'A', and I now point at a man, saying 'This is A'. Here the expression is a definition, but this can only be understood if he has already gathered what kind of object it is through his understanding of the grammar of the proposition 'A is ill'. But this means that any kind of explanation of a language presupposes a language already. And in a certain sense the use of language cannot be taught, i.e. I cannot use language to teach it in the way in which language could be used to teach someone to play the piano. – And that of course is just another way of saying: I cannot use language to get outside language. (*Philosophical Remarks*, 6)

Here Wittgenstein introduces two new ideas. The 'grammar' of a sentence is what shows what kind of 'object' is designated by the names which fit into the sentence in certain grammatical positions. 'Grammar is a "theory of logical types"' (ibid., 7). Grammar – sense – determines what possibilities are left open by the denial of a proposition, and it also, and thereby, determines an ontology: it determines the logical type of the objects designated by the names in the proposition. We have thus passed from the 'absolute' ontology of the *Tractatus*, given extra-linguistically as a condition of the possibility of language, through the possibility of a 'logical space', to an ontology determined 'from within' language as a by-product of determining the sense of propositions. But how is sense determined? Wittgenstein occasionally speaks in the *Remarks* of 'my view' of language. But what is his view? My suggestion is as follows. What Wittgenstein has seen is that, if the truth conditions of propositions are intrinsically connected, then of course we cannot give sense to propositions singly: we must give them sense collectively *as* intrinsically connected sets of propositions.

This idea is presented clearly enough, as we have already seen in Wittgenstein's new conception, in the *Philosophical Remarks*, of the system of propositions, rather than the single proposition, as the 'yardstick' we lay against reality.

What the institution of a system of measurement involving measuring rods does, in other words, is precisely to establish intrinsic connections between the truth conditions of different statements about the length of objects arrived at by the use of such rods. If 'one inch' denotes the modulus of a measuring system, if there are measuring rods marked according to this modulus, and if we introduce statements of the form 'x is ϕ inches long' by appeal to measuring procedures carried out by such rods, then clearly 'x is four inches long' and 'x is five inches long' will possess intrinsically related truth conditions, in the sense that 'x is five inches long' will be one of the possibilities left open by the denial of 'x is four inches long', and not a totally unrelated statement. In the same way, the system allows us to speak of a category of objects – *lengths* – and to introduce designating expressions such as 'five inches', 'four inches', and so on, which designate *lengths*.

Wittgenstein is often taken to be defending a form of operationalism. That is, he is taken to be defending something like the physicist P. W. Bridgman's claim (1926) that the meaning of a term is given by some specific operation or procedure, the outcome of which determines the application of the term.[6] The parallel is particularly attractive since the concept of length is one of Bridgman's standard illustrations of his thesis.

Bridgman's operationalism, however, is a theory about the meanings of single terms, or single propositions. Wittgenstein, on the contrary, introduces the notion of a procedure, or operation, if I have interpreted him correctly, not to explain how we define truth conditions for single propositions, but to explain how the truth conditions of different propositions come to be intrinsically connected: how it is that in knowing the truth conditions of Fx a competent speaker necessarily knows what possibilities are left open by the denial of *Fx*.

Setting up a sense-determining procedure of this kind – defining a way of *using* words – has two aspects. On the one hand there is a set of conventions – the conventions which determine the modulus of a measuring system, for example, the gradations on measuring rods, and so on. On the other hand there are the natural features of reality which allow us to set up the conventions in question.

The union of the conventions and the underlying features of reality which allow us to set them up is now, I think, essentially what Wittgenstein means by a *language game*, or a form of life. In answer to Strawson's query about the criteria of individuation of a language game, we can reply on Wittgenstein's behalf – and I am not unaware of the presumptuousness of this proceeding – that there are at least two criteria of identity for a language game. The first identifies the limits of a language game with the limits of a collection of propositions the truth conditions of which are intrinsically connected with one another. The second identifies the limits of the language game by appeal to the power of a certain operation (measuring, for example, or arranging colours in series or checking to see whether two samples are samples of the same substance) to organise language into sets of propositions the members of which are related to one another by possessing intrinsically related truth conditions. Presently we shall add a third criterion.

The conception of a language game, if the interpretation is correct, allows Wittgenstein to answer two of the most puzzling questions about language.

(1) How can it be possible to learn a language?
(2) How can one speaker be sure that other speakers attach the same meaning as he does to expressions in their common language?

The answers to both questions have to do with the relationship between the conventions which set up a language and the underlying features of reality which make it possible to set up the language game in question.

We cannot, obviously, describe in the language thus set up the natural features of the world which make it possible to set up the conventions of a language. Wittgenstein gives the reason in paragraph 4 of the *Philosophical Remarks*:

Saying 'x is red and x is blue' is [n]physically impossible
is not ruled out by any convention of grammar, e.g.
'x is red & x is blue' is "nonsense" ⟨ Sinnlos / Unsinnig ⟩

This is just a metaphysical muddle

If I could describe the point of grammatical conventions by saying that they are made necessary by certain properties of the colours (say) then that would make the conventions superfluous, since in that case I would be able to say precisely that which the conventions exclude my saying. Conversely, if the conventions were necessary, i.e. if certain combinations of words had to be excluded as nonsensical, then for that very reason I cannot cite a property of colours that makes the conventions necessary, since it would then be conceivable that the colours should not have this property, and I could only express this by violating the conventions.

The natural features in question simply 'show themselves' in the fact that in a given context certain sorts of assertion succeed, in the sense that in making them we actually say something, while others, which may look equally grammatical and sensible, fail, in the sense that in making them we succeed in saying nothing.

It is this train of thought which is at stake, in the *Philosophical Remarks*, in the connection that Wittgenstein draws between willing and understanding the sense of a proposition, and in the remark, in paragraph 43, that 'The essence of what we call the will is immediately connected with the continuity of the given.'

At intervals throughout the *Philosophical Remarks* Wittgenstein returns to the exploration of the 'continuity of the given'. For the sake of simplicity I shall confine the present discussion to his treatment of colour.[7] Thus, for example, he says (45):

A black colour can become lighter but not louder. That means that it is in light/dark space but not loud/soft space. – But surely the object just stops being black when it becomes lighter. But in that case it was black and just as I can see movement (in the ordinary sense), I can see a colour movement.

Later he says (220),

If I say in the ordinary sense that red and yellow make orange, I am not talking here about a *quantity* of the components. And so, given an orange, I can't say that yet *more* red would have made it a redder orange (I'm not of course speaking about pigments), even though there is of course a sense in speaking of a redder orange. But there is, e.g., no sense in saying this orange and this violet contain the same amount of red. And how much red would *red* contain?[8]

There is, that is, no process of 'adding more red' which would make *this* particular orange redder, since if a redder orange were displayed at the same point in space, *this* orange would not be displayed there. The language of quantitative addition and subtraction can be partly transferred to the description of colour, but not entirely. The transfer has its limits, and the limits are limits of sense. What sets them is the pure phenomenology of colour. 'Grammar' and 'phenomenology', in Wittgenstein's mind, are so closely connected as to be almost aspects of one another. 'Isn't the theory of harmony at least in part phenomenology and therefore grammar? The theory of harmony isn't a matter of taste' (4).

In the *Remarks on Colour*, which consists of manuscripts written in 1950–1, shortly before Wittgenstein's death, the 1930–1 treatment of colour in the *Philosophical Remarks* is carried considerably further, and the notion of a language game, developed in the *Philosophical Investigations*, is introduced in a way which, I think, along the lines I have already sketched in at the opening of this section, throws considerable light upon the vexed question of what Wittgenstein means by it. The book opens with the following paragraph:

A language-game: Report whether a certain body is lighter or darker than another. – But now there's a related one: State the relationship between the lightness of certain shades of colour (Compare with this: Determining the relationship between the lengths of two sticks – and the relationship between two numbers.) – The form of the propositions in both language-games is the same: '*X* is lighter than *Y*.' But in the first it is an external relation and the proposition is temporal, in the second it is an internal relation and the proposition is timeless.

The limits of language games are pinned down, in other words, by the *differences* between the two language games. A report on the relative lightness of two shades of colour has different consequences from a report on the relative lightness of two objects. In the second case, for example, the person who receives the report (perhaps he is trying to co-ordinate the lighting for a stage production) could respond to it by saying 'Right! Now make the first one darker.' But in the first language game this move would have no sense, because it would have no *place*. What would the expression 'the first one' refer to? The first *shade of colour*? But *that* could not be darker without being a different shade of colour, and thus not the one referred to. One or another move in discourse thus fits, or fails to fit, with other moves. This gives us the third criterion of identity for a language game, promised a few paragraphs ago. A language game is thus a system of moves which fit one another, and which exclude other moves.

The pattern of exclusions and compatibilities of moves in discourse which define the limits of language games also makes possible the learning of language. At paragraph III. 110 of the *Remarks on Colour*, Wittgenstein describes the process of colour-name learning which we have discussed in chapter 7.

learning

> If you are not clear about the role of logic in colour concepts, begin with the simple case of, e.g. a yellowish red. This exists, no one doubts that. How do I learn the use of the word 'yellowish'? Through language-games in which, for example, things are put in a certain order. Thus I can learn, in agreement with other people, to recognise yellowish and still more yellowish red, green, brown and white.
>
> In the course of this I learn to proceed independently just as I do in arithmetic.

This passage needs to be read, I think, in the light of Wittgenstein's argument in the *Tractactus* to the effect that there can be no propositional explanation of the meanings of propositions; his frequent remarks to the effect that explanation of meanings must come to an end somewhere; and remarks such as the one from *On Certainty* quoted in the last section, that it is not 'certain propositions striking us immediately as true', but 'our acting, which lies at the bottom of the language game'. In learning the language game in which expressions such as 'yellowish' have a place, Wittgenstein's child learns to do something: to 'put things [shades of colour] in a certain order'. Words are given roles in a structure of *activity*: gradually 'I learn to proceed independently, just as I do in arithmetic.'

This, it seems to me, is Wittgenstein's ultimate answer to the puzzle generated both by the remarks on ostensive definition in the *Philosophical Investigations* and by the remarks on 'elucidations' in the *Tractactus*. Both sets of remarks seem to embody an argument to the effect that language can never be taught or learned, since in order to learn the meaning of words by any such process as ostensive definition the child needs to know their logical category – how they are to

function in sentences – while in order to grasp the meanings of
sentences he needs to have grasped the meanings of their component
words.

The solution Wittgenstein offers is that learning language is learning a set of ways of manipulating the world, into which linguistic
moves fit in various ways. It is not necessary at first for the child to
learn either word meanings or sentence meanings, because what he
has to learn first is something more fundamental than either, in which
both are rooted: a way of proceeding. The ways of proceeding, the
moves in language, taken together with the phenomenological
basis upon which they are erected, define by their patterns of compatibility and exclusion distinct language games. But the same
geography of exclusion and compatibility can also be taken as
defining logical category, or logical type, and thus reveals to the child
the nature of the ontology observed by adult speakers of his language.
What makes a word a colour word is the way in which moves in
language which employ it fit, or fail to fit with other moves in
language. To Wittgenstein's remark that harmony, being in part a
matter of phenomenology, is therefore in part a matter of grammar,
we can add his remark in *Philosophical Remarks*,[7]: 'Grammar is a
"theory of logical types".'

The general coherence of discourse, as it reveals itself in the way in
which speakers observe the discontinuities between language games,
also gives us our evidence for supposing that others understand the
sense of linguistic expressions as we do. 'I say: The person who cannot
play *this* game does not have *this* concept.'[9]

The claim that an expression such as 'reddish green' has a reference
is a claim about what the speaker who wishes to use such an
expression can do with it, and whether he can do anything.

Someone who is familiar with reddish green should be in a position
to produce a colour series which starts with red and ends with green
and constitutes for us too a continuous transition between the two.
We might then discover that at the point when we perhaps always
see the same shade of brown, this person sometimes sees brown and
sometimes reddish green. It may be, for example, that he can
differentiate between the colours of two chemical compounds that
seem to us to be the same colour, and he calls one 'a brown' and the
other 'reddish green'.[10]

We could not, of course, play that language game. But that is precisely the evidence the person would have for thinking that he saw things differently from us and had, at this point, different colour concepts.

> Can't we imagine people having a geometry of colours different from our normal one? And that, of course, means: can we describe it, can we immediately respond to the request to describe it, that is, do we know *unambiguously* what is being demanded of us?
> The difficulty is obviously this: isn't it precisely the geometry of colours that shows us what we're talking about, i.e. that we are talking about colours?[11]

6. *Language games, truth conditions and linguistic autonomy*

In the *Philosophical Remarks* the Fregian connection between meaning and truth conditions is preserved: 'To understand the sense of a proposition means to know how the issue of its truth or falsity is to be decided' (43). Is this connection retained or broken in the *Philosophical Investigations*, where Wittgenstein's technical vocabulary shifts decisively from talk of propositions, and even from talk of systems of propositions, to talk of language games? The relatively smooth transition of themes and problems from the *Tractatus* to the *Remarks on Colour* and the *Investigations* which we have just traced would suggest the contrary. And I think a case can be made out for the view that Wittgenstein appeals to the concept of a language game precisely to explain how speakers can possess a public and determinate understanding of the truth conditions of statements.

In order to see how this can be so, however, we must look again briefly at the variety of meanings which philosophers have attached to the phrase 'the truth conditions of a proposition'. There is, to begin with, the broad distinction we noted earlier between a Fregian, or realist, conception of truth conditions as conditions for the truth of a proposition, and the verificationist conception of truth conditions as the conditions which *warrant assertion* of a proposition. Verificationism, as we have seen, has serious defects. But, if we try to state the truth conditions of a sentence in a realist way, the best we can achieve, it seems, is a Davidsonian T sentence, which gives the truth conditions of a sentence S' in terms of the very same sentence, or a translation of it. And even then, when we try to give a Davidsonian description of the truth conditions attaching to the sentences of an actual natural language, we find that no unique description can be given: the best we can achieve is a holistic description controlled by a 'principle of charity' based on the maximisation of truth-telling and true belief.

All of this discussion, however, whether we take a classically verificationist stance, or the more sophisticated one developed by Quine and Davidson, reposes on the assumption that the truth conditions of a proposition include, *inter alia*, all the sensory evidence that could ever be relevant to the truth or falsity of the proposition in question.

Putnam and Kripke have argued, very persuasively, that stating the meaning of a proposition cannot involve stating its truth conditions in that sense. The truth conditions of a proposition cannot, that is, be construed as a description of the sensory events the occurrence of which constitutes a sufficient and necessary condition for the truth of the proposition. And their discussion connects with the reflections on the autonomy of the sentential sign with which we began this book. Perceptual discrimination and linguistic discrimination are entirely distinct processes; in this sense, the ability to make perceptual discriminations is insufficient to account for the capacity of one speaker to predict the linguistic judgement of another competent speaker.

We suggested earlier on, in chapter 9, that Putnam's account of the meaning of natural-kind terms such as 'water' bears a strong resemblance to Wittgenstein's treatment of meaning in terms of language games. The ostensive indication of samples of water in Putnam's account takes on meaning as an indication of samples of a *substance* (rather than, say, as an indication of samples of a *potable liquid*) in terms of the structure of investigation by appeal to which we link the samples in question to other samples also called 'water'. What seems quite clear from Putnam's account is that the *perceptual marks* by which we *recognise* samples of water have no intrinsic connection with the *meaning* of 'water'. Recognising water may involve just smelling and tasting it, or it may, as in Putnam's Twin Earth, involve observing the results of chemical analyses designed to establish whether the molecular formula of the substance is H_2o or XYZ. Whether any of these perceptual marks is a condition for the truth of 'x is water', in other words, depends on the progress of a certain pattern of investigation taken together with certain original acts of baptism. It is this structure of pattern-of-investigation-plus-baptisms which, if anything, deserves to be identified as the meaning, or *sense*, of 'water'. It seems appropriate to use Frege's term 'sense', because what the structure of pattern of investigation plus baptisms enables us to do is to locate the reference of 'water': to determine the extension of the term across possible worlds. But it does not do this by exhaustively specifying what sensory events are relevant to the truth or falsity of 'x is water': it does it by giving us a *criterion by appeal to which we can recognise* new kinds of sensory event as relevant to the truth or falsity of 'x is water'.

This, now, is exactly what happens when we teach a child to use colour words such as 'yellowish', 'reddish' and 'bluish', according to Wittgenstein's account of the 'language game' into which these words fit. We teach him to arrange colours in series of progressively more yellowish or more bluish reds. 'Pure' reds then emerge for him linguistically as reds which are no more yellowish than they are bluish, and *vice versa*. Once he knows this game, he can 'place' shades of colour he has never encountered before in the series. That is, a *new* perceptual event – one which he has never encountered before – can become for him a ground for the *linguistic* judgement 'x is red' or 'x is yellowish' or 'x is bluish'.

The effect of the language game in both cases, now, is to 'make the sense of ϕ_x determinate'. The language game makes sense 'determinate' in the sense that it shows us 'what possibilities are left open' when we assert $\sim\phi_x$. In the case of $\sim x$ is red, the open possibilities are that x is yellowish or bluish; in the case of $\sim x$ is water, the possibilities left open are that x is one or another different *substance*. To put it another way, the language game gives us a criterion for dividing sensory events into those that are relevant to the truth of ϕ_x, those that are relevant to the truth of $\sim\phi_x$, and those that are irrelevant to 'the issue of its truth or falsity'.

But, in addition, Wittgenstein's final account of the determinacy of sense also at last throws some light on the problems of the autonomy of the linguistic sign and the creativity of language use with which we began this book. Because the language game provides a public criterion for deciding whether a sensory event is relevant to the truth or falsity of ϕ_x, it provides a public criterion by appeal to which one speaker can determine how another, independent speaker, appealing to the same criterion, will determine the truth or falsity of ϕ_x in unfamiliar circumstances. The distinction between knowledge of criteria and knowledge of the relevance of particular sensory events to the truth or falsity of a proposition thus provides a theoretical basis for the distinction between linguistic discrimination and perceptual discrimination which we drew intuitively in chapter 1.

We are, now, perhaps, in a position to see the force of the distinction between *criteria* and *symptoms* which Wittgenstein draws repeatedly throughout his later work. *Symptoms* are perceptual marks which happen to be relevant to the truth or falsity of ϕ_x. *Criteria* concern the language games which determine the relevance of symptoms to questions of the truth or falsity of propositions. Criteria, that is, comprise a mode of procedure (arranging colours in series; investigating the chemical composition of a substance; and so on), together with the natural background conditions, the specific mode of 'continuity of the given' which makes that mode of procedure publicly usable, teachable and learnable.

Truth conditions, for the later Wittgenstein, are given by criteria. If we wish to *state* truth conditions, the best we can do, perhaps, is to say that, for example, '"x is gold" is true just in case x is the *substance* called "gold"'; '"x is red" is true just in case x is the *colour* called "red"'; '"x is Nixon" is true just in case x is the *man* called "Nixon"'; and so on. We cannot give any more informative *statement* of truth conditions, because we cannot 'use language to get outside language'.

7. Language games and objects

To refer to *colours* or *substances*, is, of course, to refer to one category of objects, and the conditions of reference to objects has been a constant theme of our discussion. Frege's treatment of number is memorable in one way because it shows us how we can avoid thinking of numbers as objects: either as objects in the sense of constituents of the spatio-temporal world, or as mental entities (ideas). The trick, as we saw earlier, is to introduce reference to number not by giving rules for singling out numbers as a class of objects in the physical world, or as psychological entities, but by giving procedures (involving one-to-one correlation) which fix the sense – the truth conditions – of certain fundamental kinds of statement about number.

As we remarked at the start of the chapter, Wittgenstein's later work contains frequent injunctions to look for the meaning of an expression not as an *object* corresponding to the expression but as a pattern of use. Here, I think, is one more point of Fregian influence upon Wittgenstein's later work. The truth conditions of a statement are given when we know *what to do with it* – by the language game in which it is to function. And it is through knowing the truth conditions of a statement – knowing its *use*, in other words – that we know what category of objects it is a statement about. Language, for Wittgenstein as for Quine, determines ontology. But in the case of Wittgenstein's account the determination of ontology by language is not the purely conventional affair that Quine supposed it to be.

8. *Criteria and confirmation*

Something more needs to be said about Wittgenstein's distinction between criteria and symptoms, if only because the account I have offered is a relatively controversial one. A more usual account of the distinction is given, for example, by P. M. S. Hacker in his book *Insight and Illusion*. Hacker suggests that Wittgenstein meant by a criterion 'those conditions which non-inductively justify the use of application of a sentence'.[12] Hacker suggests also that criteria so defined are 'conventionally fixed', and that they constitute part of what Wittgenstein calls the 'grammar' of a sentence.

This account of Wittgenstein's intentions seems to me highly dubious, if only because the concept of a 'non-inductive justification' for the application of a sentence seems, *prima facie*, to be incoherent. The 'use' of a sentence is equated by Hacker with its 'application', and 'applying' a sentence seems to mean using it to make an assertion in some specific context of use. But surely what 'justifies' me in making any assertion is always some natural feature of the world. What justifies me in saying 'There is a skylark' may be any one of an indefinite number of things: the bird's song, its characteristic appearance seen close up, a flash of brown and a scurry in the downland grass, and so on. But none of *these* 'criteria' are 'conventionally fixed' and none can by any stretch of the imagination be regarded as any part of the 'grammar' of 'There is a skylark.' Moreover, all such criteria are presumably in Hacker's terms 'inductive': that is to say, their status as criteria rests upon my past experience of skylarks. But that merely points the obvious question: how can there, outside mathematics and logic, be non-inductive grounds for *asserting* a sentence? An assertion, unless it concerns some formal subject matter, records an empirical judgement: what could it possibly be to have *non-inductive* grounds for such a judgement?

One may reasonably wonder, therefore, whether Wittgenstein ever really entertained any such conception of a criterion. To be fair,

Hacker himself holds the conception so explained to be problematic. He lists[13] the extraordinarily diverse and heterogeneous array of things which Wittgenstein says are criteria (behaviour, facts, propositions, 'evidences') and the equally heterogeneous array of things (phrases, sentences, sentential functions, words, facts, states of affairs, concepts) which can have criteria. He discusses the difficulties of establishing the exact nature of the contrast between criteria and symptoms, or between criteria and sets of sufficient conditions. His position, in fact, is the modest and reasonable one that some such concept is at work in Wittgenstein's later writings, that it organises, in some obscure way, arguments of great power, and that therefore, although it is very difficult to make sense of the concept of non-inductive grounds for assertion, the attempt to do so is likely to prove an important philosophical enterprise.

What I doubt, however, is whether the concept of a criterion conceived as a non-inductive ground of assertion rests on anything more than mistaken exegesis.

One major locus for the concept is Wittgenstein's discussion on pp. 24–6 of the *Blue Book*;[14] another is his discussion of first-person and third-person ascriptions of pain at *Investigations*, I. 243–315. In the *Blue Book* Wittgenstein begins by considering a series of questions about x's toothache. We begin by asking 'How do you know X has toothache?' I may answer, 'Because X is holding his cheek and grimacing', or perhaps 'Because X has a réd spot on his cheek.' Wittgenstein wants to say, now, that the red spot is a *symptom*. I know it means toothache, even though I have no other reason for thinking that X has toothache, because whenever X has toothache the red spot appears. The red spot, in other words, is an inductive sign of toothache, and that is what Wittgenstein means by a symptom.

In order to know that the red spot is an inductive sign of toothache, however, I have to have some reason, distinct from the red spot, for supposing that X has toothache on each occasion when the spot appears. Wittgenstein's argument is that this reason, whatever it is, cannot also be regarded as a symptom, for that leads to a vicious regress (ibid., 153). We might, says Wittgenstein, ask 'How do you know that he has got toothache when he holds his cheek?' And one answer might be, 'I say, *he* has toothache when he holds his cheek because I hold my cheek when I have toothache.'

What Wittgenstein now goes on to say is crucial, and must be quoted in full.

But what if we went on asking: – 'And why do you suppose that toothache corresponds to his holding his cheek just because your toothache corresponds to your holding your cheek?' You will be at a loss to answer this question, and find that here we strike rock bottom, that is we have come down to conventions. (If you suggest as an answer to the last question that, whenever we've seen people holding their cheeks and asked them what's the matter, they have answered, 'I have toothache', remember that this experience only co-ordinates holding your cheek with saying certain words.)[15]

Much depends, I think, on what sort of 'conventions' we have come down to. Could there be, for example, a convention that when one has toothache one holds one's cheek? Holding one's cheek, in other words, would not be an *involuntary* response to toothache. One might imagine a convention according to which, when a man tastes a particularly fine wine, he holds up his right hand. The connection between cheek-holding and toothache, on our assumption that it is governed by convention, would be as *external* as that: there would be nothing intrinsic to the sensation of toothache to *make* one want to hold one's face. But – I think this is evident – if the connection between pain and behavioural responses to pain such as face-holding were as external as that, we should simply not have a concept of pain. People who found themselves quite free to make any behavioural response they liked, or to make none at all, according as *convention* might direct, when the C fibres in the nerves of their carious teeth fired would not, that is, have our concept of pain. But where is the difference between saying *that* and saying that they would not be *in pain*?

Again, suppose one of those people makes a practice of putting his hand to his cheek when he finds (by means of some cognitive process which presumably does not involve feeling pain) that the C fibres in his teeth are firing; and, when I ask him why he does that, says, 'I have toothache.' We now have exactly the situation which Wittgenstein describes in the parenthetical sentence at the end of the passage quoted above (that is, the *only* reason we have for thinking the speaker in pain is that he says he is). I think it is plain that in such circumstances we should not be at all disposed to believe the speaker to be in pain. He would just be 'saying certain words'; perhaps because, unlike Wittgenstein, he takes a behaviourist view of these matters and supposes (he is doing his *very best* to learn our language!) that what it *means* to say of someone that he has toothache is that he holds his cheek and says, 'I have toothache.'

Let us reflect, now, that if I say that your face-holding is a *symptom* rather than a *manifestation* of your toothache, what I am saying is that I can see no reason why having toothache should make you hold your face. Symptoms are merely inductive correlates of the conditions of which they are symptomatic. But we cannot say that face-holding is inductively correlated with *pain*, because, as we have just seen, the moment we say that, we cut away the foundations of our ordinary concept of pain. In other words, the idea that behaviour which manifests pain is *symptomatic* of pain is incoherent, because, given the ordinary meaning of the word 'symptom', a person who exhibited only *symptoms* of pain could not be said to be *in pain*.

One of the consequences of Wittgenstein's argument is that it enables us to see how what is sometimes called the 'argument from analogy' puts the cart before the horse. The argument from analogy goes like this: 'When I hold my cheek it is because I feel pain; therefore his holding his cheek is a good reason for supposing that he feels pain.' It has often been observed that the argument as it stands is invalid, indeed a *non sequitur*; but there are still plenty of philosophers who continue to believe that unless we are prepared to grant it some force we have no choice but to accept either solipsism or some form of behaviourism.

Let us put the matter the other way round. Suppose I have never felt pain, but notice that other people sometimes hold their faces, groan, and so on, and that this behaviour seems to be involuntary; that it debars them, often at the cost of some inconvenience to themselves, from pursuing their ordinary occasions. When I ask them politely why they do not stop holding their cheeks and get on with whatever they are supposed to be doing, they reply, gritting their teeth, 'Don't be a fool! I am in pain!' Up to this point, face-holding in others is, for me, merely a symptom of some unknown condition which (again from my point of view) is inductively correlated with it and which people appear to call 'pain'. At this point, however, I suddenly get an attack of toothache (no doubt, if there is a just God in heaven, a severe one). At once 'all becomes clear' to me. I 'see *why*' the others were holding their faces, for I see now what it is about toothache that makes it very difficult to do otherwise. This is the point at which I grasp the concept of pain; and it is the point at which the pain behaviour of others ceases to be *symptomatic* of something unknown called pain, and becomes, for me, a manifestation – or, as Wittgenstein would say, a criterion – of pain. One might also say that at this point the pain behaviour of others has become *intelligible* to me.

Thus, I no longer need to *infer* a person's pain from his pain behaviour, because pain behaviour is no longer, for me, merely a symptom of some unknown interior cause. No *argument*, and thus no argument from analogy, is now necessary to justify me in concluding that a man who holds his cheek is feeling the pain of toothache. To say that I know what *X* feels because I have had toothache too (which is the grain of truth in the idea that we know another's inner states by recourse to the argument from analogy) is not at all the same thing as saying that, on the basis of my own experience, I construct a hypothesis about the nature of certain interior states of *X*'s which, because they *are* interior states of *his*, are necessarily unknowable to me. The pain of toothache, alas, is very far from unknowable.

The sceptic wishes to take his stand *between* language and the world ('For how can I go so far as to try to use language to get between pain and its expression?' – *Investigations*, I. 245). But there is no gap between language and the world: if there were the sort of gap the sceptic requires, language would not be possible. In the *Investigations* (I. 256) Wittgenstein speaks of sensation words as being 'tied up with' natural manifestations of sensation.

> *How* do I use words to stand for my sensations? – As we ordinarily do? Then are my words for sensations tied up with natural criteria of sensation? In that case my language is not a 'private' one. Someone else might understand it as well as I.

One can see how this whole structure of argument depends upon a distinction between symptoms and criteria, and how, in a certain sense, the crucial feature of that distinction is that symptoms are inductive signs, while criteria are not. And one can see, too, the force of the temptation to sum up the whole argument by saying that a criterion is a 'non-inductive ground of assertion'.

And yet, I think, such a form of words is misleading, and should be resisted. On the one hand it suggests that the judgement that someone is in pain is not, for Wittgenstein, an empirical judgement. This, I think, is clearly wrong. The sceptic's view is, precisely, that empirical considerations (the fact that someone cries out, holds his cheek, and so on) cannot determine the judgement that someone is in pain. To define criteria as non-inductive grounds of assertion suggests that Wittgenstein, too, thought that there was a gap between judging someone to be exhibiting pain behaviour and judging him to be in pain, but believed that there were special 'non-inductive' (hence, presumably, non-empirical) considerations enabling us to bridge that gap. In reality, of course, Wittgenstein believed that there was no such gap, and that the appearance of such a gap is created when we treat pain behaviour as symptomatic, rather than criterial, of pain; an assumption destructive, in its implications, of the very possibility of language.

Matters are made still worse if we say not merely that criteria are non-inductive grounds of assertion, but that they acquire this status by virtue of *linguistic convention*.[16] What kind of linguistic convention, one wonders, could possibly *make* something a ground upon which to base an empirical assertion? If it is only 'by virtue of linguistic convention' that I can assert that another person feels pain, as distinct from exhibiting pain behaviour, then surely that is tantamount to saying that I have no real grounds for making any such assertion. Such an interpretation of Wittgenstein is, as I trust I have shown, a gross vulgarisation of his argument. But what, then, are we to make of Wittgenstein's remarks which apparently assert a close connection of some sort between criteria and convention: for example (in the passage from the *Blue Book* quoted a little earlier), 'You will be at a loss to answer this question, and find that here we strike rock bottom, that is we have come down to conventions.'

What are the conventions in question? (We have already seen that they cannot include a convention to the effect that when someone has toothache he holds his cheek!) Or, to put it another way, using other key words of Wittgenstein's, what are the *rules* which determine the *use* of expressions such as 'in pain', 'has toothache', 'is feeling pretty low because of his teeth', and so on? Wittgenstein's readers often strain every exegetical sinew to extract from his apparently bafflingly aphoristic text clear and straightforward definitions of such terms as 'use', 'rule' or 'convention'. Or, alternatively, when they cannot persuade themselves that they have found such definitions, they throw the book aside and dismiss Wittgenstein's argument as mystification or charlatanry.

Let us assume that Wittgenstein was neither a charlatan, nor a fool, nor a man incapable of expressing his thoughts clearly and precisely in the lucid, trenchant German which was his natural medium of expression. Then it may pay us to look around for some general reason, inherent in Wittgenstein's position, why it is not possible to give a straightforward definition of terms such as 'use', 'rule' or 'convention'. In fact, such a reason is quite easy to discover. Suppose the conventions for using the word 'pain' could be stated and understood without any need to feel pain. Then the word 'pain' would not be the name of a sensation: it would be, perhaps, a name for certain sorts of behaviour (Wittgenstein explicitly rejects – for example, at *Investigations*, 1. 304 – the suggestion that he is a behaviourist): that is to say, words for sensations would not be '*tied up with* natural criteria of sensation' (emphasis added), they would *be* names for the natural (i.e. behavioural) criteria of sensation, which would therefore, by that very fact, no longer function as *criteria of sensation* at all. It is not easy to see how a language containing names for the kinds of behaviour which manifest sensations but no names for sensations would work: certainly, it would be very unlike our language. But, if, on the other hand, the conventions for using the word 'pain' cannot be stated without appeal to the felt character of pain, then they cannot be *stated* – that is, *fully conveyed by means of words* – at all. One can 'assemble reminders' of the use of 'pain', as I have been doing in this section (for example, by asking at what point someone who had never felt pain but who had grasped the compulsive character of other people's pain behaviour could be said to acquire a full grasp of the concept of pain), but the function of these 'reminders' can only be to get the reader to reflect upon his own unverbalised (and ultimately unverbalisable) grasp of how language works: it cannot be to contribute to a verbal formulation of the 'rules of use' of English, say. Certainly Wittgenstein wants to say that some statements, including most that philosophers find puzzling, are not 'about the world' but about 'grammar'. But such statements are not prescriptive; are not statements of 'rules' or 'conventions'. As we remarked earlier, what Wittgenstein says about them is curiously redolent of what he says about the sentences of the *Tractatus*, that they are in a certain way senseless. Statements 'about grammar' are statements marking, by the way they skim the verges of absurdity and incoherence, the common limits of our language and of our world.

> 'Only you can know if you had that intention.' One might tell someone this when one was explaining the meaning of the word 'intention' to him. For then it means: *that* is how we use it.
>
> (And here 'know' means that the expression of uncertainty is senseless).   (*Investigations*, I. 247)

What Wittgenstein is arguing for, in short, is the existence of a fundamental unity or continuity between the conventions of language and the nature, or 'continuity', of the world. The demand for such a unity makes its appearance very early on in the *Philosophical Remarks*, in a passage (4) which we have already quoted:

> If I could describe the point of grammatical conventions by saying they are made necessary by certain properties of the colours (say), then that would make the conventions superfluous, since in that case I would be able to say precisely that which the conventions exclude my saying. Conversely, if the conventions were necessary, *i.e.* if certain combinations of words had to be excluded as nonsensical, then for that very reason I cannot cite a property of colours that makes the conventions necessary, since it would then be conceivable that the colours should not have this property, and I could only express that by violating the conventions.

We cannot, that is, describe the relationship between language and the world by first describing certain determinate features of reality, then in a quite independent way describing certain features of language, and finally, and again independently of the first two descriptions, describing a determinate relationship between the two. The fundamental conclusion of the *Tractatus*, 'Whereof one cannot speak, thereof one must be silent', remains (although resting upon vastly altered theoretical foundations) the *leitmotiv* of Wittgenstein's later work: 'I cannot use language to get outside language.'

We are now finally in a position to connect Wittgenstein's account of the logic of the expression 'pain' to the exegetical reconstruction of the distinction between criteria and symptoms which we offered in the preceding sections. We suggested that, for Wittgenstein, setting up a criterion for the use of a set of expressions involves connecting those expressions to one another *via* some operation or procedure which we perform with respect to 'things in the world' (in an ontologically neutral sense of 'thing') in such a way that the truth conditions of propositions employing the expressions in question come to be, in certain respects, intrinsically connected.

In the case of pain we find – for example, when we prick ourselves – that there is a sensation which, by its very nature, makes it very difficult for us not to do certain things in response to it: cry out, withdraw, rub the spot, and so on. If we do not, as yet, know why other people do such things when they are pricked, then we can *find out why* by pricking ourselves. Here is a pattern of procedures with consistent results which anyone can obtain by performing the procedures in question. Now, by convention, we 'station' the word 'pain', as Wittgenstein would say, at a certain 'post' or 'place' in this system of procedures and results: pain is what makes people cry out, and so on, when they are hurt. To grasp how 'pain' functions in language we need to know the relationships I have just, briefly, indicated. We could not introduce the term 'pain' into the language just by 'pointing at' the sensation and bestowing a name on it. One can, indeed, put Wittgenstein's general point about ostensive definition with extra force in this case: if I *could* just point at a pain, with perfect equanimity, it would not *be* pain.

We can see now, too, the implications for philosophy, and for linguistic semantics in general, of Wittgenstein's general maxim that we cannot 'use language to get outside language'. We cannot give a verbal definition of 'pain'. Nor can we *state the truth conditions* of 'I am in pain', except by way of a Davidsonian *T* sentence. But we can describe, or indicate, or 'remind' each other, how the truth conditions of the various things we say about pain and pain behaviour come to be intrinsically related in the way that they are. And we can indicate how 'things in the world' must be in order for that to happen. And we can thus delimit the roles played by nature, convention, and what I have called 'procedures' or 'operations', in the formation of such intrinsic relationships. The whole formed by nature, convention and modes of procedure working together in this sort of way is what, I believe, Wittgenstein meant by a 'form of life'.

Notes and References

1. The Autonomy of the Linguistic Sign
1. Saussure (1916)
2. Berlin and Kay (1969)
3. Bornstein (1973)
4. Lloyd (1977)
5. Berlin and Kay (1969); Lloyd (1977); Lenneberg (1967)
6. Price (1963) *passim*
7. Ogden and Richards (1923)
8. Skinner (1957)
9. Chomsky (1969)

2. Reference and Generality
1. Locke (1961), III, ii, 1
2. Ibid.
3. Ibid., II, i, 1
4. Ibid.
5. See, for example, in favour of this project, Brown, R. W. (1956) and Price (1953); and against it, Harrison (1963)
6. Locke (1961), III, iii, 6
7. Ibid.
8. Ibid., III, iii, 1
9. Ibid., III, iii, 11
10. Ibid., III, iii, 9
11. Ibid., II, xii, 1
12. Ibid., III, iv, 4
13. Ibid., III, iv, 6–7
14. Locke (ibid., III, iv, 6) notices this problem in so far as it affects the relationship between the concepts 'red' and 'colour', but does not see that exactly the same difficulties arise as between 'red' and 'crimson'. His solution, which is to say that 'coloured' stands for the

way in which ideas of colour get into the mind (viz. by way of sight), thus cuts no ice at all.

15. I should not wish to suggest that this is all that is wrong with abstractivism. Geach (1957), in his excellent discussion of abstraction, shows convincingly that there are no concepts for which a plausible abstractionist account can be given. This discussion should be treated as essential further reading

16. Hume (1888), I, i, 7

17. The logically astute feminist will stay her wrath at this, reflecting that you can take it with equal propriety as a male chauvinist dig at women or as a feminist dig at ordinary English

18. Locke (1916), III, iii, 15

19. Ibid., III, iii, 13

20. Ibid., III, iii, 15. It is perhaps worth mentioning that throughout these chapters I use the term 'sortal' as in 'sortal concept', 'sortal name', 'sortal of wider generality', and so on, exactly as Locke defines it here. Strawson (1959) has recently reintroduced the term in a newer and narrower sense: he distinguishes between 'sortal' and 'characterising' universals. My use of the term has nothing to do with Strawson's usage, but conforms to the older, Lockian use

21. Though it might equally well be called 'weak nominalism', Aaron (1967) remarks of the term 'nominalist' that it seems to have come into general usage in the late fourteenth and fifteenth centuries. A realist was a person who gave an affirmative answer to Porphyry's question whether genera and species really existed outside the mind. Those who, for one reason or another, gave a negative answer to the question were all dubbed 'nominalist'. Yet most of them were in fact 'conceptualist'

It seems to me that one reason for this confusion of terms, which was still going strong in the seventeenth century (the conceptualist Locke certainly thought of himself most of the time as a nominalist), is that strict nominalism and conceptualism share a strong structural similarity, in that they both appeal (though at different points) to arbitrary convention as alone providing the principle of unity of a group or collection of things, the radical nominalist opting for conventionalism about the principle of unity of groups of particulars, the conceptualist for conventionalism about the principle of unity of groups of properties or resemblances taken as constituting criteria for the application of general names to particulars

22. Locke (1961), III, v, 3

23. Ibid., III, v, 6
24. Ibid., III, v, 3
25. Ibid., III, vi, 28
26. Ibid.

3. General Names and Particulars

1. Caution counsels against a more definite attribution. It is never certain that a position commonly regarded as Wittgensteinian was in fact ever held by Wittgenstein
2. For this argument see Bambrough (1961), or the clear and incisive summary in Staniland (1972)
3. Strawson (1959), p. 171
4. Russell (1946), p. 101
5. This account of the distinction between proper and general names follows Strawson's observation that particulars can be introduced into discourse only by appeal to 'distinguishing empirical facts' (see Strawson (1959) *passim*)
6. Ibid., ch. 5
7. Ibid.
8. Russell (1918), reprinted in Russell (1956)
9. Ibid., p. 204

4. Sense, Reference and Truth

1. In 'Is Semantics Possible?', in Putnam (1975). See especially pp. 150–1
2. Frege (1953)
3. Ibid., p. 35
4. Ibid.
5. Frege (1972), pp. 83–4
6. Frege (1953), p. 59e
7. Dummett (1973), pp. 192–3
8. Frege 'On Sense and Reference', trans. Max Black in Frege (1960)
9. 'What is a Function?' in Frege (1960)
10. 'Thoughts' in Frege (1977)
11. Ibid., p. 6
12. Ibid., p. 16
13. 'On Concept and Object' in Frege (1960). See especially pp. 15–16
14. Ibid., p. 54

15. Ryle (1971), p. 58
16. Frege 'On Sense and Reference', in Frege (1960), p. 63
17. Ibid., pp. 62–3
18. Frege (1977), p. 12
19. Noam Chomsky (1976), pp. 56–7
20. Strawson (1970), pp. 171–2 reprinted in Strawson (1971)
21. Ibid., p. 176

5. *Meaning and Verification*
1. Michael Dummett (1976), p. 135f
2. Ayer (1946), p. 31
3. Alston (1974)
4. Ayer (1946), p. 38
5. Church (1949), pp. 52–3
6. Ayer (1946), p. 10
7. Ibid.
8. Ayer subsequently acknowledged this difficulty, and discusses it at length in *The Problem of Knowledge* (1954), ch. 1

6. *Logic and Ordinary Language*
1. Davidson (1975b), p. 26
2. Tarski (1943), especially pp. 352–3
3. Davidson (1975b)
4. For an account of the origins of this development of logical empiricism see for example, Hempel (1950), reprinted in Ayer (1959), p. 117; and Carnap (1956a)
5. Tarski, p. 235
6. Strawson (1950)
7. Frege (1977), p. 12
8. Yehoshua Bar-Hillel (1954b), pp. 359–79
9. Frege, 'Sense and Reference', in Frege (1960)
10. W. Van Orman Quine (1960), sect. 36 *et seq.*
11. See, for example, Ulrich (1977)
12. Russell (1905); now available in many anthologies and most easily in Russell (1956)
13. Ibid., p. 46
14. Montague (1970a), pp. 194–5
15. Church (1951), pp. 3–24
16. Carnap (1956b)
17. Føllesdal (1968), pp. 147–57
18. Putnam (1975), pp. 263–4

7. Meaning, Translation and Ontology

1. Quine (1951), reprinted in Quine (1953); reissued in Harper Torchbooks, (1963). Subsequent page references are to the 1963 edition
2. Ibid., p. 20
3. W. V. Quine, 'Epistemology Naturalised', in Quine (1961), p. 75
4. Ibid.
5. Ibid.
6. Ibid., pp. 80–1
7. Dummett (1974), p. 355
8. Quine (1953), p. 34
9. Dummett (1974), pp. 91–7
10. Gochet (1978), p. 23
11. Duhem (1906), pp. 303-28
12. Grice and Strawson (1956)
13. Ibid. 'We are not . . . concerned, or called upon, to elaborate an adequate theory of conceptual revision, any more than we were called upon . . . to elaborate an adequate theory of synomy'
14. Dummett (1974), pp. 352–3
15. Quine (1960), pp. 29–30
16. Ibid., p. 32
17. Quine (1961), pp. 85–6
18. Ibid., pp. 78–9
19. Quine (1960), pp. 41–2
20. Ibid., p. 68
21. Ibid., p. 52
22. Quine (1974), p. 399
23. See Gochet (1978), pp. 203–4
24. Quine (1961), p. 26
25. Ibid., p. 48
26. Ibid., p. 50
27. Ibid., p. 83
28. Ibid., p. 6
29. Dummett (1974), p. 395
30. Hesse (1976), p. 197
31. Quine (1961), p. 89
32. Ibid., p. 87
33. Ibid., p. 31
34. Ibid.
35. Ibid.
36. Quine (1960), p. 43

37. Ibid., p. 42

38. Ibid

39. As will appear in a later chapter, I owe this way of formulating the point to Wittgenstein's discussion in the *Philosophical Remarks*. The point itself seems to me of the highest importance

40. This paragraph and the next are extracted from Harrison (1979), where a fuller treatment of this argument will be found

41. Quine (1961), p. 5

42. Quine (1960), p. 97

43. Ibid

44. Wittgenstein (1977), part III, para. 110. My own book *Form and Content* (1973), although it was independently conceived, develops this suggestion of Wittgenstein's in detail, and contains a much fuller version of the theory offered here

45. Quine (1960), p. 100

8. Truth and Interpretatation

1. Strawson (1970), in Strawson (1971)

2. See Davidson (1973a)

3. Davidson (1969), pp. 158–74

4. Davidson (1970), in Davidson and Harman (1975), p. 23

5. Ibid., p.19

6. Ibid

7. Ibid

8. Ibid., p. 21

9. Davidson (1974), p. 310

10. Ibid., p. 311

11. Davidson (1973b), p. 324

12. Ibid

13. Davidson (1973a)

14. Davidson (1973b), p. 321

15. In Putnam, 'The Meaning of Meaning', in Putnam (1975), p. 261

16. Ibid., p. 262

9. Naming, Necessity and Natural Kinds

1. Bennett (1972)

2. Mill (1886), I, ii, 3

3. See, for example, Russell (1946), pp. 55ff

4. Searle (1958), in Caton (1963)

5. Dummett (1973), p. 40

6. Kripke (1972)

7. Searle (1958), in Caton (1963), p. 160

8. For a more extended version of this argument, see Kripke (1972), p. 297

9. Ibid., pp. 291–2

10. Ibid., pp. 298–9

11. Kovesi (1967)

12. Putnam, 'Is Semantics Possible?', in Putnam (1975), p. 139

13. Ibid., p. 141

14. Putnam, 'The Meaning of "Meaning"', in Putnam (1975), p. 218

15. Ibid., p. 149

16. Ibid

17. Leibniz, *Nouveaux Essais*, III, xi, 25

18. Putnam, in 'Language and Reality', in Putnam (1975)

10. Speech Acts

1. Strawson (1970), in Strawson (1971), pp. 184ff

2. Chomsky (1976), p. 71

3. Searle (1970), p. 17; see also, for example, Føllesdal (1975)

4. See, for example, Ricoeur (1971). I owe this point to Maurita Harney of the Australian National University

5. 'This dissociation of the verbal meaning of the text and the mental intention is what is really at stake in the inscription of discourse' – Ricoeur (1971), p. 534

6. Strawson (1971), p. 189

7. Searle (1970), p. 17

8. Austin (1962)

9. Ibid., Lecture 1

10. Ibid., pp. 92–3

11. Ibid., p. 95

12. Ibid., p. 98

13. Searle (1970), p. 18

14. Austin (1962), p. 138

15. Ibid., p. 141

16. Searle (1970), p. 17

17. Hart (1948), in A. G. N. Flew (ed.), *Logic and Language*, series 1 (Basil Blackwell, Oxford: 1955)

18. Strawson (1964b), in Searle (ed.) (1971), p. 27

19. Ibid., p. 27

20. Noam Chomsky (1976)
21. Searle (1976), for example

11. Meaning and Speakers' Meaning

1. Grice (1957, 1968 and 1969)
2. See, for example, Grice (1969)
3. Bennett (1976), p. 9
4. Grice (1957), reprinted in Rosenberg and Travis (1971), p. 442
5. Ziff (1967a), pp. 1–8
6. Searle (1970), pp. 44–5
7. Wilson (1970), p. 298
8. Ziff (1969), p. 7
9. Bennett (1976), especially sections 6 and 54–63
10. Lewis (1969)
11. Bennett (1976), p. 16
12. Ibid., p. 136
13. Ibid., p. 138
14. See Harrison (1963)
15. Gottlob Frege, 'On Concept and Object', in Frege (1960)

12. Interlude: Stalemate and Revision

1. Dummett (1976), p. 135
2. Gasking and Jackson (1967), p. 54
3. Hacker (1972), pp. 103–7

13. Objects and the Determinateness of Sense

1. Wittgenstein (1961b) 3.23, p. 23. All passages quoted in this chapter are taken from this translation of the *Tractatus*
2. Schlick (1934)
3. Frege, 'Negation' in Frege (1977)
4. Ibid., p. 32
5. Ibid., pp. 35–6
6. Wittgenstein (1929)

14. Meaning and Use

1. Wittgenstein (1975). Bracketed numbers in the text refer to paragraph numbers in this edition
2. Wittgenstein (1961a)
3. Ibid., p. 3
4. Wittgenstein (1969), para 204

5. Strawson (1954), pp. 70–99

6. Bridgman (1926). An operationalist interpretation of Wittgenstein can be found in C. S. Chihara and J. A. Fodor (1965)

7. A somewhat different, though closely related, treatment of colour language will be found in my *Form and Content* (Blackwell, 1973). At the time of writing the book, in 1971–2, neither the English translation of the *Philosophical Remarks* nor the much later *Remarks on Colour* (dating from 1951 but only published in 1977) had yet appeared, and I was quite unaware of the close similarity between my treatment of colour and Wittgenstein's, though much other work of Wittgenstein's was certainly active in my mind

8. Wittgenstein (1977), III, 115

9. Ibid., III, 115

10. Ibid., III, 163

11. Ibid., III, 86

12. Hacker (1972), p. 111

13. Ibid., pp. 285–6

14. Wittgenstein (1960)

15. 'Symptoms are discovered in experience, but criteria are fixed by convention' (Hacker (1972), p. 290). See also Chihara and Fodor (1965), p. 287: 'But ultimately, according to Wittgenstein, we must come upon . . . definitions or conventions which determine criteria for applying the relevant predicates.' Throughout their paper, too, Chihara and Fodor take Wittgenstein to be offering 'an operationalistic analysis of *confirmation*' [author's italics]

Bibliography

SELECT BIBLIOGRAPHY

I have listed here a brief selection of further reading appropriate to
each section of the book. Details of publication, etc. will be found in
the main bibliography which follows. (The place of publication is
London unless otherwise stated.)

Abbreviations
ASP   *Proceedings of the Aristotelian Society*
ASS   *Supplementary Proceedings of the Aristotelian Society*

General Books
ALSTON, W. P., *Philosophy of Language*
BLACK, M., *The Labyrinth of Language*
BROWN, R. W., *Words and Things*
COOPER, D. E., *Philosophy and the Nature of Language*
HACKING, IAN, *Why does Language Matter to Philosophy?*
KEMPSON, RUTH M., *Semantic Theory*
LYONS, JOHN, *Semantics*, vol. 1
URMSON, JOHN, *Philosophical Analysis*

Part I: Names
CHOMSKY, NOAM, review of B. F. Skinner, *Verbal Behaviour*
GEACH, P. T., *Mental Acts*, especially paras 1–11
HARRISON, B., *Meaning and Structure*, chs 1–7
LOCKE, JOHN, *Essay Concerning Human Understanding*, Bk III
LYONS, JOHN, *Semantics*, ch. 5
MORRIS, C. W., *Signs, Language and Behaviour*
PEARS, D. F., *Bertrand Russell and the British Tradition in Philosophy*
PRICE, H. H., *Thinking and Experience*

RUSSELL, BERTRAND, *The Philosophy of Logical Atomism*
RYLE, G. 'The Theory of Meaning'
SKINNER, B. F., *Verbal Behaviour*
STANILAND, H., *Universals*

Part II: Meaning and Truth
AYER, A. J., *Language, Truth and Logic*
CHIHARA, C. S., 'Davidson's Extensional Theory of Meaning'
DAVIDSON, D., 'Truth and Meaning'
—— 'Radical Interpretation'
DUMMETT, M. and FREGE, G., *Philosophy of Language*, especially
    chs 1, 5 and 6
—— 'What is a Theory of Meaning? (II)'
FREGE, G., *Logical Investigations*
—— 'On Sense and Reference', in Frege (1960)
—— 'On Concept and Object', in Frege (1960)
—— 'On the Scientific Justification of a Conceptual Notion', in Frege
    (1972)
HACKING, IAN, *Why does Language Matter to Philosophy?*, ch. 12 (on
    Davidson)
HEMPEL, G. C., 'The Empiricist Criterion of Meaning'
KATZ, J. J., 'Logic and Language, an Examination of Recent Criti-
    cisms of Intentionalism'
KEMPSON, RUTH M., *Semantic Theory*, ch. 3
KRIPKE, S., 'Naming and Necessity'
MORAVCSIK, J. M. E., *Understanding Language*
PUTNAM, H. 'The Meaning of "Meaning"', in Putnam (1975)
QUINE, W. V., *Word and Object*
—— 'Two Dogmas of Empiricism', in Quine (1953)
—— 'Ontological Relativity', in Quine (1961)
RUSSELL, BERTRAND, 'On Denoting'
SEARLE, J. R., 'Proper Names'
STRAWSON, P. F., 'On Referring'
—— 'Meaning and Truth'
TARSKI, A., 'The Semantic Conception of Truth'
WIGGINS, D., 'On Sentence-Sense, Word-Sense and a Difference of
    Word-Sense. Towards a Philosophical Theory of Dictionaries'

Part III: Communication and Intention
ALSTON, W. P., 'Meaning and Use'
—— 'Linguistic Acts'

AUSTEN J. L., *How To Do Things With Words*
BENNETT, J., *Linguistic Behaviour*
CARTWRIGHT, R., 'Propositions'
CHOMSKY, N., *Reflections on Language*, especially ch. 2.
COHEN, L. J., 'Do Illocutionary Forces Exist?'
GRICE, H. P., 'Meaning'
—— 'Utterer's Meaning, Sentence-Meaning, and Word Meaning'
—— 'Utterer's Meaning and Intentions'
LEMMON, E. J., 'Sentences, Statements and Propositions'
LEWIS, D., *Convention*
RYLE, G., 'Use, Usage and Meaning'
SEARLE, J. R., *Speech Acts*
—— 'Austin on Locationary and Illocutionary Acts'
STRAWSON, P. F., 'Intention and Convention in Speech Acts'
WILSON, N. L., 'Grice on Meaning: the Ultimate Counter-Example'
ZIFF, P., 'On H. P. Grice's Account of Meaning'

Part IV: Language and the World
ANSCOMBE, G. E. M., *An Introduction to Wittgenstein's 'Tractatus'*
GEACH, P. T., 'Saying and Showing in Frege and Wittgenstein'
HACKER, P. M. S., *Insight and Illusion*
HARRISON, B., *Form and Content*
ISHIGURO, HIDE, 'Use and Reference of Names'
LYONS, A., 'Criteria and Evidence'
McGUINNESS, B., 'The *Grundgedanke* of the *Tractatus*'
PEARS, D. F., *Wittgenstein*
WINCH, P., 'The Unity of Wittgenstein's Philosophy'
WITTGENSTEIN, L., *Tractatus Logico-Philosophicus*
—— *Philosophical Investigations*
—— *Philosophical Remarks*
—— *On Certainty*
—— *Remarks on Colour*

MAIN BIBLIOGRAPHY

AARON, R. I. (1967), *The Theory of Universals* (2nd edn Oxford and New York: Oxford University Press).
ALBRITTON, ROGERS (1959), 'On Wittgenstein's Use of the Term "Criterion"', *Journal of Philosophy*, LVI, 845–57; and in Pitcher (1966).

ALDRICH, VIRGIL (1955), 'Mr Quine on Meaning, Naming and Purporting to Name', *Philosophical Studies*, VI, 17–26.

ALSTON, W. P. (1958), 'Ontological Commitment', *Philosophical Studies*, IX, 8–17.

—— (1963), 'Meaning and Use', *Philosophical Quarterly*, XIII, 107–24.

—— (1964a), 'Linguistic Acts', *American Philosophical Quarterly*, I, 138–46.

—— (1964b), *Philosophy of Language* (Englewood Cliffs, N.J.: Prentice-Hall).

—— (1974), 'Semantic rules', in Munitz and Unger (1974).

AMBROSE, A. (1967), 'Wittgenstein on Universals', in Fann (1967).

ANSCOMBE, G. E. M. (1959), 'Mr Copi on Objects, Properties and Relations in the "Tractatus"', *Mind*, LXVIII, 404; and in Copi and Beard (1966).

—— (1963), *An Introduction to Wittgenstein's 'Tractatus'* (2nd edn Hutchinson).

—— (1976), 'The Question of Linguistic Idealism', in Hintikka (1976).

ARMSTRONG, D. M. (1971), 'Meaning and Communication', *Philosophical Review*, LXXX, 427–47.

AUSTIN, J. L. (1940), 'The Meaning of a Word': paper read to Cambridge Moral Sciences Club and Oxford Jowett Society, in Austin (1961).

—— (1953), 'How to Talk – Some Simple Ways', *ASP*, LIV; and in Austin (1961).

—— (1956), 'Performative Utterances': unscripted talk for the Third Programme of the BBC, in Austin (1961).

√ —— (1958), 'Performative-Constative': paper presented at Royaumant Conference, English trans. in Caton (1963).

—— (1961), *Philosophical Studies* (Oxford: Clarendon Press).

—— (1962), *How To Do Things With Words* (Oxford: Clarendon Press).

AYER, A. J. (1946), *Language, Truth and Logic* (2nd edn Gollancz).

—— (1950), 'Basic propositions', in Black, Max (eds), *Philosophical Analysis* (Cornell University Press); and in Ayer (1954a).

√ —— (1952), 'Negation', *Journal of Philosophy* X/IX; and in Ayer (1954a).

—— (1954a), *Philosophical Essays* (Macmillan).

—— (1954b), 'Can there be a Private Language?', *ASS*; and in Ayer (1963).

—— (1955), 'What is Communication?': lecture to the University College, London, Communication Research Centre, in Ayer (1969).

—— (1958). 'Meaning and Intentionality', *Proceedings of the 12th International Congress of Philosophy*; and in Ayer (1969).

—— (1959), *Logical Positivism* (Glencoe, Illinois: Free Press).

—— (1960a), 'Names and Descriptions', *Studia Filozoficzne*, 5.20; and in Ayer (1963).

—— (1960b), 'Philosophy and Language': inaugural lecture, Oxford, in Ayer (1963).

—— (1963), *The Concept of a Person* (London, New York: Macmillan).

—— (1969), *Metaphysics and Common Sense* (Macmillan).

BAMBROUGH, RENFORD (1961), 'Universals and Family Resemblances', *ASP*, LXI, 207–22; and in Pitcher (1966).

—— (1974), 'How to read Wittgenstein', in Vesey (1974).

BARFIELD, OWEN (1928), *Poetic Diction* (Faber).

—— (1967), *Speaker's Meaning* (Rudolf Steiner Press).

BAR-HILLEL, Y. (1954a), 'Logical Syntax and Semantics', *Language*, XXX, 230–7.

—— (1954b), 'Indexical expressions', *Mind*, LXIII, 359–76.

—— (1967a), 'Dictionaries and Meaning-Rules', *Foundations of Language*, III, 409–14.

—— (1967b), review of Fodor and Katz (1964), *Language*, XLIII, 526–50.

—— (1970), *Aspects of Language* (Jerusalem: Magnes).

BARTHES, R. (1964), *Eléments de sémiologie* (Paris: Seuil); English trans., *Elements of Semiology* (Cape, 1962).

BARTSCH, R. and VENNEMANN, T. (1972), *Semantic Structures* (Frankfurt: Athenaeum).

BEEBE, MICHAEL (1976), 'The Basis of Semantic Structure', *Dialogue*, XV, 624–41.

BENNETT, JONATHAN (1959), 'Analytic–Synthetic, *ASP*, LIX, 163–88.

—— (1961), 'On Being Forced to a Conclusion', *ASS*, XXXV, 15–34.

—— (1972), 'The Age and Size of the World', *Synthèse*, XXIII, 127–46.

—— (1973), 'The Meaning–Nominalist Strategy', *Foundations of Language*, X, 141–68.

—— (1975), 'Stimulus, Response, Meaning', in Rescher, N., *Studies in Epistemology* (*American Philosophical Quarterly Monograph No. 9*), 55–8.

BENNETT, JONATHAN (1976), *Linguistic Behavior* (Cambridge: Cambridge University Press).

BERLIN, B. and KAY, P. (1969), *Basic Color Terms* (Berkeley: University of California Press).

BERLIN, I. (1939), 'Verification', *ASP*, XXXIX, 225–48.

BICKERTON, D. (1969), 'Prolegomena to a Linguistic Theory of Metaphor', *Foundations of Language*, V, 34–52.

BLACK, MAX (1939), 'Some Problems Connected with Language', *ASP*, XXXIX, 43–68; and in Copi and Beard (1966).

—— (1949), *Language and Philosophy* (New York: Cornell University Press).

—— (1964), *A Companion to Wittgenstein's 'Tractatus'* (Cambridge: Cambridge University Press).

—— (1968), *The Labyrinth of Language* (New York: Praeger; British publication, Harmondsworth: Penguin Books, 1972).

BOGEN, JAMES (1972), *Wittgenstein's Philosophy of Language* (Routledge).

BOLINGER, D. L. (1965), 'The Atomization of Meaning', *Language*, XLI, 555–73.

—— (1968), *Aspects of Language* (New York: Harcourt, Brace and World).

BOORSE, CHARLES (1975), 'The Origins of the Indeterminacy Thesis', *Journal of Philosophy*, 72, 369–87.

BORNSTEIN, M. H. (1973), 'Color Vision and Color Naming: A Psychophysiological Hypothesis', *Psychological Bulletin*, LXXX, 257–85.

BOTHA, R. (1973), *The Justification of Linguistic Hypotheses* (The Hague: Mouton).

BRAITHWAITE, R. B. (1954), review of Quine, W. V., *From A Logical Point of View*, *Cambridge Review*, LXXV, 417–18.

BRÉAL, M. (1900), *Essai de sémantique* (Paris), English trans., *Semantics: Studies in the Science of Meaning* (Holt).

BRIDGMAN, P. W. (1926), *The Logic of Modern Physics* (New York: Macmillan).

BROOKE-ROSE, C. (1958), *A Grammar of Metaphor* (Secker and Warburg).

BROWER, R. A. (1959), *On Translation* (Cambridge, Mass.: Harvard University Press).

BROWN, R. (1962), 'Meaning and Rules of Use', *Mind*, LXXI, 494–511.

BROWN, R. W. (1958), *Words and Things* (Glencoe, Ill.: Free Press).

BURKS, ARTHUR W. (1951), 'A Theory of Proper Names', *Philosophical Studies*, II, 36–45.

CARNAP, RUDOLF (1936), 'Testability and Meaning', *Philosophy of Science*, III, 419–71: IV (1937), 1–40.

—— (1955), 'Meaning and Synonymy in Natural Languages', *Philosophical Studies*, VII, 33–47.

—— (1956a), 'The Methodological Character of Theoretical Concepts', in Feigl, H. and Scriven, M., *Minnesota Studies in the Philosophy of Science*, vol. I.

—— (1956b), *Meaning and Necessity* (2nd edn Chicago: University of Chicago Press).

—— (1959), *Introduction to Semantics* (Cambridge, Mass.: Harvard University Press).

CARROLL, J. (1966), 'Words, Meanings and Concepts', in Ewig, Flemming and Popp, *Language and Learning* (New York: Harcourt, Brace and World).

CARTWRIGHT, R. (1962), 'Propositions', in Butler, R., *Analytical Philosophy* (Oxford: Blackwell).

CASSIN, C. (1970), 'Russell's Discussion of Meaning and Denotation: A Re-examination', in Klemke, E., *Essays on Bertrand Russell* (University of Illinois Press).

CATON, C. E. (1962), 'An Apparent Difficulty in Frege's Ontology', *Philosophical Review*, LXXI, 462–75.

—— (ed.) (1963), *Philosophy and Ordinary Language* (Urbana, Ill.: University of Illinois Press).

CAVELL, STANLEY (1958), 'Must We Mean What We Say?', *Inquiry*, I: 172–212; and in Cavell (1969).

—— (1969), *Must We Mean What We Say: A Book of Essays* (London, New York, Melbourne, Cambridge: Cambridge University Press).

CHAFE, W. L. (1971), *Meaning and the Structure of Language* (Chicago and London: Chicago University Press).

CHAPPELL, V. C. (ed.) (1964), *Philosophy of Language* (Englewood Cliffs, N.J.: Prentice-Hall).

CHERRY, C. (1975), 'Games and Language', *Mind*, LXXXIV, 528–47.

CHIHARA, C. S. (1960), 'Wittgenstein and Logical Compulsion', *Analysis*, XXI, 136–140; and in Pitcher (1966).

—— and FODOR, J. A. (1965), 'Operationalism and Ordinary Language', *American Philosophical Quarterly*, II, 281–95; and in Pitcher (1966).

CHIHARA, C. S. and FODOR, J. A. (1975), 'Davidson's Extensional Theory of Meaning', *Philosophical Studies*, XXVIII, 1–15.

CHOMSKY, N. (1957), *Syntactic Structures* (The Hague: Mouton).

—— (1960), 'Explanatory Models in Linguistics', in Nagel *et al.*, *Logic, Methodology and Philosophy of Science, Proceedings of the 1960 International Congress on History and Philosophy of Science* (Stanford), 528–50.

—— (1959), review of Skinner, B. F., 'Verbal Behavior', *Language*, XXXV, 26–58.

—— (1965), *Aspects of the Theory of Syntax* (Cambridge, Mass: MIT Press).

—— (1968a), 'Quine's Empirical Assumptions', *Synthèse*, XIX, 53–68.

—— (1968b), *Language and Mind* (New York: Harcourt, Brace and World, enlarged edn, 1972).

—— (1976), *Reflections on Language* (New York, London: Temple Smith/Fontana).

CHRISTENSEN, N. (1965), *On the Nature of Meanings* (Munksgaard).

CHURCH, A. (1949), review of A. J. Ayer, 'Language, Truth and Logic', *Journal of Symbolic Logic*, XIV, 52–3.

—— (1951), 'A Formulation of the Logic of Sense and Denotation', in Henle, Paul, *et al.*, *Structure, Method and Meaning* (New York: Liberal Arts Press).

—— (1958), 'Ontological commitment', *Journal of Philosophy*, LV, 1008–14.

CLARK, H. H. and CLARK, E. V. (1977), *Psychology of Language* (New York: Harcourt Brace Jovanovich).

COHEN, L. J. (1962), *The Diversity of Meaning* (Methuen).

—— (1964), 'Do Illocutionary Forces Exist?', *Philosophical Quarterly*, XIV, 118–37.

—— and MARGALIT, A. (1970), 'The Role of Inductive Reasoning in the Interpretation of Metaphor', *Synthèse*, XXI, 469–87.

—— (1971), 'Some Remarks on Grice's Views About the Logical Particles of Natural Languages' in Barr-Hillel, Y. (ed.), *Pragmatics of Natural Languages* (Dordrecht: Reidel).

COLE, P. and MORGAN, J. (eds) (1975), *Syntax and Semantics 3: Speech Acts* (New York: Academic Press).

CONKLIN, H. C. (1962), 'Lexicographical Treatment of Folk Taxonomies' in Householder, F., and Saporta, J. (eds), *Problems in Lexicography* (The Hague: Mouton).

COOPER, D. E. (1972a), 'Meaning and Illocutions', *American*

Philosophical Quarterly, IX, 69–78.

—— (1972b), 'Searle on Intentions and Reference', *Analysis*, XXXII, 159–63.

—— (1973), *Philosophy and the Nature of Language* (Longman).

—— (1975), *Knowledge of Language* (Prism Press, New York: Humanities Press).

COPI, IRVING M. (1958), 'Objects, Properties and Relations in the *Tractatus*', *Mind*, LXVII, 145–65; and in Copi and Beard (1966).

—— and BEARD, ROBERT W. (1966), *Essays on Wittgenstein's 'Tractatus'* (Routledge and Kegan Paul).

CULLER, JONATHAN (1976), *Saussure* (Fontana/Collins).

DAVIDSON, D. (1965), 'Theories of Meaning and Learnable Languages', in Barr-Hillel, Y. (ed.), *Logic, Methodology and Philosophy of Science, Proceedings of the 1964 International Congress* (Amsterdam), 383–94.

—— (1967), 'Truth and Meaning', *Synthèse*, XVII, 304–23.

—— (1968), 'On Saying That', *Synthèse*, XIX, 130–46.

—— (1969), 'True to the Facts', *Journal of Philosophy*, LXVI, 748–64.

—— (1970), 'Semantics for Natural Languages', in Visentini, B. (ed.), *Linguaggi Nella Società e Nella Tecnica* (Milan: Edizioni di Communità); and in Davidson and Harman (1975); and in Harman (1974a).

—— (1973a), 'In Defense of Convention T', in Leblanc, H. (ed.), *Truth Syntax and Modality, Proceedings of the Temple University Conference on Alternative Semantics* (Amsterdam: North Holland Publishing Company).

—— (1973b), 'Radical Interpretation', *Dialectica*, XXVII, 313–27.

—— (1974), 'Belief and the Basis of Meaning', *Synthèse*, XXVII, 309–23.

—— (1975a), 'Thought and Talk', in Guttenplan (1975).

—— (1975b), 'The Logical Form of Action Sentences', in Davidson and Harman (1975).

—— (1976a), 'Mental Events', in Foster, L. and Swanson, J. W. (eds), *Experience and Theory* (Duckworth).

—— (1976b), 'Replies to Foster', in Evans and McDowell (1976).

—— and HARMAN, G. (eds) (1972), *The Semantics of Natural Language* (Dordrecht: Reidel).

—— and —— (eds) (1975) *The Logic of Grammar* (Encino, California: Dickenson Publishing Co.).

—— and HINTIKKA, J. (eds) (1969), *Words and Objections: Essays on the Work of W. V. Quine* (Dordrecht: Reidel).

DEAN, J. D. (1977), *Semantics: Theories of Meaning in Generative Linguistics* (New York: Crowell).

DECKERT, M. (1973), 'Quine, Strawson and Logical Truth', *Philosophical Studies*, 54–6.

DONELLAN, K. (1966), 'Reference and Descriptions', *Philosophical Review*, LXXV, 281–304.

—— (1970), 'Proper Names and Identifying Descriptions', *Synthèse*, XXI, 335–58.

DUDMAN, V. H. (1969), 'A Note on Frege on Sense', *Australasian Journal of Philosophy*, XLVII, 119–22.

—— (1972), 'Frege on Assertion', *Philosophical Review*, XXII, 61–4.

DUHEM, P. (1914), *La Théorie physique* (2nd edn Paris: Rivière).

DUMMETT, M. (1955), 'Frege on Functions: A Reply', *Philosophical Review*, LXV, 229–30.

—— (1967), 'Gottlob Frege', in Edwards, P. (ed.), *The Encyclopedia of Philosophy* (N.Y., London: Macmillan), 225–37.

—— (1973), *Frege: Philosophy of Language* (Duckworth).

—— (1974), 'The Significance of Quine's Indeterminacy Thesis', *Synthèse*, XXVII, 351–97.

—— (1975), 'What is a Theory of Meaning?', in Guttenplan (1975).

—— (1976), 'What is a Theory of Meaning? (II)', in Evans and McDowell (1976).

EVANS, J. (1953), 'On Meaning and Verification', *Mind*, LXII, 1–19.

EVANS, GARETH and MCDOWELL, JOHN (1976), *Truth and Meaning: Essays in Semantics* (Oxford: Clarendon Press).

FANN, K. (1967), *Wittgenstein, the Man and his Philosophy* (New York: Dell).

—— (1969), *Symposium on J. L. Austin* (Routledge and Kegan Paul).

FEYERABEND, PAUL (1955), review of Wittgenstein, *Philosophical Investigations*, *Philosophical Review*, LXIV, 449–83; and in Pitcher (1966).

FIELD, H. (1972), 'Tarski's Theory of Truth', *Journal of Philosophy*, LXIX, 347–75.

FINDLAY, J. (1961), 'Use, Usage and Meaning', *ASS*, XXXV, 229–42.

FLEW, A. G. N. (1963), 'Philosophy and language', in Flew (ed.), *Essays in Conceptual Analysis* (Macmillan).

FODOR, J. A. (1960), 'What Do You Mean?', *Journal of Philosophy*, LVII, 499–506.

—— and KATZ, J. J. (1964), *The Structure of Language: Readings in the Philosophy of Language* (Englewood Cliffs, N.J.: Prentice-Hall).

FODOR, J. D. (1977), *Semantics* (New York: Crowell).

FØLLESDAL, D. (1966), *Referential Opacity and Modal Logic* (Oslo: Universitets Forlaget).

—— (1968), 'Quine on Modality', *Synthèse*, XIX, 147–57.

—— (1973), 'Indeterminacy of Translation and Underdetermination of the Theory of Nature', *Dialectica*, XXVII, 289–301.

—— (1975), 'Meaning and Experience', in Guttenplan (1975).

FOSTER, J. A. (1976), 'Meaning and Truth Theory', in Evans and McDowell (1976).

FRANKENA, W. (1958), '"Cognitive" and "Non-cognitive"', in Henle, Paul, *Language, Thought and Culture* (Ann Arbor: University of Michigan Press).

FREGE, GOTTLOB (1953), *The Foundations of Arithmetic*, trans. J. L. Austin (Oxford: Blackwell).

—— (1960), *Philosophical Writings*, ed. Peter Geach and Max Black, (2nd edn Oxford: Blackwell).

—— (1972), *Conceptual Notation and Related Articles*, trans. and ed. Tyrrell Ward Bynum (Oxford: Clarendon Press).

—— (1977), *Logical Investigations*, ed. P. T. Geach, trans. P. T. Geach and R. H. Stoothoff (Oxford: Blackwell).

FRIEDMAN, M. (1975), 'Physicalism and the Indeterminacy of Translation', *Noûs*, XI, 353–74.

FRIES, C. (1954), 'Meaning and Linguistic Analysis', *Language*, XXX, 57–68.

FURBERG, M. (1969), 'Meaning and Illocutionary Force', in Fann (1969).

GABBAY, DOV, and MORAVCSIK, J. M. E. (1970), 'Sameness and Individuation', *Journal of Philosophy*, LXX, 513–26.

GARNER, R. T. (1974), 'Grice and MacKay on Meaning', *Mind*, LXXXIII, 417–21.

GASKING, D. A. T. and JACKSON, A. C. (1967), 'Wittgenstein as Teacher', in Fann (1967).

GEACH, P. T. (1950), 'Russell's Theory of Descriptions', *Analysis*, X, 84–8.

—— (1951), 'Frege's Grundlagen', *Philosophical Review*, LX, 535–44.

—— (1957), *Mental Acts* (Routledge and Kegan Paul).

—— (1962), *Reference and Generality* (New York, Cornell University Press).

—— (1963), 'Frege', in Anscombe, G. E. M. and Geach, P. T., *Three Philosophers* (Oxford: Blackwell).

—— (1965), 'Assertion', *Philosophical Review*, LXXIV, 449–65.

GEACH, P. T. (1969), 'Russell on Meaning and Denoting', *Analysis*, XIX, 69–72.

—— (1975), 'Names and Identity', in Guttenplan (1975).

—— (1976), 'Saying and Showing in Frege and Wittgenstein', in Hintikka (1976a).

GELLNER, E. (1975), 'The Last Pragmatist', *Times Lit. Supp.*, 25 July.

GEWIRTH, ALAN (1953), 'The Distinction Between Analytic and Synthetic Truths', *Journal of Philosophy*, L, 397–426.

GIEDYMIN, J. (1972), 'Quine's Philosophical Naturalism', *British Journal for the Philosophy of Science*, 45–55.

GINET, CARL (1976), 'Wittgenstein's claim that there could not be just one occasion of obeying a rule', in Hintikka (1976a).

GOCHET, P. (1972), *Esquisse d'une théorie nominaliste de la proposition* (Paris: Colin).

—— (1978), *Quine en perspective* (Paris: Flammarion).

GODDARD, L. and ROUTLEY, R. (1966), 'Use, Mention and Quotation', *Australasian Journal of Philosophy*, XLIV, 1–49.

GOGUEN, J. A. (1969), 'The Logic of Inexact Concepts', *Synthèse*, XIX, 325–73.

GOODMAN, N. (1949), 'On Likeness of Meaning', *Analysis*, X, 1–7.

—— (1953). 'On Some Differences About Meaning', *Analysis*, XIII, 90–6.

—— and QUINE, W. V. (1947), 'Steps Toward a Constructive Nominalism', *Journal of Symbolic Logic*, XII, 105–22.

GREIMAS, A. (1965), *La Sémantique structurale* (Paris: Larousse).

—— *et al.*, (eds) (1970a), *Sign, Language, Culture* (The Hague: Mouton).

—— (1970b), *Du Sens: essais sémiotiques* (Paris: Seuil).

GRICE, H. P. (1957), 'Meaning', *Philosophical Review*, LXVI, 377–88.

—— (1968), 'Utterer's Meaning, Sentence-meaning, and Word-meaning', *Foundations of Language*, IV, 225–42.

—— (1969), 'Utterer's Meaning and Intentions', *Philosophical Review*, LXXVIII, 147–77.

—— and STRAWSON, P. F. (1956), 'In Defense of a Dogma', *Philosophical Review*, LXV, 141–58.

GUTTENPLAN, SAMUEL (ed.) (1975), *Mind and Language: Wolfson College Lectures 1974* (Oxford: Clarendon Press).

HACKER, P. M. S. (1972), *Insight and Illusion* (Oxford: Clarendon Press).

HACKING, IAN (1975), *Why Does Language Matter to Philosophy?* (Cambridge: Cambridge University Press).

HAMPSHIRE, STUART (1957), 'The Interpretation of Language: Words and Concepts', in C. A. Mace (ed.), *British Philosophy in the Mid-Century* (Allen and Unwin).

HARE, R. M. (1957), 'Are Discoveries About the Uses of Words Empirical?', *Journal of Philosophy*, LIV, 741–50.

—— (1970), 'Meaning and Speech Acts', *Philosophical Review*, LXXIX, 3–24.

HARMAN, G. (1968), 'Three Levels of Meaning', *Journal of Philosophy*, LXV, 500–602.

—— (1972), 'Logical Form', *Foundations of Language*, IX, 38–65.

—— (ed.) (1974a), *On Noam Chomsky* (New York: Doubleday).

—— (1964b), 'Meaning and Semantics', in Manitz and Unger (1974).

HARRIS, ROY (1973), *Synonymy and Linguistic Analysis* (Toronto: University of Toronto Press).

HARRISON, BERNARD (1963), 'Meaning and Mental Images', *ASP*, LXIII, 237–50.

—— (1965), 'Category-Mistakes and Rules of Language', *Mind*, LXXIV, 309–25.

—— (1967), 'On Describing Colours', *Inquiry*, X, 38–52.

—— (1972), *Meaning and Structure: An Essay in the Philosophy of Language* (New York: Harper and Row).

—— (1973), *Form and Content* (Oxford: Blackwell).

—— (1974), review of J. J. Katz, 'Semantic Theory', *Mind*, LXXXIII, 599–606.

—— (1977a), Review of Jonathan Bennett, 'Linguistic Behavior', *Mind*, LXXXVI, 600–5.

—— (1977b), 'On Understanding a General Name', in Vesey (1977).

—— (1979), 'Epistemological Relativism', in N. Mouloud (ed.), *Les Codes signifiants et les opérations de traduction* (Lille: Publications de l'Université de Lille 3).

—— (forthcoming), *The Anatomy of Sense*.

HART, H. L. A. (1948), 'The Ascription of Responsibility and Rights', *ASP*, XLIX, 171–94.

HARTNACK, JUSTUS (1965), *Wittgenstein and Modern Philosophy* (New York: Doubleday).

HEMPEL, G. C. (1950), 'The Empiricist Criterion of Meaning', *Revue internationale de philosophie*, IV, 41–63; and in Ayer (1959).

—— (1952), 'Fundamentals of Concept Formation', *International Encyclopedia of Unified Science*, II.7 (Chicago: University of Chicago Press).

HERZBERG, LARS (1976), 'On the Factual Dependence of the Language Game', in Hintikka (1976a).

HESSE, MARY (1976), 'Duhem, Quine and a New Empiricism', in Harding, S. (ed.), *Can Theories be Refuted?* (Dordrecht: Reidel).

HILL, THOMAS E. (1974), *The Concept of Meaning* (Allen and Unwin).

HINTIKKA, J. (1968), 'Behavioral Criteria of Radical Translation', *Synthèse*, XIX, 69–81.

—— (1969a), *Models for Modalities* (Dordrecht: Reidel).

—— (1969b), 'Semantics for Propositional Attitudes', in Davis, J. *et al.*, *Philosophical Logic* (Dordrecht: Reidel).

—— (1969c), 'Wittgenstein on Private Language: Some Sources of Misunderstanding', *Mind*, LXXVIII, 423–5.

—— (1972), 'The Semantics of Modal Notions and the Indeterminacy of Ontology', in Davidson and Harman (1972).

—— (1973), 'Grammar and Logic: Some Borderline Problems', in Hintikka, Moravcsik and Suppes (1973).

—— (1976a), *Essays on Wittgenstein in Honour of G. H. von Wright, Acta Philosophica Fennica*, XXVIII, issues 1–3 (Amsterdam: North Holland Publishing Co).

—— (1976b), 'Language Games', in Hintikka (1976a).

—— (1976b), 'Possible-Worlds Semantics as a Framework for Comparative and Critical Philosophy', in G. Ryle (ed.), *Contemporary Aspects of Philosophy* (Oriel Press).

MORAVCSIK, J. M. E. and SUPPES, P. (eds) (1973), *Approaches to Natural Languages* (Dordrecht: Reidel).

HOCHBERG, H. (1957), 'On Pegasizing', *Philosophy and Phenomenological Research*, XVII, 551–4.

HOFSTADTER, A. (1954), 'The Myth of the Whole: An Examination of Quine's View of Knowledge', *Journal of Philosophy*, LI, 397–417.

HOLDCROFT, D. (1964), 'Meaning and Illocutionary Acts', *Ratio*, VI, 128–43.

HOOK, S. (1969), *Language and Philosophy* (New York: New York University Press).

HUGHES, G., and CRESSWELL, M. (1968), *An Introduction to Modal Logic* (Methuen).

HUME, DAVID (1888), *A Treatise of Human Nature*, ed. L. A. Selby-Bigge (Oxford: Clarendon Press).

HUNTER, J. F. M. (1973), *Essays After Wittgenstein* (Allen and Unwin).

HYMES, D. (1970), 'On Communicative Competence', in Gumperz, J. and Hymes, D. (eds), *Directions in Sociolinguistics* (New York: Holt, Rinehart and Winston).

ISHIGURO, HIDE (1969), 'Use and Reference of Names', in Winch (1969).

JACOBSON, A. (1970), 'Russell and Strawson on Referring', in Klemke (1970).

JACKSON, HOWARD (1970), 'Frege's Ontology', *Philosophical Review*, LXIX, 394–5.

JARDINE, N. (1975), 'Model-Theoretic Semantics and Natural Language', in Keenan, E. (ed.), *Formal Semantics of Natural Language* (Cambridge: Cambridge University Press).

KAMBARTEL, E. (1976), 'Symbolic Acts: Remarks on the Foundations of a Pragmatic Theory of Language', in G. Ryle (ed.), *Contemporary Aspects of Philosophy* (Oriel Press).

KASHER, A. (1972), 'Sentences and Utterances Reconsidered', *Foundations of Language*, VIII, 313–45.

KATZ, J. J. (1964), 'Analyticity and Contradiction in Natural Language', in Fodor and Katz (1964).

—— (1966), *The Philosophy of Language* (New York: Harper and Row).

—— (1967), 'Some Remarks on Quine on Analyticity', *Journal of Philosophy*, LXIV, 36–52.

—— (1971), *Linguistic Philosophy* (Allen and Unwin).

—— (1972), *Semantic Theory* (New York: Harper and Row).

—— (1975), 'Logic and Language: An Examination of Recent Criticisms of Intensionalism', in Gunderson, K., *Language, Mind and Knowledge* (University of Minnesota Press).

—— and MARTIN, E. (1967), 'The Synonymy of Actives and Passives', *Philosophical Review*, LXXVI, 476–91.

—— and NAGEL, R. (1974), 'Meaning Postulates and Semantic Theory', *Foundations of Language*, XI, 311–40.

KEMENY, J. G. (1952), review of W. V. Quine, 'Two Dogmas of Empiricism', *Journal of Symbolic Logic*, XVII, 281–3.

KEMPSON, RUTH M. (1977), *Semantic Theory* (Cambridge: Cambridge University Press).

KENNY, A. (1967), 'Criterion', in P. Edwards, *Encyclopedia of Philosophy* (New York: Macmillan 1967).

—— (1971), 'The Verification Principle and the Private Language Argument', in *The Private Language Argument*, ed. O. R. Jones (Macmillan).

KENNY, A. (1974), 'The Ghost of the *Tractatus*', in Vesey (1974).

—— (1976), 'From the Big Typescript to the *Philosophical Grammar*', in Hintikka (1976a).

KEYT, D. (1966), 'Wittgenstein's Notion of an Object', in Copi and Beard (1966).

KHATCHADOURIAN, H. (1956), 'Frege on Concepts', *Theoria*, XXII, 85–100.

—— (1957), 'Common Names and "Family Resemblances"', *Philosophy and Phenomenological Research*, XVIII, 341–58; and in Pitcher (1966).

KLEMKE, E. D. (1968), *Essays on Frege* (Urbana: University of Illinois Press).

KNEALE, WILLIAM C. (1956), 'Gottlob Frege and Mathematical Logic', in G. Ryle (ed.), *Revolution in Philosophy* (Macmillan).

—— (1962), 'Frege's General Logic', in W. Kneale and M. Kneale, *The Development of Logic* (Oxford: The Clarendon Press).

KOVESI, JULIUS (1967), *Moral Notions* (Routledge and Kegan Paul).

KRIPKE, S. (1963), 'Semantical Considerations on Modal Logic', *Acta Philosophica Fennica*, XVI, 83–94.

—— (1971), 'Identity and Necessity', in M. Munitz (ed.), *Identity and Individuation* (New York: New York University Press).

—— (1972), 'Naming and Necessity', in Davidson and Harman (1972).

LAKOFF, G. (1970), 'Linguistics and Natural Logic', *Synthèse*, XXII, 151–271.

LAMBERT, K. and FRAASSEN, B. C. VAN (1970), 'Meaning Relations, Possible Objects and Possible Worlds', in Lambert (ed.), *Philosophical Problems in Logic* (Dordrecht: Reidel).

LEHRER, A. (1974), *Semantic Fields and Lexical Structure* (Amsterdam: North-Holland).

—— and LEHRER, K. (eds) (1970), *Theory of Meaning* (Englewood Cliffs, N.J.: Prentice-Hall).

LENNEBERG, E. (1967), *Biological Foundations of Language* (New York: Wiley).

LEMMON, E. (1966), 'Sentences, Statements and Propositions', in Montefiore, A. and Williams, B. (eds), *British Analytical Philosophy* (Routledge and Kegan Paul).

LÉVI-STRAUSS, C. (1962), *La Pensée sauvage* (Paris: Plon); English trans., *The Savage Mind* (Weidenfeld and Nicolson, 1966).

LEWIS, C. I. (1943), 'The Modes of Meaning', *Philosophy and Phenomenological Research*, IV, 236–50.

LEWIS, D. (1969), *Convention* (Cambridge, Mass.: Harvard University Press).

—— (1970), 'General Semantics', *Synthèse*, XXII, 18–67; and in Davidson and Harman (1972).

—— (1974), 'Languages, Language and Grammar', in Harman (1974a).

—— (1975), 'Radical Interpretation', *Synthèse*, XXVII.

LINSKY, L. (1952), *Semantics and the Philosophy of Language* (Urbana: University of Illinois Press).

—— (1967), *Referring* (Routledge and Kegan Paul).

LLOYD, BARBARA (1977), 'Culture and Colour Coding', in Vesey (1977).

LOAR, B. (1972), 'Reference and Propositional Attitudes', *Philosophical Review*, LXXXI, 43–62.

LOAR, D. (1976), 'Two Theories of Meaning', in Evans and McDavell (1976).

LOCKE, JOHN (1961), *Essay Concerning Human Understanding*, ed. John W. Yolton (Everyman).

LYON, A. (1974), 'Criteria and Evidence', *Mind*, LXXXIII, 211–27.

LYONS, JOHN (1963), *Structural Semantics* (Oxford: Blackwell).

—— (1968), *Introduction to Theoretical Linguistics* (London and New York: Cambridge University Press).

—— (1977), *Semantics* (Cambridge: Cambridge University Press).

MACDONALD, M. (ed.) (1954), *Philosophy and Analysis* (Oxford: Blackwell).

MCGUINNESS, B. (1956), 'Pictures and Form in Wittgenstein's *Tractatus*', in E. Castelli (ed.), *Filosofia e Simbolismo: Scritti di T. W. Adorno, et al.* (Rome: Fratelli Bocca).

—— (1974), 'The Grundgedanke of the *Tractatus*', in Vesey (1974).

MCKAY, A. (1972), 'Grice's Theory of Meaning', *Mind*, LXXXI, 57–66.

MALCOLM, N. (1951), 'Philosophy and Ordinary Language', *Philosophical Review*, LX, 329–40.

—— (1954), 'Wittgenstein's *Philosophical Investigations*', *Philosophical Review*, LXIII, 530–559; and in Pitcher (1966).

—— (1963), 'The Verification Argument', in Black, M. (ed.), *Philosophical Analysis* (Englewood Cliffs, N.J.: Prentice-Hall).

MANSER, A. (1969), 'Pain and Private Language', in Winch (1969a).

MARSHALL, W. (1953), 'Frege's Theory of Functions and Objects', *Philosophical Review*, LXII, 374–390.

—— (1956), 'Sense and Reference: A Reply', *Philosophical Review*, LXV, 342–61.

MARTIN, R. (1967), 'On Proper Names and Frege's *Darstellungsweise*', *Monist*, LI, 1–8.

—— (1970), 'Some Thoughts on the Formal Approach to the Philosophy of Language', in Bar-Hillel, Y. (ed.), *Pragmatics of Natural Language* (Dordrecht: Reidel).

MATES, B. (1952), 'Synonymity', in L. Linsky (ed.), *Semantics and the Philosophy of Language* (Urbana: Illinois University Press).

—— (1958), 'On the Verification of Statements about Ordinary Language', *Inquiry*, I, 161–212.

—— (1973), 'Descriptions and Reference', *Foundations of Language*, X, 409–18.

DE MAURO, T. (1967), *Ludwig Wittgenstein* (Dordrecht: Reidel).

—— (1969), *Une Introduction à la sémantique* (Paris: Payot).

MAYNARD, P., FREED, B. and MARRAS, A. (1975), *Forms of Representation* (Amsterdam: North Holland Publishing Co).

—— and PEARCE, G. (eds) (1973) *Conceptual Change* (Dordrecht: Reidel).

MERLEAU-PONTY, MAURICE (1969), *La Prose du monde* (Paris: Gallimard); English trans., *The Prose of the World* (Heinemann, 1974).

MEPHAM, JOHN (1973), 'The Structuralist Sciences and Philosophy', in Robey, D. (ed.), *Structuralism: An Introduction: Wolfson College Lectures 1972* (Oxford: Clarendon Press).

MILL, JOHN STUART (1886), *System of Logic* (8th edn, Longmans Green & Co).

MILLER, G. A. and JOHNSON-LAIRD, P. N. (1976), *Perception and Language* (Cambridge, Mass.: Harvard University Press).

MISES, RICHARD VON (1951), *Positivism* (New York: Dover).

MONTAGUE, R. (1969), 'On the Nature of Certain Philosophical Entities', *Monist*, XXXV, 159–94.

—— (1970a), 'English as a Formal Language' in Visentini, B. (ed.), *Linguaggi nella società e nella tecnica* (Milan: Edizioni di Communità).

—— (1970b), 'Universal Grammar', *Theoria*, XXXVI, 373–98.

—— (1970c), 'Pragmatics and Intensional Logic', *Synthèse*, XXII, 68–94.

—— (1973), 'The Proper Treatment of Quantification in Ordinary English', in Hintikka, Moravcsik and Suppes (1973).

MORAVCSIK, J. M. E. (1965), 'The Analytic and the Nonempirical', *Journal of Philosophy*, LXV, 415–30.

—— (1969), 'Competence, Creativity and Innateness', *Philosophical Forum*, N.S. I, 407–37.

—— (1974), 'Linguistics and Philosophy', in Sebeok (ed.), *Current Trends in Linguistics, 12* (The Hague: Mouton).

—— (1975a), review of Harrison, 'Meaning and Structure', *Language*, LI, 178–85.

—— (1975b), *Understanding Language* (The Hague: Mouton).

MORRIS, C. W. (1939), 'Foundations of the Theory of Signs', in Neurath *et al., International Encyclopedia of Unified Science* (Chicago: Chicago University Press).

—— (1946), *Signs, Language and Behaviour* (Englewood Cliffs, N.J.: Prentice-Hall).

—— (1971), *Writings on the General Theory of Signs* (The Hague: Mouton).

MOULOUD, N. (1969), *Langage et structure* (Paris: Payot).

—— (1976), *L'Analyse et le sens* (Paris: Payot).

MULDER, J. and HERVEY, S. (1972), *Theory of the Linguistic Sign* (The Hague: Mouton).

MUNITZ, M. and UNGER, P. (1974), *Semantics and Philosophy* (New York: New York University Press).

NAESS, A. (1953), *Interpretation and Preciseness, A Contribution to the Theory of Communication* (Oslo: Universitats Forlaget).

NIDA, E. (1975), *Exploring Semantic Structures* (Munich: Fink).

OGDEN, C. J. and RICHARDS, I. A. (1923), *The Meaning of 'Meaning'* (Kegan Paul).

ÖHMAN, S. (1953), 'Theories of the Linguistic Field', *Word*, IX, 123–34.

OSGOOD, C. (1964), 'A Behaviouristic Analysis of Perception and Language as Cognitive Phenomena', in Harper, R., *et al.* (eds), *The Cognitive Process* (Englewood Cliffs, N.J.: Prentice-Hall).

PAP, A. (1955), 'Belief, Synonymity and Analysis', *Philosophical Studies*, VI, 11–15.

PAP, A. (1958), *Semantics and Necessary Truth* (New Haven and London: Yale University Press).

PARKINSON, G. (ed.) (1968), *The Theory of Meaning* (Oxford: Clarendon Press).

PARSONS, C. D. (1965), 'Frege's Theory of Number', in Black, M. (ed.), *Philosophy in America* (Allen and Unwin).

PARTEE, B. (1972), 'Opacity, Reference and Pronouns', in Davidson and Harman (1972).

PASSMORE, J. (1961), *Philosophical Reasoning* (Duckworth).

PEARS, D. F. (1967), *Bertrand Russell and the British Tradition in Philosophy* (Fontana).

—— (1971), *Wittgenstein* (Fontana).

PITCHER, G. (1964), *The Philosophy of Wittgenstein* (Englewood Cliffs, N.J.: Prentice-Hall).

—— (1966), *Wittgenstein, the Philosophical Investigations: A Collection of Critical Essays* (New York: Doubleday).

PLATO, *Cratylus*, in Jowett (1953), *The Dialogues of Plato* (Oxford: Clarendon Press).

POTTS, T. (1976), 'Montague's Semiotic: A Syllabus of Errors', *Theoretical Linguistics, 1976*, 191–208.

—— (1977), 'The Place of Structure in Communication', in Vesey (1977).

PRICE, H. H. (1953), *Thinking and Experience* (Hutchinson).

PRIOR, A. N. (1963), 'Is the Concept of Referential Opacity Really Necessary?', *Acta Philosophica Fennica 1963: Modal and Many-Valued Logics*, 189–99.

PUTNAM, H. (1954), 'Synonymity and the Analysis of Belief Sentences', *Analysis*, XIV, 114–122.

—— (1962), 'The Analytic and the Synthetic', *Minnesota Studies in the Philosophy of Science, 3* (University of Minnesota Press).

—— (1975), *Mind, Language and Reality: Philosophical Papers* vol. 2 (Cambridge: Cambridge University Press).

—— (1976a), 'What is Realism?', *ASP*, LXXVI, 177–94.

—— (1976b), '"Two Dogmas" Revisited', in Ryle (1976).

QUINE, W. V. (1951), 'Two Dogmas of Empiricism', *Philosophical Review*; and in Quine (1953).

—— (1953), *From a Logical Point of View* (Cambridge, Mass.: Harvard University Press; Harper Torchbooks, 1963).

—— (1959), 'Meaning and Translation', in Brower (1959).

—— (1960), *Word and Object* (New York: John Wiley & Sons).

—— (1961), *Ontological Relativity and Other Essays* (New York: Columbia University Press).

—— (1966), *The Ways of Paradox* (New York: Random House).

—— (1967a), 'On a Suggestion of Katz', *Journal of Philosophy*, LXIV, 52–54.

—— (1967b), 'On the Reasons for the Indeterminacy of Translation', *Journal of Philosophy*, LXIV, 178–83.

—— (1969), 'Reply to Chomsky', in Davidson and Hintikka (1969).

—— (1970), *Philosophy of Logic* (Englewood Cliffs, N.J.: Prentice-Hall).

—— (1972), 'Methodological Reflections on Current Linguistic Theory', in Davidson and Harman (1972).

—— (1974), 'Comment on Michael Dummett', *Synthèse*, XXVII.

—— (1975a), 'The Nature of Natural Knowledge', in Guttenplan (1975).

—— (1975b), 'Mind and Verbal Dispositions', in Guttenplan (1975).

—— (1976), 'Worlds Away', *Journal of Philosophy*, LXXIII, 863.

QUINTON, A. (1963), 'The *a priori* and the Analytic', *ASP*, LXIV, 31–54.

REICH, P. (1969), 'The Finiteness of Natural Language', *Language*, XLV, 831–43.

RESCHER, N. (1968), *Topics in Philosophical Logic* (Dordrecht: Reidel).

RHEES, R. (1960), 'Miss Anscombe on the *Tractatus*', *Philosophical Quarterly*, X, 21–31.

—— (1969), '"Ontology" and Identity in the *Tractatus*', in Winch (1969).

—— (1970), *Discussions of Wittgenstein* (Routledge and Kegan Paul).

—— (1976), 'Wittgenstein on Language and Ritual', in Hintikka (1976a).

RICHARDS, T. (1975), 'The Worlds of David Lewis', *Australasian Journal of Philosophy*, LIII, 105–18.

RICHMAN, R. J. (1956), 'Neo-pragmatism', *Methodos*, VIII, 35–45.

RICOEUR, PAUL (1971), 'The Model of the Text: Meaningful Action Considered as a Text', *Social Research*, XXXVIII, 529–62.

ROBINSON, IAN (1975), *The New Grammarians' Funeral* (Cambridge: Cambridge University Press).

ROGERS, ROBERT (1963), 'A Survey of Formal Semantics', *Synthèse*, 15, 17–56.

290   BIBLIOGRAPHY

ROMMETVEIT, R. (1974), *On Message Structure: A Framework for the Study of Language and Communication* (London and New York: Wiley and Sons).

ROSENBERG, JAY F. and TRAVIS, CHARLES (eds) (1971), *Readings in the Philosophy of Language* (Englewood Cliffs, N.J.: Prentice-Hall).

ROSS, J. R. (1972), 'Act', in Davidson and Harman (1972).

—— (1975), 'Where to Do Things with Words', in Cole and Morgan (1975).

RUSSELL, B. (1905), 'On Denoting', *Mind*, XIV, 479–43.

—— (1946), *The Problems of Philosophy* (reset edn, Oxford University Press).

—— (1918), 'The Philosophy of Logical Atomism', *Monist*; and in Russell (1956).

—— (1940), *An Inquiry into Meaning and Truth* (Allen and Unwin).

—— (1956), *Logic and Knowledge: Essays 1901–56*, ed. Robert C. Marsh (Allen and Unwin).

—— (1957), 'Mr. Strawson on Referring', *Mind*, LXVI, 385–389.

RYLE, G. (1939), 'Are There Propositions?', *ASP*, XXX, 91–126.

—— (1955), 'Categories', in A. G. N. Flew (ed.), *Logic and Language* (2nd ser., Oxford: Blackwell).

—— (1957), 'The Theory of Meaning', in C. A. Mace (ed.), *British Philosophy in the Mid-Century* (Allen and Unwin).

—— (1961), 'Use, Usage and Meaning', *ASS*, XXXV, 223–29.

—— (1971), 'Letters and Syllables in Plato', in *Collected Papers*, vol. 1 (Hutchinson).

—— (ed.) (1976), *Contemporary Aspects of Philosophy* (Oriel Press).

RYNIN, D. (1956), 'The Dogma of Logical Pragmatism', *Mind*, LXV, 379–91.

SAMPSON, G. (1973), 'The Concept "Semantic Representation"', *Semiotica*, VII, 97–134.

—— (1975), *The Form of Language* (Weidenfeld and Nicolson).

SAUSSURE, F. DE (1916), *Cours de linguistique générale* (Paris: Payot); English trans.: *A Course in General Linguistics* (New York: Philosophical Library).

SAVIGNY, E. VON (1976), 'Some Elements of the Form of a Theory Perhaps Useful in Describing a Language', in Ryle (1976).

SCHAFF, A. (1964), *Introduction to Semantics* (Pergamon).

SCHEFFLER, I. and CHOMSKY, N. (1958), 'What is Said To Be', *ASP*, LIX, 71–82.

SCHILPP, P. A. (1963), *The Philosophy of Rudolf Carnap* (La Salle, Ill.: Open Court).

SCHLICK, M. (1934), 'Form and Content, An Introduction to Philosophical Thinking', in *Gesammelte Aufsätze* (Vienna: Gerold).

—— (1936), 'Meaning and Verification', *Philosophical Review*, XLV, 339–69.

SCHULDENFREI, R. (1972), 'Quine in Perspective', *Journal of Philosophy*, LXIX, 5–16.

SCHWYZER, H. R. G. (1962), 'Wittgenstein's Picture-Theory of Language', *Inquiry*, V, 46–63; and in Copi and Beard (1966).

SEARLE, J. R. (1957–58), 'Russell's Objections to Frege's Theory of Sense and Reference', *Analysis*, XVIII, 137–43.

—— (1958), 'Proper Names', *Mind*, LXVII, 166–71; and in Caton (1963).

—— (1962), 'Meaning and Speech Acts', *Philosophical Review*, LXXI, 423–32.

—— (1965), 'What is a Speech Act?', in Black, M. (ed.), *Philosophy in America* (Allen and Unwin).

—— (1966), 'Assertions and Aberrations', in Williams, B. and Montefiore, A. (eds), *British Analytical Philosophy* (Routledge and Kegan Paul).

—— (1968), 'Austin on Locutionary and Illocutionary Acts', *Philosophical Review*, LXXVII, 405–24.

—— (1970), *Speech Acts* (Cambridge: Cambridge University Press).

—— (ed.) (1971), *The Philosophy of Language* (Oxford: Clarendon Press).

—— (1975a), 'A Taxonomy of Illocutionary Acts', in Gunderson, K. (ed.), *Language, Mind and Knowledge* (University of Minnesota Press).

—— (1975b), 'Indirect Speech Acts', in Cole and Morgan (1975).

—— (1976), review of Noam Chomsky, 'Reflections on Language', *Times Lit. Supp.*, 10 September.

SELLARS, W. (1963), 'On Abstract Entities in Semantics', in Schilpp (1963).

—— (1966), 'Naming and Saying', in Copi and Beard (1966).

SEUREN, P. (ed.) (1974), *Semantic Syntax* (Oxford: Clarendon Press).

SHIBLES, W. (1971), *Metaphor: an Annotated Bibliography and History* (Whitewater, Wisconsin).

SCHIFFER, S. (1972), *Meaning* (Oxford: Clarendon Press).

SCHWAYDER, D. S. (1969), 'Wittgenstein on Mathematics', in Winch (1969).

SKINNER, B. F. (1957), *Verbal Behavior* (New York: Appleton-Century-Crofts).

SOMMERS, F. (1963), 'Types and Ontology', *Philosophical Review*, LXXII, 327–63.

SPARCK JONES, K. (1964), *Synonymy and Semantic Classification* (Cambridge: Cambridge University Press).

SPERBER, DAN (1964), *Rethinking Symbolism* (Cambridge: Cambridge University Press).

STAAL, J. F. (1969), 'Formal Logic and Natural Languages', *Foundations of Language*, V, 256–84.

STANILAND, H. (1972), *Universals* (Macmillan).

STALNAKER, R. C. (1972), 'Pragmatics', in Davidson and Harman (1972).

STAMPE, D. W. (1968), 'Towards a Grammar of Meaning', *Philosophical Review*, LXXVII, 137–74.

—— (1975), 'Meaning and Truth in the Theory of Speech Acts', in Cole and Morgan (1975).

STEINER, GEORGE (1975), *After Babel* (Oxford: Clarendon Press).

STENIUS, E. (1963), 'Wittgenstein's Picture Theory', *Inquiry*, VI, 184–95; and in Copi and Beard (1966).

—— (1967), 'Mood and Language-Game', *Synthèse*, XVII, 254–74.

—— (1976), 'The Sentence as a Function of its Constituents in Frege and in the *Tractatus*', in Hintikka (1976a).

STOCK, G. (1974), 'Wittgenstein on Russell's Theory of Judgement', in Vesey (1974).

STRAWSON, P. F. (1950), 'On Referring', *Mind*, LIX, 320–44; and in Strawson (1971).

—— (1954), review of Wittgenstein, 'Philosophical Investigations', *Mind*, LXIII, 70–99; and in Pitcher (1966).

—— (1957), 'Propositions, Concepts and Logical Truth', *Philosophical Quarterly*, VII, 15–25; and in Strawson (1971).

—— (1959), *Individuals* (Macmillan).

—— (1964a), 'Identifying Reference and Truth Values', *Theoria*, XXX, 96–118; and in Strawson (1971).

—— (1964b), 'Intention and Convention in Speech Acts', *Philosophical Review*, LXXIII, 439–60; and in Searle (1971); and in Strawson (1971).

—— (ed.) (1967), *Philosophical Logic* (Oxford: Clarendon Press).

—— (1970), 'Meaning and Truth', Inaugural Lecture (Oxford: Clarendon Press), and in Strawson (1971).

—— (1971), *Logico-Linguistic Papers* (Methuen).

—— (1974), 'On Understanding the Structure of One's Language', in *Freedom and Resentment* (Methuen).

STROUD, BARRY (1965), 'Wittgenstein and Logical Necessity', *Philosophical Review*, LXXIV, 504–18; and in Pitcher (1966).

SUPPES, PATRICK C. (1973), 'Congruence of Meaning', *Proceedings of the American Philosophical Association*, vol. 46 (Yellow Springs: Antioch Press).

TARSKI, ALFRED (1943), 'The Semantic Conception of Truth', *Philosophy and Phenomenological Research*, 4, 341–75; and in Feigl, H. and Sellars, W., *Readings in Philosophical Analysis* (New York: Appleton-Century-Crofts, 1949).

THOMASON, R. H. and STALNAKER, R. C. (1968), 'Modality and Reference', *Noûs*, II, 359–72.

TRAVIS, C. (1975), *Saying and Understanding: A Generative Theory of Illocutions* (Oxford: Blackwell).

TUGENDHAT, ERNST (1970), 'The Meaning of "Bedeutung" in Frege', *Analysis*, XXX, 177–89.

URBAN, W. (1939), *Language and Reality* (Allen and Unwin).

ULRICH, WILLIAM (1977), 'Redundancy and Frege's Chosen Object Theory', *Philosophical Studies*.

URMSON, J. O. (1956), *Philosophical Analysis* (Oxford: Clarendon Press).

——, HAMPSHIRE, S. and QUINE, W. V. (1969), 'A Symposium on Austin's Method', in Fann (1969).

VENDLER, Z. (1967), *Linguistics in Philosophy* (Ithaca, N.Y.: Cornell University Press).

VESEY, G. N. A. (ed.) (1974), *Understanding Wittgenstein: Royal Institute of Philosophy Lectures*, vol. 7, 1972–3 (Basingstoke: Macmillan).

—— (ed.) (1977), *Communication and Understanding: Royal Institute of Philosophy lectures*, vol. 10 (Hassocks: Harvester Press, 1975–6).

WEINBERG, JULIUS R. (1935), 'Are There Ultimate Simples?', *Philosophy of Science*, II, 387–99; and in Copi and Beard (1966).

WAISMANN, F. (1945), 'Verifiability', *ASS*, XIX, 119–50.

—— (1965), *The Principles of Linguistic Philosophy* (Macmillan).

WEINREICH, U. (1963), 'On the Semantic Structure of Language', in

Greenberg, J. (ed.), *Universals of Language* (Cambridge, Mass.: MIT Press).

WELDING, S. O. (1971), 'Frege's Sense and Reference Related to Russell's Theory of Definite Descriptions', *Revue internationale de philosophie*, XXV, 389–402.

WHEATLEY, J. (1970), *Language and Rules* (The Hague: Mouton).

WHITE, A. (1954), 'A Note on Meaning and Verification', *Mind*, LXIII, 66–69.

—— (1958), 'Synonymous Expressions', *Philosophical Quarterly*, VIII, 193–207.

WHITE, R. M. (1974), 'Can Whether One Proposition Makes Sense Depend on the Truth of Another? (*Tractatus*, 2. 0211–2)', in Vesey (1974).

WHORF, B. L. (1956), *Language, Thought and Reality* (Cambridge, Mass. and New York: MIT Press and John Wiley).

WIGGINS, D. (1961), 'On Sentence-Sense, Word-Sense and a Difference of Word-Sense. Towards a Philosophical Theory of Dictionaries', in Steinberg, D. and Jakobivits, L. A., *Semantics, An Interdisciplinary Reader in Philosophy, Linguistics and Psychology* (Cambridge: Cambridge University Press).

WILLIAMS, BERNARD (1974), 'Wittgenstein and Idealism', in Vesey (1974).

WILSON, D. (1975), 'Presuppositions and Non-Truth Functional Semantics' (New York: Academic Press).

WILSON, N. L. (1959a), *The Concept of Language* (Toronto: Toronto University Press).

—— (1959b), 'Substances Without Substrata', *Review of Metaphysics*, XII, 521–39.

—— (1967), 'Linguistic Butter and Philosophical Parsnips', *Journal of Philosophy*, LXIV, 55–7.

—— (1970), 'Grice on Meaning: The Ultimate Counter-Example', *Noûs*, IV, 295–302.

WINCH, PETER (ed.) (1969a), *Studies in the Philosophy of Wittgenstein* (Routledge and Kegan Paul).

—— (1969b), 'The Unity of Wittgenstein's Philosophy', in Winch (1969a).

WITTGENSTEIN, L. (1929), 'Some Remarks on Logical Form', *ASS*, IX, 162–71; and in Copi and Beard (1966).

—— (1956), *Remarks on the Foundations of Mathematics*, ed. G. H. von Wright, R. Rhees and G. E. M. Anscombe; trans. G. E. M. Anscombe (Cambridge, London: MIT Press).

—— (1958), *Philosophical Investigations* (2nd edn [revised] Oxford: Blackwell).

—— (1960) *The Blue and Brown Books* (Oxford: Blackwell).

—— (1961a), *Notebooks 1914–16*, trans. G. E. M. Anscombe (Oxford: Blackwell).

—— (1961b), *Tractatus Logico-Philosophicus*, trans. D. F. Pears and B. F. McGuinness (Routledge and Kegan Paul).

—— (1967), *Zettel*, ed. G. E. M. Anscombe and G. H. von Wright, trans. G. E. M. Anscombe (Oxford: Blackwell).

—— (1969), *On Certainty*, ed. G. E. M. Anscombe and G. H. von Wright, trans. Denis Paul and G. E. M. Anscombe (Oxford: Blackwell).

—— (1975), *Philosophical Remarks*, ed. Rush Rhees, trans. Raymond Hargreaves and Roger White (Oxford: Blackwell).

—— (1974), *Philosophical Grammar*.

—— (1976), *Lectures on the Foundations of Mathematics, Cambridge, 1939, edited from the notes of R. G. Bosanquet, Norman Malcolm, Rush Rhees and Yorick Smithies, by Cora Diamond* (Hassocks: Harvester Press).

—— (1977), *Remarks on Colour*, ed. G. E. M. Anscombe, trans. Linda L. McAllister and Margarete Schätle (Oxford: Blackwell).

YOUNG, J. (1972), 'Rabbits', *Philosophical Studies*.

ZIFF, P. (1964), 'About Ungrammaticalness', *Mind*, LXXIII, 204–14.

—— (1967a), 'On H. P. Grice's Account of Meaning', *Analysis*, XXVIII, 1–8.

—— (1967b), *Semantic Analysis* (Ithaca, N.Y.: Cornell University Press).

—— (1969), 'Natural and Formal Languages', in Hook (1969).

Index